Father Michael, Ernest Farnol

Father Ignatius in America

Father Michael, Ernest Farnol

Father Ignatius in America

ISBN/EAN: 9783337322137

Printed in Europe, USA, Canada, Australia, Japan

Cover: Foto ©ninafisch / pixelio.de

More available books at **www.hansebooks.com**

FATHER IGNATIUS

IN AMERICA.

BY

FATHER MICHAEL, O.S.B.

WITH A PREFACE BY

ERNEST A. FARNOL.

JOHN HODGES,
AGAR STREET, CHARING CROSS, LONDON.
1893.

TO
HER GRACE
"THE DUCHESS OF TANGLEWOOD,"
who was
the first to befriend and shelter
THE WELSH MONKS
on their arrival in a strange land,
THIS BOOK IS DEDICATED,
As a small token of gratitude for the interest and kindness in countless ways she displayed in their work for "THE MASTER'S GLORY" and the Salvation of Souls on the shores of Magnificent America.

PREFACE.

THE object of this little work, written by one of the Monks of Llanthony, is to describe, in simple narrative, the Rev. Father Ignatius' travels in the United States and Canada, and to present a record of the heaven-blest labours of love, for Christ's sake, which were there undertaken by him.

In the pages of God's immutable Word it hath been written that, "He who spake as never mortal man ever spake," once declared: "That a prophet is not without honour, save in his own country and in his own house;" and if ever this saying of our Lord could be applied to any, it might be most appropriately so to the Rev. Father Ignatius, until the last few years. During the earlier part of his most wonderful career of the past thirty years, he had heaped upon him, by many of his countrymen and co-religionists (to their shame be it said), all kinds of obloquy and slander. He has nevertheless received, as the following pages will fully show, the most cordial receptions at the hand of almost all the representative Evangelical communities of North America. Many a chapel and mission hall belonging to the

Presbyterians, Methodists, Baptists, and Independents, as well as of High Church and Low Church Episcopalians, has resounded oft with the soul-stirring proclamation of the "Old, old Gospel Story" by the eloquent Benedictine Monk.

Great and almost innumerable were the spontaneous kindnesses shown to the Rev. Father Ignatius by all ranks and degrees of American Society during his thirteen months' stay in the United States, incidental references to which are interspersed with interesting effect in the pages of this book. Be it also noted, that not a few of Columbia's most illustrious personages, including President Harrison, offered the Benedictine Monk their most kindly and cordial greetings; while from certain notable Ecclesiastics, the most friendly receptions were granted him, together with their prayers that the work of the Lord might prosper abundantly in his hands.

It might very naturally be asked by readers uninformed of Father Ignatius' antecedent history, why and wherefore is it that he who has given such signal proofs of his Divine authority and commission as a Preacher and Ambassador of "Jesus Christ and Him Crucified," by reason of the wonderful and numerous conversions which have attended his Evangelistic labours, and was accorded so genial a reception by the representative Churches of the United States and Canada—why should he have been subjected in earlier years amongst his fellow-countrymen to so prolonged a series of persecutions, enduring at their hands so severe an ordeal of suffering for conscience sake? Now to those who from the meagre reports which have from time to time appeared in sundry papers and petty publications of the life and extraordinary career of this man, have therein gleaned what little knowledge of the Benedictine Monk and his great work they may possess, an answer to such inquiries is neither hard or very far to seek, for truly it may be embodied in a single word, and that is " Monasticism," and Father Ignatius's relation thereto, as its Nineteenth Century Restorer in the English Church.

The storms of persecution which have raged around the pathway of this devoted servant of Christ, have been almost solely raised by intolerant, semi-Christian opponents, because of his unswerving adherence to deep seated convictions and his bold profession of the same, viz.:—that the system of Monasticism, as it existed in the pre-Reformation times, and in its best and purest form, if once again and thoroughly revived, would prove an inestimable boon, a tower of strength, and a spiritual glory to the Church of England. It is not too much to say that all the contumely, mis-representation, and opposition which the Rev. Father Ignatius has received, has been undeniably on account of his unwearying efforts to restore Monasticism within that branch of the Church militant, of which he is Limself, one of its truest, ablest and most faithful representatives.

Yet utterly regardless of all the unrelenting persecutions, which his nobly unfaltering fidelity to principle, as the Nineteenth Century Apostle of Monasticism within the pale of the English Church, have already cost him, he has not for more than half his lifetime swerved one jot or tittle from pursuing the solitary path to which he believes the Master has called him. With unflagging energy he still presses forward, rejoicing like the Saints of old that he has been accounted worthy of suffering so many, and such great things for the Lord's Name's sake.

Whatever may be the personal feelings and opinions of the readers of this book with regard to the system of Monasticism, and its revival within the pale of the English Church, it can neither be denied or disproved by those, who, with minds unprejudiced, have made themselves acquainted with the Ecclesiastical history of England, especially with the historical records bearing upon Monasticism as it flourished in primitive times, that it verily constituted the mightiest mainstay —the most efficient conservator of simple and unaffected piety in Christendom, and proved itself indeed a very bulwark and stoutest stronghold of the Ancient British Church.

Monasticism, like many other Ecclesiastical institutions, had within its pale men whose inconsistency brought discredit upon themselves, with dishonour and defame upon the institution itself. But to condemn the system of Monasticism, because of the unworthy lives of misdemeanants within the monastic fold, would alike be unwise, as indeed it would be most unreasonable. Whatever the monks of the Ancient British Churches were in themselves, regarding them collectively, they were at all times in life and character superior to their contemporaries, as historic records well attest.

Let those who have nought but Anathemas for Monasticism, remember, that to it we owe the lights of liberty and literature; that it was there that "Learning trimmed her lamp and Contemplation pruned her wings." It was the Benedictines who instituted schools; whilst to them we owe the guardianship of the Holy Scriptures and the Classics of Greece and Rome; besides other learned lore. It was they, who, as the greatest scholars of their day, were the copyists of the Ancient Manuscripts, and the principal custodians of the literature of their times. Be it also remembered, that to the monks their age owed all the beneficent institutions of their day. Many of our glorious Cathedrals we owe to the Benedictines and Augustinians—we may specially mention Canterbury, Peterborough, Gloucester, Worcester, St. Alban's, Bristol and Exeter.

Although to the general reader this brief expatiation upon the system of Monasticism might be considered a somewhat irrelevant digression, I have been so thoroughly convinced that such blind prejudices prevail amongst the representatives of Evangelical denominations, with regard to Monasticism, particularly in its bearing upon the life and labours of the Rev. Father Ignatius, that I have felt it my most pleasurable duty to write what I have written, not for defensive purposes merely, either for the system or the man, but simply to bring before the mind of any uninitiated reader a few of the cardinal facts relating to English Monasticism.

In the various reports of the Rev. Father's labours in the United States and Canada, as contained in the following pages, will be found the fearless and uncompromising stand which this valiant Knight of the cross of Christ has made against infidel doctrines so insidiously yet shamelessly disseminated by divers clergymen in the American Church. These stealthy encroachments are undermining the faith of many; blinding the spiritual eyesight of multitudes; whilst producing a very widespread decadence from the vital truth of "The Faith once delivered to the Saints." The noble vindication which the Rev. Father made for the Faith of Christendom, will be found embodied in the great controversy he had with several notable Clergymen of the United States, an abbreviated report of which is given in this volume.

It may come perhaps as a surprise to not a few of our readers, that such has been the increasing spread of heterodoxy amongst the religious communities of

North America, and to their utter shame be it said, amongst some of the most exalted Ecclesiastics in the United States, that disbelief in the foundation truths of Christianity abounds; and a vaunting scepticism has emasculated, yea, well nigh destroyed the spiritual life of many. This falling away from the Faith has resulted in a Pseudo-Christianity, and a degenerated system of theology, without creed or dogma, utterly at variance with all Historical Christianity.

Of these sad defections in the religious life of America, the Rev. Father was an indignant witness; and against them both with voice and pen he hurled unyielding protestations, and contended earnestly for the pure and undefiled religion of Jesus Christ as set forth in the oracles of God's inspired Word.

Amongst the various incidents recorded in this volume, none perhaps will prove more interesting to the Christian reader than those which narrate certain particular instances of Conversion wrought by the Holy Spirit's power, under the faithful presentation of Gospel Truth, by the Benedictine Monk. Of such conversions, particulars of only a few have here been given; for both manifold and abundant were the blessed fruits of his labours, in souls regenerated, backsliders restored, and weakly, wavering Christians confirmed and strengthened in their most Holy Faith.

Finally, I would now commend this book to all into whose hands it may fall, with the earnest hope that it may be abundantly blessed to the Glory of Jesus, and that to many a reader it may come as a message of light and life " through the tender mercy of our God."

ERNEST A. FARNOL,

An old member of
the Rev. Father's London Congregation.

November, 1892.

East Putney, S.W.

INTRODUCTION.

On putting this book of American experiences before the public, I feel a few words, explanatory of my reasons for so doing, will be only right and necessary.

In these pages, it has not been my object to enter into any of the controversies, caused by the Father's work in "the United States," but rather to give a full and authentic account (gathered from newspapers and private letters of blessing and thanksgiving) of the teaching and results of his Missions in America, and the various parts of "the States" we visited.

Though my intention originally was to write these articles (now framed into chapters) solely for "*The Church Chronicle,*" a paper at that time devoting a page every week to our work, wishes have been expressed by members of *all* grades of society, at home and abroad, to know something of the Father's Mission work, and the good resulting from his sermons, so that I now put them forth in this form, the majority of the following chapters having been especially and entirely written for this book.

His recent campaign against " Infidelity and Worldliness IN the Episcopal Church of America " in this *great* crisis of her history, has increased the desire for an authentic account of the Father's American experiences.

Since this book went to press one of the prominent characters in it, " America's King of Preachers," Dr. Philips Brooks, Bishop of Massachusetts, has passed away from earth, to the presence of his God. It is doubtful if ever before the death of a citizen has so plunged Boston in sorrow and mourning, and called forth such *laudatory* paragraphs in the Press of the *whole* world. He was a man *without* his peer to those who *knew* him, and to those who *cared* but LITTLE about the preservation and uplifting of the *pure* " Bible Christianity,"—a man whose aim was to *better* humanity and to *bridge over* the gulf between Sectarianism and the Church—a man broad to the extreme, and as " *The Boston Transcript* " of January 23rd, 1893 calls him, (apparently) "*more* powerful than *all* the Churches." His power of attracting immense crowds wherever he preached was great in the extreme. In these pages the greatness of his Latitudinarianism, and the lack of his preaching " the Gospel of Salvation," has been prominently brought forward. The assertion of his Unitarian parentage and that he has brothers in the "Unitarian" Ministry, though obtained FROM *Boston*, appears to be false, unless used in a sarcastic manner for "Episcopalian."

It had been intended at the *close* of these American Experiences to have *appended* several interesting articles that appeared in the American papers, respecting the Father's Life History, Llanthony Abbey, etc., but the unforeseen size of the book itself *at the last moment* prevented it, and compelled an interesting chapter on "The Seminole Indians" of Florida (in whom the Father was much interested whilst at Fort Myers,) to be *altogether* omitted.

Lest any of the readers of the following pages should run away with the idea that owing to my monastic vow of obedience, this book has been written by the Rev. Father's orders, and has been revised by him, I wish to say "*right here*" that not only was the MSS. first put into the publisher's hands before he even had read but half-a-dozen chapters, and that, when they formerly appeared in the columns of "*The Church Chronicle*" and "*The Church Review*," but that the GREATER part of the book the Rev. Father has *never* seen, and will *not* see, until it is in the hands of the public, therefore HE is *not* responsible for anything contained in the following pages. The book is put forth by his *permission*, NOT his command.

From a *literary* point of view this book is worthless, and its pages will afford *ample* scope for the critic. If it, however, succeeds in helping to lead souls *into* the Peace of God, and to bring them Home to the Feet of the Good Shepherd as *lost* sinners, my wish will be fully realized. Should it, besides this, break down the wall of prejudice and misconception that exists in many minds respecting the preaching, doctrines, and orthodoxy of the Welsh Monk. I shall be amply rewarded for my work in compiling these experiences of our visit to America in 1890.

My thanks are, in a great measure, due to Mr. Ernest Farnol, for the preface he has kindly written, and the unselfish way in which he has given up his leisure time, in order to arrange for the placing of this book before the reading public. The unforeseen delay in its publication has been unavoidable, and when orders and subscriptions were first solicited in June last, a few weeks at the most were expected to see the work " on the market." When the publication of this book was first proposed, a wish was expressed that it should be illustrated, but owing to the extra expense of illustrations and the necessary rise it would compel in the published price of the work, this scheme was found quite unfeasible.

MICHAEL DAVID, O.S.B.,
Monk.

March 8th, 1893.
  Llanthony Abbey,
    Abergavenny.

CONTENTS.

CHAPTER I.
The Departure—Voyage—Arrival in New York .. 1

CHAPTER II.
Landing in the New World—First Sermons in New York 13

CHAPTER III.
The Pilgrim Land—Falmouth 33

CHAPTER IV.
Falmouth Continued—More Services—Falmouth Boys —Lost in the Woods 55

CHAPTER V.
NEWPORT, RHODE ISLAND 68

CHAPTER VI.
Canada—Magog—Quebec 84

CHAPTER VII.
BOSTON 96

CHAPTER VIII.
First New York Mission 126

CHAPTER IX.
GREEN COVE SPRINGS, FLORIDA 158

CHAPTER X.
S. AUGUSTINE.
Lent Services—The Town—Visit to North and South Beaches 173

CHAPTER XI.
S. JAMES ON THE GULF OF MEXICO.
Punta Gorda—Sailing down Charlotte Harbour—Pine Island 185

CHAPTER XII.
FORT MYERS.
Mission in Methodist Church—Blessings—Children—Hospitality Experienced 193

CHAPTER XIII.
WASHINGTON, D. C. 207

CHAPTER XIV.
PHILADELPHIA.
Services—Visit to Indian Schools—Sioux Indians .. 215

CHAPTER XV.

NEW YORK.

Second Mission—Infidelity of the Episcopal Church—Reception by the Welsh 231

CHAPTER XVI.

Cornwall-on-Hudson—The Highlands of the Hudson—Sermons—Beauties of Nature 255

CHAPTER XVII.

THE FALLS OF NIAGARA 271

CHAPTER XVIII.

CHICAGO.

The City of "The World's Fair"—Crowded Services—Mission Results 281

CHAPTER XIX.

Last Sermons—Farewell to New York—Homeward Bound 301

CHAPTER XX.

IRELAND.

Queenstown—Cork—Dublin—Tara 328

CHAPTER XXI.

Return to Wales.

Bala—Llangollen—Abergavenny..   347

CHAPTER XXII.

Conclusion   366

FATHER IGNATIUS IN AMERICA.

CHAPTER I.

The Departure—Voyage—Arrival in New York.

NOT having had any real rest for over 20 years, in spite of the doctor's frequent orders, a number of the members of his Kensington congregation having by public subscription made up a purse of £437 to defray his expenses, the Rev. Father at length decided to visit America. He hoped there, as the doctors prophesied, to obtain better rest, and return stronger than ever to his work at the end of six months. So all arrangements having been made for the safety and prosperity of the little community at Llanthony Abbey during his absence, berths were engaged* in the Nordeutscher Lloyd s.s. Trave, to sail on June 12. His last sermons in England were preached at the Drill Hall, Hay, and for Archdeacon Mason at Longcross Church. It was soon after nine when we left Virginia Water by train for Waterloo, where numbers of sorrowing friends and sad hearts were gathered to bid the Father good-bye. Whilst

---

*The party consisted of the Reverend Father, Father Michael, Brother David, Henry Fitzhardinge Berkeley and Sister Annie.

waiting on the platform at Virginia Water for our train we met Father Benedict (the Roman Franciscan Friar from Ascot), in his brown habit and sandalled feet, going on to Weybridge. Remarking on the conspicuity of the Father's Book of Common Prayer which he carried, he asked if Brother David and I were going to found branch Monasteries in America, as he considered we were far too young. At last our train arrived, and we were soon en route for Waterloo. As we steamed out of the familiar old station, on looking out we saw all our friends at the windows of the hotel we had just left, waving their adieus, to which our little party replied with handkerchiefs till the bridge hid them from our sight. Arrived at Waterloo, we found we had an hour to wait before the boat train started, so having found Platform One, the Father retired to the waiting room to rest. There many of his faithful children had come to spend a last few minutes with him, and bid him "God's speed" before he sailed. As a few papers had erroneously stated that Llanthony's Abbot was about to sever all connection with the Monastery, several doubtless felt a sad uncertainty whether he would ever return to the shores of Albion, or they behold his face again.

At last time was up and we were off. As the train steamed out of the station, the tearful faces and sorrowful looks of the faithful few left behind was indeed most touching. On arriving at Southampton we found another band of friends and spiritual children (some of whom had for this purpose crossed from the Isle of Wight) gathered, for a last look at, and a last word from, him they loved so well. Some of these came off on the tender with us to the steamer, to embark on which we had to go out into the Solent. Just before leaving the tender, on which our friends were to return to the shore, the Father admitted three of them as Associates of our order. As the magnificent Trave steamed down the Solent towards us, the band on board was playing gaily, and all her passengers seemed gathered on deck to see the new additions to their company. At half-past three the anchor was up and we were off. Being a German ship, its nationality prevailed among the passengers, though there were a few Americans returning home. The steerage passengers were a large band of 600 Polish emigrants about to try their fortunes in the New World. These Poles, who were all in their various coloured and stylish national costumes, presented a most picturesque appearance. On Sunday, though there was a Deacon on board from the American Church in Paris who was on his way to receive his Priest's Orders from the Bishop of Tennessee, there seemed no arrangement for a service, so several gentlemen sent to ask the Father, if the captain consented, if he would hold a service and preach. This all being satisfactorily arranged, notices were posted on the decks announcing service for 10.30. A large congregation of the ship's passengers having assembled in the 1st Class Saloon, the service commenced with the singing of the Old Hundredth, the Father presiding at the piano. The prayers were read by Mr. Massey, the American Deacon, the Father taking the lessons and starting the Glorias after the Psalms. That old familiar hymn, " How Sweet the name of Jesus sounds," was sung before the sermon, which the Welsh Monk preached on the text (taken from the Gospel of the Day), " Come, for all things are now ready." He showed from a human point of view the utter foolishness of Paul preaching Christ a crucified Jewish carpenter on Mars Hill at Athens, or before the polished scientific Greeks and Romans at Ephesus. Why did he? How could a man believe it possible that he could gain the ear of such philo- sophers, and wean them from their classic gods to serve a dead Jew? What, indeed, must his faith not have been in daring to proclaim a crucified Jewish malefactor as the Saviour of the world? His message was divine. He *knew* it, and trusted to the power of its divinity, in the *strength* of which, wherever he went, he formed Churches of believers.

Look at the Church nowadays—eaten up with discordant sects and controversies of Church ritual, instead of one and all uniting, Catholics and Protestants alike, in preaching the simple message of the love of Christ, crucified for poor fallen humanity. Then, if one and all did this, there would be no room for infidelity and worldliness within our Church. Oh for the faith of Paul! Determined to know nothing but Christ crucified! To many it seems difficult to believe that the great Father God, who made the universe, and in whose sight this sea is but a speck, though to the eyes of men it appears a mighty ocean, *can* love such a poor, sinful, rebellious little world as ours. Though countless far larger worlds spangle space, yet He reveals to us His love in Christ, and His doing so proves the immensity of the love of God. Behold the birds of the air, the wild beasts of the forests, the fishes of the sea, and contemplate the immensity of God's love and forethought. He satisfies all their cravings, and supplies their every need. Look at the bird that lives on seed. God supplies the means to satisfy its craving, as also that of the bird that lives on flesh. Now look at Man! Man is a being with an instinct which rules his whole existence, an instinct that craves after something far higher and surpassing anything to be found below. It is a God-given instinct, which God alone can, will, and does supply for those who trust Him as their Life, and their Hope, and their *All*. " Come, for all things are now ready." A marriage feast of good things is ready; the Bridegroom bids you come. The feast awaits your acceptance, and you are invited, if you will, to feed there and be *filled*. Jesus is the feast. In Him, and Him alone, you will find ALL good things, everything necessary to satisfy the very inmost cravings of your soul—*rest* for the weary, *joy* for the sorrowful, *peace*—peace that passeth *all* understanding for the restless—*sympathy* for the lonesome, and *grace* sufficient to help in *every* time of need.

Have *you* ever looked on Jesus as the Bread of Life? "If any man eat of Me he shall *never* hunger; and he that cometh to Me shall *never* thirst." " He that believeth on Me *hath* everlasting life." "*I* am *the Bread of Life*." Do you say you are too bad to come to Jesus; you must wait until you are better? No, come now; just as you are. " Cast all your care upon Him, for He careth for you ; " and " The Blood of Jesus Christ His Son cleanseth from all sin." He came to save the *sinner*, and none are too bad for Jesus. Only trust Him with a simple, childlike faith, and hear His tender words of love, " I will blot out as a thick cloud their transgressions, and their sins and their iniquities will I remember no more."

In conclusion, the Father told an anecdote of how sometime ago, after a sermon at Bournemouth, a lady came to the waiting-room to ask him if he would go and speak to her husband, who was in the front seat crying bitterly. On the Father going to him, and asking what he could do for him, the poor sinner replied, "Jesus Christ has won my heart, but not my intellect." The Father said, " Thank God if He has won your *heart*. It is all He asks—' Give Me thine heart.' He does not ask for your brains. Give Him your heart, and the Holy Ghost will take care of your intellect." Before leaving him, he prayed that the Holy Ghost would enlighten him. At the next Mission, which was in Edinburgh, what was the Father's surprise to find this gentleman in the front seats. He was all right *then*, and so anxious was he that others might find what he had found, that he had some large Mission placards printed at his own expense, and drove about Edinburgh *with* a bill-poster and pastepot, putting them up in the most conspicuous places. Now he has gone home to rest, safe on the bosom of Jesus, in His everlasting arms.

The service over, some little time after on our going on deck, the expressions of thanks and enjoyment to which the Welsh Evangelist was subjected on all hands were most profuse. Many expressed a wish that he would preach again in the evening, and next day a number of passengers asked him to hold prayers every day on board. It was a surprise at the morning service to find the saloon so full, on account of so many of the passengers being foreigners. Instead of an evening service the Father held a small Bible meeting, which was very well attended, in the Ladies' Saloon. The portion of Scripture chosen was 1 St. John v. 9-13, on which he spoke after reading. The following are a few notes thereon, which I wrote out from memory next day:—" Here in the portion of Scripture we have just read we see the vast difference between God's and man's witness, and of how very much greater value the former is than the latter. I am going to speak to Christians to-night, *i.e.*, those who have come to Christ as lost sinners. As a little band of Christians at this close of another Sabbath day we are met together at the Feet of Jesus, waiting to be fed, as the Prophet Jeremiah says, 'Thy words were found, and I did eat them, and they were to me the very joy and rejoicing of my heart.' We are very hungry and are waiting to be fed, and Jesus will feed us and satisfy us before we part to-night. Here in our reading St. John tells us what 'The Witness of God' is, how it may be obtained, and who are those that possess it. It is only 'he that *believeth* on Me that 'hath Everlasting Life,' and then when a soul has 'the witness' in himself won't he be anxious and eager to proclaim it to all? We Christians are living witnesses for Christ and should glorify Him in all we do; in our daily lives, our every thought, word or action. 'Whether ye eat or drink or whatever you do, do all to the glory of God.' How easy it is, whatever position one holds in society, whether it be in the merchant's office, in the bank, on the quay, or in society, whatever one's vocations may be, how easy it is to glorify and witness for Christ, and so lay up treasure in Heaven, where neither moth nor rust doth corrupt, by a loving smile, a kind action, or a gentle word. Then how happy are the witnesses—safe in the Arms of Jesus—for they have received Eternal Life and have entered into the peace of God which passeth all understanding. They are QUITE safe now—oh! *so* safe, having believed the Witness of God, for the Shepherd not only finds and saves, but 'keeps' the sheep as alone they cannot keep themselves. Were the Shepherd to leave them for a minute, or the sheep to try to keep themselves, they could not fail to come to grief. As on our Welsh mountains at home, it is the Shepherd who day and night watches over the sheep and protects them from harm, so our Heavenly Shepherd keeps us. In the 1st Epistle of St. Peter we learn the Christian is 'kept by the power of God.'* God keeps him. Jesus Christ takes hold of his hand directly he accepts Him by a simple act of faith, and He will never let him go—nothing can pluck the believer 'out of His Hand.' Some people call it presumption, and Calvinism, others Erastianism to believe this, but the Christian will not trouble what 'ism' the world calls it, for Jesus Christ has spoken, and so *we* will believe and trust His Word. Consider the solemn words the Apostle gives us in the portion we have read to-night, that 'if we believe NOT the Record that God gave of His Son, we make *Him* a liar.'"

When our minds throughout the day had been filled with thoughts of God, and of the quiet happy Sabbath hours spent at home in the house of God, it was very saddening to the Christian to find a secular concert given in the evening by the German band. Though up to this time our voyage had been delightful, few, I think, will ever forget that Sunday night at sea. Rough weather had begun, sleep was out of the question, and many were agonizing in the throes of seasickness. The wind was high, the ship tossing and rolling, huge waves breaking on the deck, crashing

---

* Vide "KEPT BY THE POWER OF GOD." A Penny Tract published by the Monks of Llanthony.

like thunder over our heads. The saloon at meal times was comparatively deserted, and many of the passengers were invisible from now to the end of the voyage. The effect of this weather on the Father, combined with the movement of the screw, was very painful, causing him sleepless nights and suffering from his head. Sometimes he was so bad that we had to migrate in the small hours of night to the saloon to see if he could obtain any better rest on the couches there. My readers, no doubt, know the experience when below, of the ship continually rolling and plunging. Next day we were able to get on deck a little and enjoy the sea, which was gloriously rough, though of a beautiful greeny-blue appearance, with lovely white breakers. The spray was lively, breaking occasionally as it did over the deck, and subjecting one, if too near, to a shower-bath *gratis*. To-day we heard we had come eighty miles out of our way, as the captain was anxious to avoid the icebergs which were now breaking up and coming down from the North Pole. In the evening we had a splendid specimen of a glorious sunset at sea, the sky looking beautiful with its streaks of blue, crimson, yellow, and grey, the crimson being reflected on the waves all round. The next day, Tuesday, we sighted the *Britannic* on her way home. The sailors, who are a very superstitious set of men, and do not like having a cat, corpse, or priest on board, were heard to remark that another sermon like the Father preached on Sunday would " sink the ship!" Amongst our fellow-passengers was a gentleman, whose brother (a priest in San Francisco) walked over from Newport to our Abbey, and spent three days there in 1883, and an American owning a large ranche at Duluth, who most hospitably invited Bro. David and a friend to go and spend a month with him in August, when he promised to give them some splendid shooting. He said if you went far enough in those parts wild ducks, geese, prairie hens, deer, foxes, squirrels, rabbits, cheetahs, and wolves were to be found. On waking next morning, and looking out of our porthole, a most glorious sight met our eyes, and one never to be forgotten—a huge magnificent iceberg, about a mile away, and quite 200ft. high, sailing past in the brilliant sunlight. The sea was a bright blue, and the iceberg, glistening with all the colours of the rainbow in the golden sunshine, was a most beautiful sight. In the evening the decks were lit up with coloured electric lights, and cleared for a dance, the music being supplied by the band on board. Next day a Jewish gentleman on board, who had been holding an interesting conversation with the Father on the chances of salvation for the Jews, before leaving gave him two dollars to do as he liked with "for the love of humanity." He would not say for the love of Jesus, though he heard the Father preach on Sunday, when, it was stated, had there been an offertory, £100 could have been collected for our work. The next was our last day at sea, for in the afternoon, at a quarter to five, we sighted land (off

Long Island), after nine days on the ocean. From that time until we anchored for the night outside the harbour, we were running along the coast, which, as the shades of evening crept on, looked beautiful, for the electric lights of the hotels and those in the windows of the houses on shore, mingled with the crimson lights of the floating buoys, made up quite an illumination. About a quarter to nine, as we were in "the Roads," the gigantic ship ran aground for a moment, but was soon got off, and at half-past nine we anchored for the night in quarantine, with two other ocean steamers each side, just past the mammoth statue of Liberty,* at the entrance to New York Harbour. Amongst our fellow-passengers was one gentleman who had crossed the Atlantic seventy-six times. We were all very glad to get to the end of our voyage, especially, I am sure, the poor sick ones. Our Heavenly Father, in whose keeping we had been throughout, had indeed been good to us. By the sermon on Sunday morning, He had opened the heart of one American lady to provide us with a house, free of expense, for the whole summer at her own seaside resort, where her family had just built the parish church, which had only been consecrated the previous S. Barnabas Day.

* This colossal statue by Bartholdi of " Liberty enlightening the World " which faces the east is the largest of modern times. It is 151 feet high, made of *repoussee* copper, standing upon a pedestal 155 feet high built of granite and concrete. The pedestal cost 250,000 dollars, and the statue, which weighs over 25 tons, cost more than a million francs. The figure is that of a draped female crowned by a diadem, holding a tablet close

CHAPTER II.

LANDING IN THE NEW WORLD—FIRST SERMONS IN NEW YORK.

WHEN looking out of my porthole next morning (June 21st), at ten minutes past four, my eyes were greeted by a lovely crimson and yellow sunrise reflected on the water. The ship's stewards were hard at work rushing about and making such a noise that it was impossible to sleep. At half-past five the anchor was weighed and we began to slowly enter the great harbour. Having breakfasted at six, all the passengers commenced to land about seven. As the Father was very unwell, we did not go on shore till nearly ten. Brother David meanwhile got our luggage passed by the Customs House. About eight o'clock, the Rev. Dr. Wallace Neil, an American priest came on board to welcome the Father to the shores of Liberty, and to ask him to preach his first sermon in the New World at his Church the next morning at the High Mass. This the Father consented to do, if his strength permitted. This clergyman, who, with two of his choir boys, had visited our Monastery the previous summer, told us that the morning papers had already heralded the Father's arrival as "The Protestant Monk." Having landed

---

to the body in the left hand and a torch in the uplifted right hand. At night the torch is lighted by electricity, the base and pedestal by the same means. The forefinger of the goddess' right hand is 7 feet long and 4 feet in circumference at the second joint.

in New Jersey, which the river divides from New York, a horrid dirty little cab, all tumbling to pieces, and such a funny old driver were procured to take us to our resting place, which the Father had decided should be the " Hotel Normandie." To reach this house we had to cross the river in the Hoboken ferry. This was a kind of large covered moveable bridge or station capable of taking forty carriages at once. Our friend, Henry, was the first to meet with an adventure, he being quietly relieved by someone of his pocket book and its contents of bills and gold. I must pass over many points of interest, and hurry on to the Father's first American sermon at the Church of St. Edward the Martyr. The church was very hot, and what seemed strange to us, supplied with fans in every seat —people fanning themselves all through the service, which was conducted in a thoroughly Catholic manner. The singing by both congregation and choir was most hearty. The Celebrant at Mass was vested in a richly embroidered Chasuble. On the altar, which was of white marble, was a fine brass tabernacle, though not in use. The hymn sung before the sermon was, " Jesus, and shall it ever be, a mortal man ashamed of Thee?" The attention of the congregation was riveted on the Father as he preached from the Chancel steps on " The Lost Sheep "—" To-day the Gospel brings before us the Parable of the Lost Sheep. Sheep are such very silly, mischievous creatures, always getting into the most dangerous places, and meeting with disasters. Their bleating is always piteous, but more so than ever when one is lost. The bleating of the lost sheep is like the ceaseless moan of pain, sin and suffering ascending to the Throne of God from the human race. Humanity is like a lost sheep that has gone astray, and it is no use denying or attempting to hide it. This human race of ours is a very restless, pain-filled, weary, sorrow-laden race. Some of those whose whole lives are now given to politics and the worship of Mammon, or of human reason, before very long will have their thoughts distracted from this lower scene by some thrill of woe and agony, all too common in this short pilgrimage. Such men as these soon, yes, very soon, begin to look on the things of time as of little worth, and join in the bleating of the lost sheep. The human race has lost its way. There is a mighty canker gnawing at the very root of humanity. Humanity is diseased socially, domestically, physically, intellectually and morally, and is on its downward course, apart from God. Is there anyone able to restore it to its pristine beauty, purity, and holiness?—any hand able to lead it back to true liberty, true peace and an eternal perfect rest? From the earliest epochs of human history has any philosopher arisen able to do this? Did Socrates, Plato, Zoroaster, or Buddha Gautama find for the lost one the way to this Fold of rest? My brethren, human life is indeed made up of sorrows, disappointments, sufferings and pain, and earth's sons can *not* escape them. It is everyone's lot, rich or poor, to bear them sooner or later, but oh! how they are lightened when we have found the peace of Christ. Some of you in this very congregation this morning, I daresay, are going home to sick-beds, to witness the acutest suffering caused by disease of the body; some, perhaps, to the bedside of a darling parent or dearly-loved child, now sick unto death. Take Jesus home with you to them. Perhaps some of you are suffering from the blighted life of a daughter who was once the sunshine of your home, but whose name may not be mentioned now in your family circle—she has sunk so low. Or it may be a darling boy in whom once all your hopes were centered, but who is now speeding along the downward course to ruin. I daresay you know the story of that Indian chieftain who used to go outside his wigwam at night and look up into the great silent heavens and wonder if the Great Spirit had ever broken silence to this world of ours. And when at last he heard there was a white man come from the sun-rising, who professed to have a message from Him, he and his tribe packed up all their belongings, and started off to hear what the message could be, so anxious and hungry was the noble savage for rest and peace. If our world is really in the weary, helpless state it is, do you think it is at all unlikely that the great God, who is *all* love, would send a message, and bridge over the great gulf between Himself and man, between heaven and earth? I do not. When we see that there *is* a GOD who satisfies the hungerings and cravings of the bird and brute creation, I think there is every reason to suppose that that same Power will love humanity so much that He will bring Himself into touch with man, and with Himself satisfy the cravings of man's soul. Has there ever come to this little planet of ours a Power that can still the cry of suffering and sorrow going up from the human race—a voice that can raise up the sin-tossed, weary, heavy-laden, into a perfect and eternal calm? Has there ever come a Hand able to lift man up from the chains and depths of sin into a perfect purity and liberty of soul? Has there ever come a Friend who has professed to feed and satisfy the inner craving of our restless, weary race? Again I ask you, Have any of the great teachers of the past ever professed to do this, and by so doing proved themselves the shepherd of the lost sheep? No, you know they have not. None of these have ever applied the healing balm to the sore of human life. But *One* HAS come down from the heights of heaven above, to this little earth of ours, to seek and to save that which was lost. Who is this Strange One? Is He not a lunatic or imposter to dare profess Himself able to work such works as these? No, neither; for time, which proves all things, has proved, and proves on still, that the story of Christ crucified is heard to-day with the self-same power as on Mars Hill of old at Athens; and, wheresoever it is faithfully preached, the same results are manifested in the finding of the lost sheep. Jesus says, 'In Me ye might have peace,' and countless storm-tossed, weary souls *have* found, and find to-day, eternal rest in Him. Perhaps there are some even in

this little Church who are lost sheep at this moment.
Who are the lost sheep? Those who have never yet
come to Jesus, and found in Him peace, rest, life
eternal, joy unspeakable, and a perfect salvation.
The only way to come to Jesus is to accept Him as
God's gift to you by an act of simple childlike faith,
prompted by the Holy Spirit's power. Look up in
His face, and trust Him. If you have not yet found
Him, ask yourself the question, everyone of you: 'Am
I at this moment a lost, or a found sheep? If I was
the latter, surely I should be more restful and satisfied than I am.' Have I believed Christ's promises?
'None shall pluck you out of My hand;' 'Your
sins are forgiven you for His Name's sake;' 'My
sheep shall *never* perish.' A found sheep is one who
has 'embraced the promises,' and believed in
Christ's FINISHED work upon the Cross. If a soul
who has trusted Him *is* able to perish, the crucifix is
a mockery, and Christ becomes an 'open shame';
for He came on earth to accomplish our salvation
and pay the debt for our sin. On the Cross He
cried, 'It is finished'—*i.e.*, the work He had come
on earth to do; and if God says, 'It IS finished,'
there can be nothing left for us to do but to accept
the free and perfect gift. The moment you trust
Jesus you are safely reposing on His bosom, quite safe
in the everlasting arms of God. Are you there—
resting peacefully, happily, securely? If you are, then
remember your salvation does not depend on anything
you do, or can do, but solely and entirely on God

keeping His promises and 'keeping' *you*. You cannot keep yourself, but Jesus holds you fast in His nail-pierced hand. Is the Lord Jesus here in our midst? Yes, He is. He is here to seek and to save that which is lost. His loving arms are open to you who have not yet trusted Him, and He bids you come. 'Come unto Me all ye that labour and are heavy laden, and *I* will give you rest.' Will you trust Him now? The moment you do see! He takes you in His arms, and hear Him say, 'My sheep shall never perish.' He calls you His sheep. Yes, you are His now—firstly, because the Father gave you to Him; secondly, because He bought you with His own blood; and, thirdly, because you have given yourself to Him. You are redeemed, not by silver and gold, but by the precious blood of Jesus. Oh, sinner, lingering still, will you be His? Then restfully, peacefully accept Him with the faith of a little child. You will, you do, you say. Then right away through the fields of ether, beyond all the countless worlds that spangle space, there shall be rejoicing in heaven over the lost sheep, now found and safe in the Good Shepherd's fold. There is a mighty electricity betwixt earth and heaven that joins the sinner to Christ in less than a moment, directly he trusts Him. To many of you I daresay this is quite a new doctrine, but no one can teach it you to your soul's salvation, save the Holy Ghost speaking to your heart. 'Not by enticing words of man's wisdom, but by My Spirit,' saith the Lord.

If you are a Catholic, and have never yet come to Christ, you are like a building without a foundation. The same mighty power attends the preaching of the Gospel to-day as of old. Who will bow down their whole being at His feet and accept Jesus? If thou wilt, then thou shalt go out of this Church indeed totally changed. The Apostle says: 'If any man be in Christ he is a new creature; old things are passed away, all things are become new.' A sun-glow, then, from the land of glory will light your bitterest hour of trouble, sorrow, or sickness. Presently, when the priest elevates the Blessed Sacrament, some of you will be able to say for the first time from your heart 'My Jesus!' All your future joy and peace depends then, not on anything you do, but on Christ faithfully keeping and fulfilling His promises; upon Himself, who changes not; upon His finished work for your salvation."

Driving home down Fifth Avenue, past the Vanderbilt Mansion, we saw on our way the great Jewish Synagogue of "Temple Emmanuel," the magnificent Roman Catholic Cathedral of S. Patrick, the Reformed Dutch Church, S. Thomas', and the Church of the Heavenly Rest. On reaching S. Patrick's Cathedral, a fine Decorated Gothic building of 13th century work, the Father wished to go in and see it. This is supposed to be the most imposing church building in the States, and the following quotation from a guide book[*] will interest many:—"It was begun August 15th,

---

[*] "Appleton's Dictionary of New York."

1858, in presence of 100,000 people, and solemnly dedicated May 25th, 1879. It is built of white marble, and in the form of a Latin Cross. It is 306 feet long by 120 feet wide. The pillars, which are of white marble and clustered, are 36 feet high and have a diameter of 5 feet. The roof is groined with richly-moulded ribs and foliage, the bosses being 77 feet from the floor. The high altar, which is 40 feet high, was constructed in Italy of the purest marble inlaid with semi-precious stones. The Tabernacle, also of white marble, is richly decorated with Roman mosaics and precious stones, with a door of gilt bronze. The altars of S. Joseph and the Sacred Heart are of bronze, that of the Blessed Virgin of carved French walnut, and that of the Holy Family of white Tennessee marble and Caen stone. The thirty-seven stained memorial windows of the Nave were made at Chartres, in France, costing 100,000 dollars, depicting, amongst other scenes, the Life of S. Patrick, the Life of Our Lady, the Sacrifice of Abel, the Sacrifice of Noah, Melchisedeck and Abraham, the Giving of the Keys to S. Peter, S. Bernard, Martyrdom of S. Laurence, Approval of the Christian Brothers' Rule, Proclamation of the Immaculate Conception," etc. After the service at S. Edward's this morning Brother Gilbert, who was in the Vestry (in his brown habit), offered the House of "The Brothers of Nazareth " * (of which he is Superior) to the Father whilst he remained in the city. In the afternoon the newspaper reporters began to besiege the hotel. In the evening the Father

---

* A religious order for men doing a great work in the American Episcopal Church.

decided to attend Compline at the Church of S. Ignatius, which was the first church in New York to reserve the Blessed Sacrament. Finding hotel living so expensive, we were obliged next day to secure lodgings, but before moving, it having now spread that the First Monk of the Anglican Church since the Deformation of Henry Tudor, was in the City, callers began to be numerous. Amongst the earliest was Father Prescott, a priest of the Transfiguration, where Father Benson, of Cowley, had preached the previous day. He came to ask the Father to occupy their pulpit the next Sunday, and in the afternoon he received an invitation to a Magdalene Home. Directly we landed on Saturday, the Father had written (with a letter of introduction given him by the American lady on board the Trave) to the Bishop, but as yet had received no answer. Soon we heard from the good Rector of S. Edward's, that after the Father's sermon there on Sunday, he had been inundated with letters from all parts of the country. Numbers who had heard the Evangelist Monk in various places of the Old Country, were writing, eager to know when and where he would preach next. To one born and brought up in the Isle of Britain, it seemed so strange meeting such numbers of coloured people, dressed quite respectably and even fashionably, copper-coloured and even yellow people, Chinese and Hindoos, and to think that many of them are now very rich and ranking among the upper classes of New York, whereas a few years back they or their parents were slaves! In

New York every nation under the sun seems represented, it being *the* port of the country, Italians, Poles, Germans, Jews, all helping to swell the population for which Chinese laundries do all the washing. Here we were to experience our first American thunderstorm—though nothing will ever come up to a subsequent one which we witnessed at Falmouth. The Father had not been one week in the City ere the business men of Wall Street sent to ask him to come and address them, in their dinner hour, at the Old John Street prayer meeting.* Letters now began to pour in on the Father from all over the States, inviting him to preach in many of the chief churches, amongst the early ones being an invitation to S. Mark's, Philadelphia, Holy Cross Church, New York, and Mount Calvary, Baltimore.

The Historical Society of Dallas, Texas, wrote stating that they had elected him a member of their society as a mark of esteem and honour.

Now the Lyric Hall having been hired for a service on Sunday night, and the Father having promised to preach in the morning at S. Edward's, we began to

---

*This prayer meeting is held daily at noon in John Street Methodist Church, which was " the cradle of American Methodism," where the first society was organised in 1766, by Philip Embury and Mrs. Barbara Henck. Only four persons listened to the first sermon. The original pulpit and chancel rail, the pulpit Bible and brass candlesticks of the first church are still preserved, while the clock given by John Wesley still keeps good time in the church.

think about getting out of the city to some quiet little country place, to rest, for the heat in New York was unbearable, worse than anything one who has never experienced it can imagine. And the mosquitoes. Ugh ! They seemed to take a delight in livening one up. God was indeed good to us, and had already provided for our comfort by opening the liberal heart of the American lady from the Trave to secure a house for our party. On writing to her, to know if she could obtain rooms for us near her own house, she replied that she had taken a furnished cottage for the whole summer for us, and had herself defrayed the rent, besides supplying a servant and many extra articles of furniture, plate and linen. The Rector of S. Mary the Virgin, on our going there to Evensong one night, was very friendly, and said how he should like the Father to preach at his Church, which next to S. Ignatius, is the most Catholic church of the city and possesses a magnificent marble altar and reredos. On Sunday the Feast of S. Peter, when the Welsh Father preached again at S. Edwards, the little church was packed to its utmost capacity, right out into the street. Amongst the clergy was a deaf priest from S. Mary's, who had been to the Transfiguration by mistake, and had come all the way on here on purpose to hear the Father preach. The sermon was on— " Thou art Peter, and upon this *Rock* will I build My Church." In the afternoon the Rector of the Transfiguration called to offer his services to the Father in any way he could make use of them, and they were indeed useful subsequently, as it was this good priest that arranged matters with the Bishop (who was now just leaving for England), and obtained a license for the Evangelist Monk. On attending Vespers at S. Mary the Virgin's, the Rector came out into the church and invited us into Choir. Although it was not the custom to have a sermon in the afternoon, he asked the Father to read the lessons and preach, "if the Holy Spirit moved him." The Monk spoke on "The Release of S. Peter from prison." He spoke somewhat as follows: "My mission to this country is simply to bring Peter out of prison, and there are many Peters now in prison bound with the chains and fetters of sin and the world, of a clouded human reason and unbelief. To these Christ Jesus has sent me as His angel, *i.e.*, His messenger, to preach liberty to the captive, and to bring souls by the simple preaching of His Word into touch with God—into touch with the Divine Conqueror, Who has burst the bands of death and sin, paying the ransom for our debt with His own precious blood. My mission is to preach liberty to the sin-bound, and to bring some of the many Peters in our midst into the glorious liberty of the sons of God. 'If Christ shall make you free, then are ye free indeed.' Civilization will never deliver the captive, never bring peace or rest to the weary, sin-tossed soul. It only hampers it, and is one of the quaternions of soldiers surrounding Peter; but Christ can break its chains by the power of the Holy Ghost. The world now, in its high pitch of civilization, is once more as it was when the learning and civilization of mighty Rome and Greece were at the acme of perfection—yet see what little good civilization, however enlightened it is, does to the souls of men. See the vice rampant in our midst to-day; see the restless craving after something to satisfy the inmost longings of man's heart. Civilization without Jesus Christ is worthless; but with Him there comes in a liberty unspeakable—unlike the liberty contrived by man— the glorious liberty of the children of God. 'Other foundation hath no man laid than that which is in Christ Jesus.' Grafted on the Rock of Ages by a simple faith in Christ you can 'never perish,' and are a member of that 'glorious Church without spot or wrinkle, or any such thing.' This is no mere chance, your kind rector having asked me to speak now so unexpectedly. There is a soul here, I know, in which the Master has a work for me to do."

After this service a Presbyterian student, who had wandered inadvertently in to the service, came up to the Father, as he was leaving the church, most enthusiastically. He said he should never forget that sermon. He had always been set against the Ritualists and their forms and ceremonies, and would not have believed it possible that such teaching was to be heard in a church like S. Mary's. This young man, who was QUITE overcome, walked home with us to our lodgings, and kept repeating he should never forget that afternoon's service, and should bring all the students he could influence to hear the Father when he knew of his preaching again. The gist of the sermon really was the vast difference between Peter *in* prison and Peter out of prison, or the soul IN the fetters of bondage of sin and the world and the soul out of these same fetters, brought into liberty by the power of the Holy Ghost.

The address in the evening, at the Lyric Hall, on "The Power of the World and the power of Jesus Christ contrasted," for which the notice-bills had been printed by the Father's old Bristol printer, was not so well attended as he expected. But this was owing a great deal to the fact that the heat in New York had driven so many people to the Catskill and White Mountains, and to the coast. Nevertheless a fair and very enthusiastic congregation (amongst which were several clergy) greeted the Father when he ascended the platform, and announced his text in clear ringing tones as "Be of good cheer, I have overcome the world."

So strange was the monastic garb to the representatives of the New York Press that they took particular care next morning in the papers to describe it fully. Throughout the entire address the congregation listened spellbound, as if "the old, old story" of the Gospel and Christ's love had never been preached to them before.

"Be of good cheer, I have overcome the world." Yes, my brethren, Jesus Christ said many extraordinary things, and spoke words no other man ever had the boldness to utter. No philanthropist, orator, or statesman ever uttered such words as these of the poor peasant carpenter of Galilee, about to be gibbeted as a criminal, crowned with thorns, and hung upon the tree of shame born in poverty, swathed in want, when about to conclude His work on earth, though He had gathered very few disciples, yet He says: "Be of good cheer, I have overcome the world."

Was He a lunatic to speak thus? Has any mere man ever dared to use such words as these? No, my brethren, no man has ever done so. He says unless we love Him more than father and mother we are not worthy of Him. "Come unto Me, all ye that labour and are heavy laden, and I will give you rest." Did ever any man make such claims as these upon the love of humanity? Did ever man have such an ancestry as Jesus Christ? It paved the way for His appearance upon the platform of human history. The whole nation of Israel was the ancestry of Christ. The plot of ground this nation inhabited was situated midway between the two civilizations of the world. Every powerful nation of the world had tried in vain to obliterate the Jew. Antiochus, Alexander the Great, and other mighty ones of history, had been stayed by Almighty power from destroying the Jew, the mystic people who were to produce the Christ of God; thus even, before His birth in the flesh, had Jesus "overcome the world."

The Jewish nation were situated in every way in a peculiar situation. First they were possessed with the idea that they had a special mission from God. Men's hearts failed them for fear! Men's brains were restless then as now. The sighs of the human race went up unceasingly to God. This little people of the Jews, this peculiar race, so different to all the other nations of the globe, were kept together by the one idea that they should produce a Man who should bring in the Golden Age of humanity,—a Man through whom all the nations of the earth should be blessed. Their ancient prophets sang of His birth, passion, and pain, His coming as Redeemer, and even of the city where He was to be born. Was this treasure promised to the Jews unexpected amongst the other nations of the earth? No! all the nations of the world were looking for, aye, daily expecting, a Golden Age, when the poison of the serpent should be taken away, and the baneful plant should lose its bane. All looked for the New Prodigy that should descend on the Earth. So Jesus Christ had an ancestry at once both unique and peculiar. At His long-looked-for coming, the ancient seers and prophets foretold that He should create a Cosmopolitan Fraternity in which there should be neither bond nor free, Greek nor Jew, but where all should be one in Him. The glorious visions of Israel's seers, the songs of the psalmist, the resplendent foretellings by her prophets of the final vanquishment of wrong and ill, passion and pain—the glad resurrection of humanity into the liberty of the final and victorious

Kingdom of God, were all foreshadowings by the Holy Ghost of the different stages in human history, of the glad truth of the words of our Lord in the text, " I have overcome the world." Now the work of Jesus by His Holy Gospel was the taking out from the world, and in spite of the world, from all the peoples, the Church which His Father had given Him, and His Blood had bought. This is the present mystery of the work of God. Has this race of Israel ever produced such a man, who has thus gathered out a people to His name. What power was it that " Overcame the World " under Nebuchadnessar, Sennacherib or Tiglath Pileser when *they* tried in vain to obliterate the Jew? Look now at the birth of the Christmas Child in the manger of Bethlehem. The chilly wind and icy air surround the cave as a peasant maid folds her child to her bosom on that mid-winter night. As you gaze on this new-born Child, the Christmas present of Heaven to a dying, sinful, weary world, think, can that peasant child be the long-looked-for hope of humanity? In this child, is a picture of *weakness*, indeed. Now change the scene, and look at the mighty Augustus on his Throne. The Power of Rome has made the nations of the world bow down in servile homage before the Emperor's feet; but soon his throne and Empire must crumble to the dust before the new-born Child of Bethlehem. Now this peasant Child has crossed the Atlantic waves, and all your temples are erected for the adoration of the Living Son. The power of Rome is gone—a thing of the past, the glory of her former greatness is passed away for ever. The Christmas Child has conquered by His Might, which is greater than that of the world. Indeed, before our eyes His words are true: "I have overcome the world." Time tests the strength and weakness of all things, but has it, I ask you, touched the Crown of Jesus Christ? Look at Him. Of what Empire is He the King? No worldly kingdom is His, but He reigns in the hearts of His believing Chi'dren,—His Crown a wreath of Love. Time has failed to touch the Glory of the Christ. The Gospel is doing to-day what it did of old on Mars Hill at Athens, or in the palaces of Rome. It is drawing out still a people to His Name, and, according to His Promise, numbers will be sent out *to-night* new creatures in the liberty of Christ. The Jews were kept together in Palestine until they had produced the Christ. See! He weeps over Jerusalem at the zenith of her day, because Jerusalem shall crucify Him, and a few years hence shall be devastated and laid low, her children scattered over the world, unwilling witnesses to the reality of the Messiahship of the Christ. Here is a magnificent power—an historical reality. Look at Jesus Christ, as He who knows the future, beholds Jerusalem in the heyday of her beauty, in all her mirth, and weeps over it. He knows Jerusalem's day is nearly past, and He weeps for her. "Her work is done." The Father went on contrasting the Power of Christ with that of the world, and inviting sinners to lay hold of the Christian's strength, in which they should be more than conquerors.

As people were most curious to know more about this Episcopal Monk who had just dropt down in their midst, the Editor of "The New York World" asked the Father to write his autobiography,* for which they presented 25 dollars to his work, whilst "The Morning Journal" gave him 8 dollars for an article on "Monasticism." After the service on Sunday night at the Lyric Hall, a great rush was made to get at the Father by the enthusiastic audience, who were most profuse in giving their names and addresses, and offering to help make known any future services. As for the large band of reporters, they simply jumped on the platform, and took the waiting room by storm. Now the first note of the strife and opposition the Father was to meet with in the States was begun. They one and all wanted to know what "Credentials" he had brought to the Bishop. Credentials! indeed! Why we had never heard or dreamed of such things before (much less been asked for them) as being necessary for one so well known by name all over the world as "Father Ignatius," the Reviver of Monasticism in the Anglican Church. Nevertheless I replied to their enquiries in an early number of a daily paper.†

---

* Vide Appendix A.   † Vide Appendix B.

CHAPTER III.

THE PILGRIM LAND—FALMOUTH.

IT was on the last Monday in June, the day after the British Monk had proclaimed "the old, old story" of the Gospel from the Lyric Hall platform (in spite of the noise caused by the trains on the Elevated Railway), that we bade farewell to hot, sultry, dusty New York, and found ourselves *en route* for "The Pilgrim Land," Cape Cod, where our Puritan forefathers landed from *The Mayflower* ship, of historic fame.

All our goods and chattels having been packed and stowed away on the Saturday, at nine o'clock we "boarded" the drawing-room car of the first American train we had ever seen. You never find first, second, and third-class carriages when travelling in the New World, only drawing-room and ordinary cars. Instead of one carriage, as in England, being partitioned off into compartments, there the railway-carriage is just like one large English tramcar, with seats for two down the sides, one behind the other, and a passage down the centre, so, even whilst in motion, you can always walk from the one end of an American train to the other. At the two respective ends of the carriage are usually a lavatory and iced-water filter. Generally, too, on long journeys, a dining-room car is attached, where almost anything can be obtained. To many this is a far more agreeable mode of travelling than that of the old country. Every train also possesses its smoking and observation car. All these cars are warmed in winter by stoves, and generally the heat is quite unbearable to a Britisher, for the Americans go in for a tremendous amount of warmth.

Well, having at last got fairly off from New York, it was very interesting to watch our progress through a strange country, beholding with curiosity the wooden houses, and looking in vain for any sheep or cattle on the pasturage *en route*. One of the prettiest scenes on the journey, was the crossing of the broad and picturesque Connecticut river. A little before four we arrived at Boston, the city that obtained her historic fame through the emptying of the tea-chests into her harbour, which gave rise to the great war for American Independence.

Here we had to change trains, and, what is more, stations, exciting great curiosity, but meeting with nothing but respect, as we walked though the street to the old Colony Depot, where we once more "boarded" a train for Falmouth. Arriving there soon after six, we were met at the station by the kind American lady who had, "for the love of Jesus," given us a pretty quiet home for the summer. On reaching the house, or summer cottage, on the lake side, which, being unnamed, we soon designated "S. David's Retreat," we found a comfortable and refreshing meal spread, and one of this lady's own servants there ready to wait on us.

The situation was beautiful. To our left and right lovely lakes, abounding with fish; behind, wooded hills of luxuriant growth; across the lake, to our left, the village, with the church steeple just peeping through the trees; while in front the "wild sea waves" broke upon the sandy shore. Away on the horizon, the houses of which were visible on a clear day, was the island of St. Martha's Vineyard. Birds of beautiful plumage, flowers of every hue, ferns of the most delicate kinds, helped to make up the beauty of this little seaside village.

Our house, like all the others, was built of wood, with a piazza round it, on which many a pleasant hour was spent reading, writing, or watching the picturesquely-dressed and intelligent American children at their play. Having hired a boat, our leisure time was often diversified by a row on the lake, or a fishing expedition, which was often very successful, Bro. David and I having caught as many as 200 fine perch in one afternoon. For the sake of the lovers of beauty in Nature, shall I describe this lake—its luxuriant beds of white water-lilies and dark green leaves near the shore; the purple arrow-heads, white meadow-sweet, large wild yellow dahlia along its banks; and the clumps of golden rod, America's national flower, sweet-scented fern, and purple and white asters, that bloomed in the meadows, sloping down to its shores; while from the trees overshadowing the banks, festoons of the most brilliant red Virginian creeper, and clusters of the wild grape, green and blue, hung in profusion. On the opposite side of the lake was the old, long since forsaken cemetery of the Puritans, with tombstones of ancient date and quaint inscriptions.

How beautiful on this lake, the boats used to look with their white sails glinting in the sun, or quietly gliding along in the silver moonlight. Fish of all kinds abounded in these waters, from the pickerel, black bass, and perch, down to the tiny minnow. Here also was the turtle to be found, and as for the eels, it was a regular trade in the village with some, catching them for the Boston and New York markets. American blue birds, golden orioles, and marsh quails surrounded us on all sides, and of an evening the meadows all round, sparkled with the countless flashes of the golden firefly.

The village does not possess a postman, consequently there is no delivery of letters, and it seemed very strange to us at first, having to walk in twice a day to the Post Office, when the mail arrived, to fetch our letters. It was here, in this quiet little village on the sand dunes of Cape Cod, that the Welsh Monk was to experience his first opposition from an American bishop—the late Bishop Paddock, of Massachusetts—

who refused to allow him to officiate in the churches of his diocese. The Bishop wrote: "While entertaining no doubt of your piety and sincerity, such notices as have fallen under my notice of late years, concerning your teachings, services, modes of life, and institutions, have led me to the strong impression that in some very important respects, you were not in sympathy with the doctrine, discipline, and worship of the Church of which you are a minister, nor in all respects loyal thereto."

So the Father was shut out from the churches of Massachusetts, and forbidden to preach "the old, old story" of the Gospel of Christ's love, owing to certain newspaper reports, that had from time to time fallen under the Bishop's notice, but which he did not specify or give the British Monk an opportunity of explaining or replying to. So, though the kind friends who had been the means of our visiting Falmouth, wished to hear the Father preach in the new church they had built, the Bishop refused to permit it, and added, that he hoped the Father would not preach in any halls either.

The Town Hall having previously been hired for a service on July 27th, the Rector and Methodist Minister of the village were notified, and I here give for contrast of Christian spirit, the reply of each. The Methodist Brother writes:—" Dear and Reverend Sir, Your communication of July 12th is before me. The lovely Christian spirit you reveal is of sweet interest to me. I have consulted my brethren of my church, and we decide to hold our service on Sunday, July 27th, at an hour which will not conflict with your service of 8 p.m. I join in your prayers that the dear Saviour may be found of many who now know Him not. . . God bless you." In this letter the spirit of the Children of God is unmistakably manifest. Now the YOUNG Episcopal Rector, who never had an evening service of his own on Sundays after five o'clock, wrote : "I was informed during my call this p.m. that you had received from the Bishop, a letter inhibiting you from holding services in the Diocese. Doubtless it seems to you very unjust, but I trust that you will heed it; you should yield all the more, because this is not your own land, and you do not understand well the ways nor the needs of the people. I must ask you not to hold the service in the Town Hall advertised for Sunday evening. I understand the town folks better than you do, and you must believe me, when I say that you will do more real harm than good to the work of the Church here, whatever you might do in a city. I ask very earnestly that you will hold no public service in the town." This priest, from the very beginning, had been most reluctant to call on the Father, and now, not content with trying to hinder the service advertised in the town, he writes to the Rector of S. George's Church, Newport, where a ten-days' mission had been arranged to be held by the British Monk, trying to prejudice him and stop the services there also. But the Rector, who had known the Father for years, having heard him preach many times for the late Mr. Purchas, in Brighton, was not to be influenced, and showed Mr. Perry's letters to the Father. The service in Falmouth Town Hall was held as advertised, and the following is the report from the village paper, *The Falmouth Local*:—

" On Sunday evening, July 29th, long before the time appointed for the Rev. Father Ignatius to preach, numbers had already sought admission to the Town Hall, and as 8 o'clock approached, not an unoccupied seat was to be had in the hall or gallery, in fact, numbers were standing round the doors eager to hear what the Monk, whose presence in Falmouth has so long excited the curiosity of its visitors, was going to say. Vanloads of people from the Heights, East and West Falmouth, Quissett and Woods Holl, Episcopal Clergy, Methodists and Congregationalists, all had gathered to hear the Monk preach as announced ' the Gospel of the Lord Jesus ; ' but, sad to say, great numbers had to return home disappointed, unable to get in, the Hall was so full. The Episcopal Methodist and Congregationalist ministers had most kindly held their services earlier than usual in order to enable their congregations to attend the sermon of Father Ignatius, of which opportunity many availed themselves. Conspicuous among the congregation were many men, and despite the lateness of the hour for such a scattered country place, a great number of little children, who all appeared to listen with the most rapt attention, notwithstanding the intense heat, as in thrilling tones the Rev. Father spoke on 'Christ's weeping over Jerusalem.' The service began with a couple of verses of the Old 100th Psalm, sung without accompaniment, and led by Father Ignatius, followed by an extempore prayer, and then the sermon. The father was attired simply in his black serge Benedictine habit, scapular emblematical of obedience, sandals of poverty, rope of chastity, a hood, with a large crucifix and rosary hanging from his rope. The shaven head denotes renunciation of the world, the ring of the tonsure being supposed to represent the Crown of Thorns placed on Christ's head by the Roman soldiers.

"'When Jesus was come near, He beheld the City, and wept over it, saying, If thou hadst known, even thou, at least in this thy day.' The preacher began by saying that empires, nations, cities, families, individuals all have their day. Falmouth, for instance, was having its day. It was the height of its season, the summer skies, the shining sea, the laughing flowers, the singing birds, the bright and happy youths and maidens, the crowd of visitors, their fishing, bathing and cheerful games all made up a glad and joyous picture. Falmouth was having its day. But soon it would be over, the flowers would die, the birds would cease their singing, the moaning of the chill winds would sweep the once bright leaves, all sere and dead, along the ice-bound roads and fields of winter time, the houses would be empty, the visitors all gone.

Jerusalem was at the height of its gayest season when Jesus wept over it. It was in the bright Syrian spring, it was just when vast mult'tudes of rejoicing pilgrims from far and near were gathered there for her Paschal Tide. The fields were at their freshest, the hillsides gay with flowers. Jerusalem with her white stone palaces and squares, her glorious temple roofed with gold, shimmering with dazzling glory in the sunshine of that Orient Land ; the vast assemblage of snowy canvas tents spreading on every side, filling the valleys and covering the western plains as far as the eye could reach. Then the glad murmur of a million voices, the sweet songs of Sion, echoing in the long cloisters of the temple in the near distance at Jesus's feet. Wealth, fashion, gaiety, mirth, youth, laughter, beauty, joy, on every side.

" What sights, what sounds to make all hearts dance for gladness. 'And when Jesus was come near, He beheld the City, and He wept over it.' The tears of God are falling over the glad, gay City. Once before had 'Jesus wept.' It was with the weeping mourners at Lazarus' grave, when human sorrow touched the human heart of God Incarnate. But now He weeps, not for human sorrow, but for human sin. In a few short days shall Jerusalem reject her Messiah and crucify her King. He comes to His own people, the Jews, and His own received Him not ; their prophets and seers, their psalmists and patriarchs have all foretold His coming; their laws, their ceremonial worship all pointed to His coming as the 'Desire of all nations;' the Seed of Abraham, through whom 'all the nations of the earth shall be blest.' But now He has come at last, for whom so long the world has waited, and Jerusalem shall now reject and crucify Him. It is her day, she may receive Him now and be saved, but if she will she may reject Him and perish. Ah! as Jesus is beholding the bright, gay city, He sees two pictures of her guiltiness and doom, —and so 'He wept over it.' Only a short five days, and those fair, sunlit streets, thronged with life and beauty, shall ring with the cry, 'Crucify Him, crucify Him.' Only a few more days and the echo shall reach the surrounding hills, from the heart of the Jewish nation, rejecting their Messiah, their King, their God—'Away with Him, away with Him, release unto us Barabbas!'

"And then their rejected, crucified Christ shall stretch out His hands of tenderness and power to the weary people and races of the tired world, crying to them in His gospel of love, 'Come unto Me, ye weary and heavy-laden, and I will give you rest.' And forth from all the nations there shall come 'a great multitude that no man can number,' taking Him at His word, and entering into the peace of His great salvation, whom the City of Jerusalem rejects and crucifies. 'And when He beheld the City He wept over it.' He sees her guilt and folly, and so He weeps. But also He sees her *doom*—her guilt, unlike

all other guilt; so shall her doom, her awful doom—
unlike all other dooms—soon be. Jerusalem is gay,
she is laughing now; it is her *day*, but she has
wasted it; it is near its end, the gathering shadows
of an awful night are near! Hark! Jesus tells His
wondering apostles and disciples the cause, as they
marvel at His tears. He wept over it, saying: 'If
thou hadst known, even thou, at least in this thy
day, the things which belong unto thy peace, but
now they are hid from thine eyes. For the day shall
come upon thee, that thy enemies shall cast a trench
about thee, and compass thee round, and keep thee
in on every side, and shall lay thee even with the
ground, and thy children within thee, and they shall
not leave in thee one stone upon another, because
thou knowest not the time of thy visitation. Oh,
Jerusalem, Jerusalem! How often would I have
gathered thy children together, as a hen gathereth
her chickens under her wings—and ye would not.'
O, pitiful cry of the loving and mighty Shepherd,
'and ye would not.' Therefore soon, soon shall the
legions of mighty Rome surround thee; soon, soon
shall Titus and Vespasian, with their conquering
eagles, hasten to their prey; their moving towers and
battering-rams shall soon assail thee; thud after
thud, the massive balistas shall cause thy firmest
bastions to quiver, and thy most mighty battlements
to shake; thy streets shall run with blood; thy
famine shall be so sore that thy princeliest daughters
shall devour their babes in their straits so dire; and

when thy temple at length is fired by the flaming brands of the soldiers, the moaning cry of a people's broken heart shall go up to the Throne of God.

"So Jesus ' beheld the City, and wept over it.' In a few short passing years from Christ's Crucifixion day—they were but 40—Jerusalem's day sunk down in shades of darkest, woesome night. And so it is of all alike, the day must end, and night draw on. Where are the giant nations and mighty empires of the old-time? Where are Babylon and Nineveh, Greece, and Rome? They have had their day; silent and desolate are the sites of earth's proudest and wealthiest cities. Their night has come, their season, their day is over, and so it soon will be with *us*.

"Oh people, dear people, what are you doing with *your* day? Have you received or rejected Christ? Without Him you can do nothing acceptable to God, without Him your life is a wasted day. And, oh! it seems this Sabbath day, with the half-empty church and the crowds of people outside, as if Jesus was rejected and His service neglected by many. We enjoy His gifts and daily mercies—we fish in His waters, we bathe in His seas, we enjoy His fair earth and bask in His sunshine, we enjoy the breath and life He gives, but we forget or neglect Him. Yet He loves us; He would draw us *now* to His nail-pierced feet. He calls us *now*, ' Come unto Me,' by a simple faith receive Me as the Father's gift, life, pardon, righteousness, salvation, and 'you shall never perish; none shall pluck you out of My hand.' 'How often would I have gathered you as a hen gathereth her chickens under her wings.' Jesus is calling you *now*. '*Now* is the accepted time; *now* is the day of salvation,'—'this is thy *day*.'

"Old men here present, let me speak to you. Life's day for you is nearly done—your innings in life's game are nearly out—what have you done with your day? When you are dying, will you look back upon a wasted life, 'without Christ,'—Christ rejected, warnings neglected, His loving gospel invitations silenced at last for ever? 'How often would I have gathered you, and ye would not.' 'Your house is left unto you desolate.' Forth into the night of the unprepared—for eternal years, without the Christ, the Tender Shepherd, the Mighty Saviour. He called you, but 'you would not.' And now ringing in your dying ears, and for ever, you hear the last, loving words of His sad, sad voice: 'Ye would not come to Me, that ye might have life,' 'How often would I have gathered you, but ye would not.'

Then the preacher called to all, to children, to youths and maidens, rich and poor, to accept Jesus as God's gift offered to them now, as He was in the midst of them, and the power of the Holy Spirit present to enable them to come 'whosoever will.' And so the sermon of the Monk ended, and he asked " of how many of my dear hearers shall the words of my sad text come true, because they still, like Jerusalem, let life's little day run on to an eternal night? On you now, He is looking in sadness. Jesus draws near, and, as He beholds you, He weeps over you, saying: 'If thou hadst known, even thou, in this thy day, the things which belong unto thy peace, I would receive you, but ye would not.' Oh let us all look in His dear face just now, and trust Him, taking in His fulness as God's gift to us needy sinners, and say, 'Lord, now lettest Thou Thy servant depart in peace according to Thy word, for mine eyes have seen Thy Salvation.'"

Some little time after our first arrival we found ourselves for a week without a servant, so Henry and I took to the cooking, washing, and housemaiding for our party. On the sands, towards Woods Holl, the bathing was most delicious, especially on an early morning, ere the heat of the day set in, for the summer sun was very warm. The new awnings to the piazza, which our thoughtful and generous American patron had specially had put up for us, proved most welcome. In the early part of the summer, the brook to the left of the house swarmed with large fresh herrings, and boys and men used to congregate there in numbers to catch them with a net, or their hands, as bait for blue fish, which were obtainable in "the Sound."

A kind neighbour from the house opposite, who pronounced the Father (to a friend) as a "bully" old man (the American for "jolly"), brought us a present of one of these delicious fish he had caught. His younger brother and his friends around, were continually bringing presents of perch or other fish, which they were lucky enough to capture, while his little sister frequently brought fruit fresh from California. Presents were often sent the Father by the neighbours—tomatoes, lettuces, peas, melons, from one, flowers from another, ice-creams from a third, kindness and proffered hospitality from all. It was most delightful on a bright, starry, moonlight night to sit on the piazza singing hymns and litanies, to wander slowly along the seashore, or to roam listlessly round after a broiling day, called politely by the Americans " mild."

Do my readers not know the delights of mushrooming? By doing so of an early morning, directly after bathing, and thus stealing a march on our neighbours, numbers could be gathered in the fields about us, which added a delicious relish to the breakfast. Whilst in the land of the Pilgrims, invitations to preach and hold Missions continued to pour in on the Father from all parts of the country. The Rector of Dundas, near Hamilton, Canada, who used in the old days, as a boy, to attend the Monastery at Laleham, begged him to visit them. Another clergyman, the Rector of Magog, Quebec, besought a Mission, and stated he had mentioned it to his Bishop, when holding a confirmation there recently, who gave the proposed work his blessing, and stated he should be so pleased if they could persuade the Father to come. The Rector of S. Mark's, Hamilton, also in Canada, pleaded for a few services; the Priest of Methuen, Mass., begged the Father to try and give them a Mission; and the new Rector of Holy Trinity, Shagticoke, the Rector of S. John's, Montreal, Parish Priests of Toronto, Bridport, Connecticut and Providence, New Haven, likewise.

One Saturday the Father and Bro. David crossed over to Nantucket Island and Martha's Vineyard, where the great annual Methodist camp meeting is held. In crossing, on board the steamer, were several Episcopal clergy, and the minister of the Great Tabernacle of Cottage City, who begged the Father to preach for them, and stated if he consented, in spite of the short notice, he should have it packed with thousands.

Whilst resting at Falmouth, the clergy summering all around, including one of the Bishop's chaplains, called on him. From here the Father twice went forth on Missions to Newport on Rhode Island, and once to Canada. Here we spent our first "Independence Day" in the Land of Liberty, of which country the eagle is the emblem. All the shops were shut, no tradesmen called, the town all gay with flags and bunting, flags on the horses' heads, and the children round all letting off fireworks of rejoicing in the bright sunlight, instead of keeping them till night.

Such was our first Independence Day, one of the greatest holidays of the American people.

It was whilst here at Falmouth, resting and gathering strength for the work he was going to do for the Church, having heard so much of Boston's famous preacher, Philips Brooks, that the Father read and studied two volumes of his public sermons, and decided to go and hear him when he reached Boston. We read also the sermons of Heber Newton's father, the sainted priest of Philadelphia, so different to his influential heretic son of to-day.

Many of the townsfolk, who had never seen a Monk before, were quite taken by storm at our advent in their midst, and for a long time did not know what to make of us. The *Boston Globe* of July 13th, says, speaking of us as monks : " As there has never been anything of the kind in Falmouth before, the whole company presents a very striking appearance to the natives and cottagers. Indeed, some people were afraid of them when they first arrived ; " whereas, in the same paper of July 20th, appears: " It was like spirits their softly sandalled feet stepped into the quiet town, and the common dust of the village street was brushed by the monk's black gown.

" Father Ignatius rented (? no) one of the Weld Cottages on the Surf Drive, and there, in a modern seaside villa, established his temporary monastery. . . . Every morning and afternoon the monks take long walks over the sand-dunes of Cape Cod. Their stalwart tread, untrammelled by shoes, sends their black garments flying in most picturesque fashion, while the long knotted rope, impelled by the vigorous motion of their limbs, performs many impromptu gyrations in the air.... Anyone observing the Rev. Father would at once recognise that for him rest would never be for long, that he would find repose only in action.... To the quiet residents at Falmouth the Monkish party is a genuine sensation, a more than nine days' wonder. Every encyclopædia possessed in the town has been unearthed, the dust brushed from its covers, and its pages perused in the hope of finding who and what the Benedictine monks may be." The owner of the cottage where we stayed, and a next-door neighbour, possessing a fine yacht, just come up for the summer from Georgia, took us a lovely cruise along the coast to Hyannis one day.

Though there were constant clambakes held in the neighbourhood, we never experienced this truly American sort of beanfeast. Our most kind benefactress often enabled us by the use of her carriage to go most beautiful drives in the country round. One drive through the Sandwich Woods (where deer still roam in freedom) to Bonny Bray (a lovely cottage in the forest), on the banks of Long Pond or " The Lake of the Golden Cross*," I shall ever remember, as this most charmingly-situated cottage, or, as the Falmouthians call them, "camp," was once offered to us, and had

---

* For the Legend of this Lake *vide* Appendix C.

it not been for its utter seclusion, and the difficulty of access to the village, stores and food providers, I really think we should have rusticated there. On S. Michael's Day we drove to the early Communion at Woods Holl, and, oh ! such a pretty drive it was, through Quissett, with Buzzard's Bay in the distance, glistening in the sunshine. Here the clergyman who celebrated came out directly after service to speak to the Welsh Monk, and proved to be one who had been a choir boy under Father Lowder in the Father's time, and was now working among the colliers in Newfoundland. Never have I experienced such a thunderstorm as it was our lot to witness at Falmouth, never before or since. The scene, though most awful in its solemnity, was most superbly grand. Crash after crash shook the house, and made every board and rafter echo and re-echo as if it must part asunder. The earth trembled, the most gorgeous and vivid lightning lighting up all around, poured like streams of liquid fire from the black clouds above. Though magnificent to watch, the extreme bluey whiteness of the flashes, like electric light, were most dazzling to the eyes. This was indeed worthy of being called a thunderstorm, one in comparison with which all our English storms are but child's play.

A description of Falmouth and the neighbourhood, from a guide book* will, I think, be a fitting conclu-

---

* " Pilgrim Land." Published by The Old Colony Railway Company.

sion to this chapter, as we shall deal especially in the next with the "Falmouth Boys," and getting lost in the woods. "Whether one begins the traversing of the shores of Buzzard's Bay from the New Bedford or the Woods Holl termini, all the same he finds successions of the finest beach, and the fairest combination of land and water scenery, cool forest driveways; innumerable lakes and ponds for fishing and fowling, streams for 'trouting,' historic hills for climbing (for we are on the ground our Pilgrim Fathers trod) and plains for exploration; and above and beyond all, a summer climate of unequalled sanitary advantages; air bracing and invigorating like magic tonics; bubbling springs of purest water at every turn; and miles upon miles of the finest beaches anywhere to be found in existence for salt or fresh water bathing. Behold the glorious beauties of its frowning bluffs; its wooded hills coming down often to the water's edge; its white, gleaming beaches, and its bays, coves, harbours, and roadsteads. The prevailing forest growth for all the Cape below Sandwich and Falmouth is the dwarf pitch pine, the needles of which, full of highly-spiced perfumes and resinous juice, add much to the health-giving recreative qualities of the section. In Sandwich, Falmouth, and Barnstable the Quaker element abounds with all that is implied of thrift, orderly life, and those attributes of progressive, well-to-do humanity, which mean so much wherever they are found. Marshpee (the site of several large cranberry bogs, for the growth of which fruit Cape Cod is famous), is the last remaining home of the Indian representatives on the mainland of Southern Massachusetts, but the specimens left present more of the social domestic features of the white, than of their original tribes."

The little town, or, as I prefer to call it, village (as this gives a better idea of its size to the English reader) of Falmouth is rich in the possession of three churches—an Episcopal, Methodist, and Congregational or Orthodox, for the latter claim to be *the* Church of the country, and all others to be dissenters, as we shall see in our chapter on Boston. Every Sunday at service time the village street outside the two former, is always lined with a goodly stream of carriages, most Americans preferring driving to walking when they are able. It was just here that I met the first ox-waggon, drawn by four huge oxen, carrying timber. The nearest Roman Catholic place of worship where service is held once a month, is at Woods Holl.

It will interest many readers to know that besides Massachusetts being a Prohibition State, *i.e.*, where no wines, beer, spirits, or intoxicating drinks are allowed to be sold, save at chemists, in its confines, so neither are any horses allowed to have their tails or manes cut or to be otherwise ill-treated to suit the ever-varying freaks of fashionable society. The first Sunday I went to church I was very much surprised to notice that scarcely anyone kneels, or attempts to, for the prayers, in spite of the invitation "let us *kneel* before the Lord our Maker." Strange, too, it was to find in their Prayer-Books such alteration as a permission to sing the Gloria in Excelsis after the Psalms at Morning and Evening Prayer, to recite the Apostles' or Nicene Creed at either, substituting for the words, " He descended into Hell," " He descended into the place of departed spirits," in churches where the former expression is objected to. Then, too, the usual Psalms appointed for the day need not (oh dear no) be used at Matins or Evensong, but " selections," compiled specially for the American Church may be recited instead. The " Our Father," at the commencement of the Communion, may be omitted, some extra words of prayer are tacked on to the Commandments, and the Consecration Prayer, and, until recently, the Hymn of our Lady (*i.e.*, The Magnificat), was omitted entirely from the Prayer Book. At S. Barnabas there were only morning and afternoon services on Sunday, an evening one on Fridays, and Early Celebration of the Blessed Sacrament on Saints' Days, the Mid-day Mass being once a month.

CHAPTER IV.

FALMOUTH CONTINUED — MORE SERVICES — FALMOUTH BOYS—LOST IN THE WOODS.

IN response to a generally-expressed wish of the people to hear the Father preach again, the Town Hall was hired, and arrangements made for a sermon on Sunday evening, August 10th, a Devotional meeting the next night, and an oration, in answer to the question, "Why are you a Monk?"* on the Thursday.

But when the time arrived, owing to excessive wet weather, the Sunday service, at the last moment, was unable to be held, and postponed for a week, though a number had braved the elements in order to be present. This being the case, great uncertainty prevailed in the village, as to whether the subsequent addresses would be given, and consequently the congregations did not assume the proportions they otherwise probably would have done. These were the Welsh Benedictine's last public words in Falmouth. As a specimen of opinions formed at these last Falmouth services, I have culled the following from the *Boston Budget* of September 13th :—

---

*This is published by the Monks of Llanthony Abbey, 6½d., post free.

"I wish I could learn the secret of Father Ignatius's power over an audience. The hall was filled with a curious and expectant crowd. A woman, in black, with a peculiar bonnet, having a veil falling from its crown, entered from the rear of the hall. This was the one woman with the monks. She looked as if she had much determination, and intellectuality as well. She took a front seat. At the moment appointed, a handsome monk entered the hall from the side door; a little later, another (say twenty-four years old), in a long, graceful robe, with thick black hair and handsome features; in the aisles, with great modesty and gentleness of demeanour, the private secretary, dressed like other men, showed people to their seats. This, too, was a fine-looking young man.

"Well, the door on the stage opened, and a thin man, of medium height, with closely-shaven head and face, long black gown, the knotted rope and beads and cross at his waist, bare feet, and hooded cloak, stepped quickly forward. He knelt a moment in silent prayer, then arose, and asked all to join in a familiar hymn. He went to an organ, and, seizing a book, read a verse of the hymn, then played and sang, repeating this performance for each verse. The reading was strange and fascinating. His voice in singing was mellow and sweet, and he sang in a way peculiar to himself. He then read from the Bible, and preached his sermon.

"But the man! He was on fire with his subject. He was elegant in his delivery, rapid in utterance, and filled with a sort of yearning sweetness which made every one who heard him, say they loved him. His eyes lighted up beautifully, his mouth was small, and very sweet in expression. He had a way of pausing on a word, and then tripping, as it were, on other words, which gave peculiar emphasis. His enunciation was very distinct, and there was a spirituality in his very presence. But how the words poured from his lips! And always so apt and choice in expressing what he intended. His intensity gave me a headache all the next day, for it took straight hold of every nerve in my body. If monks are like Father Ignatius, let me sit at their feet."

It was here that we gained our first insight into the happy — yes, and luxuriant—life of American children. Almost every child, boy or girl, you met, though barely in their teens, possessed their own pony-carriage, pony, or horse, with which they scoured the surrounding country, and of a hot summer's afternoon enjoyed the breezes of the Surf Drive. As to their costumes, in most cases those of the fair portion were both cool-looking and simple, while their younger sisters, dressed in the quaint Old Mother Hubbard style and long dresses, was a pleasing change. The boys (oh! how nice and cool they must have been!) rejoiced in *nothing* but a white, striped, or spotted flannel blouse and knickerbockers, fastened at the waist with a cricket-belt—knickerbockers all over the States, even for youths and men, seeming to be a prevailing custom.

Talking of American children and their peculiarities, whilst travelling through the States I especially noticed that every child, no matter *how* young—just out of babyhood—wore a ring. In the cities, roller-skating and tricycling seemed to be their chief and usual amusement, this being caused in a great way probably by many newspapers and certain firms offering tricycles, &c., to all who obtained a certain number of new subscribers to their paper, &c.

Whilst in Falmouth the Father visited the school —I now really forget, whether it was called the Grammar or High School, but that does not matter— in the dinner hour, and was surprised to find it consisted of boys and girls of the middle-class, well into their teens, who were romping about together as if they were children of a much younger age.

All through the summer a small school, open for about an hour each morning, that the children of the visitors should not quite forget all their arithmetic and history, was maintained in an old ivy grown windmill, in the grounds of a cottager on the shores of the lake.

Whilst the Father was away in Newport and in Canada, Henry and I gave two tea-parties to the boys, and so, in describing our simple evening's amusements, I want to try and give you some of our own personal experiences with them. In issuing the invitations, various titles were tacked on to all their names, and when they departed homewards, after a simple tea and a number of games, they all expressed themselves as highly pleased with their evening's entertainment.

The games consisted of truly British tugs-of-war, foot-races, hide and seek in the piazzas and empty houses round, and the game, "*strike a light*," over the surrounding common and fields at night. Our hospitality was returned by an invitation for a sail on Salt Pond, the sail itself being manœuvred by a number of boys, none of whom seemed to be able to keep still, till one was made to walk the plank, and set adrift without oars or anything. After this, no day passed without a visit from them for a game, a talk, or a walk. But I must hurry on to the great adventure of our summer rest—the being lost in the woods with a tribe of three of them, one of the boys being but a child of seven; and though a full account appeared in the next issue of the local paper, instead of using the boys' proper names, we will designate them Edmund, Harold, and Wilfrid.

It was a bright autumn afternoon, a little after three, that Henry, the three boys and I, started for a ramble through the Beebee Woods (part of the Sandwich Forest, which stretches for 15 miles), on an exploring expedition, to find the renowned Punch Bowl Pond, which is hidden in a dell amongst the

thickest under-growth of the centre of the Woods.
Edmund was armed with a thick stick, Harold had a
whip with a leather lash, and Wilfred a dagger
Edmund had cut out, whereas I carried a long jumping pole as a walking staff, to keep my party in order
and to clear the way somewhat when necessary. The
woods were gay with the crimson and yellow of the
autumn foliage. " The Beauty of Dying " surrounded
us' on all sides. The luxuriant Virginian creeper,
in its blood red dress, climbing the stately pines, and
suspended in gorgeous festoons in the sunlight from
the overhanging branches, the many-hued mosses
and lichens, russet and grey, golden, red, and brown,
the crimson and purple leaves of the bramble bushes,
the green and dead-gold fern, all spoke of "the
Beauty of Dying." The autumn of life, when Man's
Immortal Soul is about to rejoin its Maker in the
Perfect Garden and Beautiful Green Pastures of the
Heavenly Home. Oh ! the beauty and brilliancy of the
autumnal tints in " the Pilgrim Land ! " How they
excel and far surpass what it is our lot to see at home,
how they glisten and flash in the distance, in masses,
of brilliant colour beneath the autumn sun. Such
blazes of beautifully blended tints as would send many
an artist into raptures, and if painted few would
believe to be real, but pronounce them overdone and
unnatural. To return to our expedition. We all
started off in the best of spirits, entering the woods
through the " Cedar Gate," wending our way up a
shady, moss-grown glade, past " The Robbers' Cave,"

and " The Old Man Clothed in Leather," leaving " The Two Ponds," and " Riddle Hill" on our left, down a soft woodland avenue, past " Unker's (the old Indian Chief) Grave," we gradually approached our destination, the far-famed Punch Bowl, the deepest pond near Falmouth, so closely-hidden and difficult to find that, though teeming with fish, they are left in peace by the anglers of the day.

As we neared the pond, the brush and undergrowth, through which a hardly-visible path wound zigzag, grew taller and denser—so thick in some parts that we had difficulty to force our way through, which was also occasionally blocked by the low boughs of a tree, beneath which we had to crawl in a most undignified manner. Overhead, the song of the birds, and the occasional screech of the catbird, woke the echoes of the woodland glades, whilst grey and black squirrels sported amongst the branches of the forest trees. Warblers of all kinds in profusion surrounded us, singing the praise of their Creator. Our path was very winding, and instead of carefully marking, or even observing our way, caution and prudence gave way to jollity, pleasure, and happy thoughtlessness. The woods were quite strange ground to Henry and me, but the boys, who had often trodden their mossy sward before and had volunteered to be our guides, now we had got into the wild thickets, far from any visible path, schemed how they might elude and forsake us. Consequently, it was necessary to keep a keen eye on the movements of these American "lovers of mischief," who would continually run off into the brush, and dodge us, until pursued, captured, and brought back. Occupied thus, and, at the same time, carrying on a most animated historical and political conversation as to the relative merits of England and America, brought out once more the learning and precociousness of American children, who, besides being never shy, are always prepared to talk on any subject, presumably on account of their reading the papers so much. Thus, at length the Punch Bowl was reached, and breaking through the brushwood that clothes the lakelet's edge, the scene before us was entrancingly lovely—the water smooth and glistening in the sun, reflecting in her mirror the crimson and yellow foliage of her autumn-dressed banks. After a rest beneath the trees on her shore we began to wend our steps homewards, but soon lost all trace of the path, or any path, and found ourselves wandering round and round back to the place we started from. The shades of night began to creep on apace. All at once the truth flashed upon us—" we were lost," and should probably have to wait till morning, or until rescued by a search party. One of the boys proposed we should listen for the whistle of the six o'clock train, so as to ascertain in which direction home lay, from which we knew we were not very far, though the forest stretched for fifteen miles. The younger members of our party now began to get frightened, but Edmund proved himself the stay and comfort of the party, cheering and caring for the younger brethren. He apparently knew no fear, and when, on having climbed a pine-clad hillock, it being too dark to see our steps any further, we were compelled to settle down for the night, he set to work to see the children comfortably and warmly settled. It was very dark—we could not see one another. The drops of rain and distant roll of thunder warned us a storm was coming on, and we should probably have a soaking wet night in the woods. At length it burst upon us, but to our joy, and in answer to a prayer we had all previously knelt to offer to our Creator and Kind Father, it soon cleared away for a time.

Though so very dark it was barely six o'clock, and we knew no search-party would be organized before nine, so three hours had to be spent in the woods, and, despite our plight, I think the whole party will agree they were a very pleasant three hours, whiled away with songs, stories, adventures, and experiences, to keep the young ones bright and happy.

It was just about nine that we caught the first sound of a horn in the distance, making known to us that searchers were out seeking us, though it was not until after we got safely home that we learned what a stir and commotion our disappearance had made in the village. Friends and neighbours had rushed from house to house, one to have all the church and chapel bells of the place rung in alarm to call the people together to organize and form search parties. Another had rushed off to a gentleman's house on the border of the woods, and though that night they had guests for a card-party, the guests dispersed to search the wood with horns and lanterns, and we heard the horns tooting in the distance long after we were safely esconced at home.

Little we thought, as we waited quietly to be found, longing for daylight, that the alarm-bells would be rung, and the village turn out a hue and cry after us. When the first notes of the horn sounded in our ears, the boys expressed disappointment at being found so soon, one declaring: "They've spoilt our fun by not leaving us till morning." As the friendly horn drew nearer, Edmund recognised its tuneful notes as his dinner-horn, and it was not long ere we saw the spark of light from a lantern—all having called in unison at the tops of their voices in reply to the horn—twinkling like a will o'-the-wisp amongst the trees, and gradually ascending our hill. Thus our adventure in the woods was over, without any untoward result; and soon we were all safe home, warming ourselves and enjoying our supper. Oh! how it rained that night. Lying in bed, and listening to the rain, what thoughts of gratitude to God filled our breast for not having left us out in it.

Next morning several callers arrived, with kind inquiries as to how we were, and, on going into the village, the whole place was found ringing with the tale, and every one asking questions, desirous of hearing our experiences. So pestered were the boys themselves with questions, that for some time after they shrunk from going into the village. Notwithstanding their adventure of the previous day, the very next morning, when they came to see us, they wanted to go in the woods again, and find the place where we were lost and slept.

Now, before concluding this chapter, I must not forget to give you a brief description of a truly local American amusement, called "Nantucket hidings," as two of these interesting games took place during our sojourn in the lovely little village on Cape Cod. The young people of the place enjoy the fun, which consists, on a certain afternoon, of all the fair portion of the families hiding together in some house or other within certain affixed limits.

Then, in the evening, the boys, with lanterns, go forth in bands and search for them. If they find them, the girls are obliged, on an early evening, to cook and give the boys a supper; whereas, if they fail, the boys have to give it to the girls. On one of these occasions some of the young searchers came and wished to search our house, as they are generally granted the right to inspect and examine any suspected house.

It was whilst here at Falmouth that a gentleman from the North wrote, begging the Father to visit Philadelphia and address the Annual Convention of

E

the S. Andrew's Brotherhood, which was about to gather there from all parts of the States and Canada; but as the date was during the already advertised Mission in Boston, it was impossible.

Some of the truly American words which we first heard here puzzled one much at first to interpret. On remarking a certain train daily whizzing past, *en route* for Boston, fancy being told, "Oh! that's the Dude's train!" So, never having heard of "the Dude," it was natural to ask what that "creature was. Imagine our surprise on being told it was our word "swell"—slangily often designated "masher" —Americanized, in fact. The train was a "subscription" one, run in the summer months by Boston business men, whose families imbibed the invigorating air of Cape Cod's seaside resorts.

Then, too, you may expect to hear our English words "bully" and "daisy" used in quite a different sense, meaning in America "jolly" and "fine; clever, etc.;" whereas, if you tell anyone to take something, and put it in your room, you must not be surprised if you are asked where they shall "locate" it. Should you wish a fire lit, or a room tidied, when done your "help" will inform you, it is "fixed." As you wend your way southwards, where warmth and hospitality to the traveller increases, when the time comes to wish your friends farewell, you will hear the quaint expression, "I must *tell* you good-bye," and the quaint "aha" of assent to everything you say.

In the country of "the Stars and Stripes," if anyone is especially pleased with anything, you will hear they were quite "enthused"; and if it is their privilege to listen to a grand sermon or interesting lecture you will be informed the orator was "a lovely man."

To many who visit Columbia for the first time these quaint American expressions *may* seem "excessively silly"; but silly or not silly, they are by no means so unpleasant and uncomfortable as to be continually "store" or stared at by everyone you meet.

Truly, as our American cousins say, Columbia, the country of which "the heagle is the hemblem," possesses "more crookeder rivers and forkeder lightnins" than it falls to the lot of "the old folks at home" ever to see.

CHAPTER V.

Newport, Rhode Island.

IT was whilst resting at Falmouth that the good Rector of S. George's, Newport, who had known the Father in by-gone days in the Old Country, sent to ask him to come and preach in the "Brighton of America," where the *elite* of the States yearly gather in summer. Nothing was said about "credentials," or the Bishop's sanction, it being taken for granted that as his Lordship, when visiting the town, was always the guest of the Rector of S. George's, he would not be likely to object to any clergyman, invited by him, officiating in the parish. Besides, as there were to be but two services in the church, and the evening service in a hall (for which purpose Evensong in Church was omitted), and as the Canons of the Anglican or mother Church permit any clergman to preach for " two consecutive Sundays " in a strange diocese without acquainting the Bishop thereof, it was hardly deemed necessary in this case, to trouble the Representative of the Apostles, and Shepherd of the Souls of Men, in the Rhode Island Diocese. So the services were held, the sermon in the morning being on " Righteousness—What is it ? " while that of the afternoon was on " Baptised into Christ, Dead indeed unto Sin ;" and the evening subject, in the Masonic Hall, was "The Song in the Land of Judah." The following little paragraph appeared in " *The Newport Daily News*" of the previous day :

" In these days of every-day preaching, which for many years may be considered to have been a lost art, or one ignored or set aside, it was refreshing and inspiring to hear a trumpet blast of graceful and impassioned eloquence from Father Ignatius. It was no downpulling or glorification of any religious sect, but a rousing appeal for the reception of the precepts, example, beatitudes and consolations of the Morning Star of Hope and Love, that for nearly nineteen centuries has pierced this old Planet with its Heavenly influence. We advise the lovers of sacred themes and the inspiring influence of a wide-awake orator to go and hear him to-morrow, when he will preach at St. George's Church, as advertised."

In his sermon on " The Song in the Land of Judah," the British Monk took for his text, Isaiah xxvi. 1, 2. He drew a most vivid picture of the remarkable ancestry of Jesus Christ—the ancestry composed of Patriarchs, Prophets, Psalmists; the ancestry that should produce One for Whom the whole world, east and west, looked, the One Who should be God Almighty; the Reformer Who should bring 'the Golden Age' into the midst of a troubled, restless, weary world. The little land of Judah was not so big as our Wales, but it contained the Kernel of the world's

Hope, and was to be the cradle from whence true Liberty, Equality, and Fraternity should spring and spread. The song in the land of Judah was a song of peace and knowledge, a song of Atonement between the poor rebel-man, and the Great Creator of the Universe; a song of reconciliation between the sinner and the All-Holy Judge; a song of Deliverance, of Perfect Peace, of Light and Everlasting Love. All the civilized world had tried to crush the people in the little land of Judah, and the song that should be sung when Christ was born. They tried in vain; no power could still the song, no power could scatter the people of the land or prevent Christ from being produced there. Babylon and Nineveh, Egypt, Syria, and Greece, all tried to crush the Jew, but Judah was under the special protection of God, and so they failed. Christ has triumphed over the mighty Cæsars, for He must do the work He came to do, and *is* doing now, spreading ' the Music of Jerusalem '—the Gospel of Peace. We have a strong city; Salvation will God appoint for walls and bulwarks. Christ is *our* City; Christ *our* Bulwarks. That little Land of Judah produced God's Christ, though not as a Monarch's Babe, but as the Child of the poor peasant maiden, Mary. Yet *That* Child was to overthrow kingdoms, conquer the world, and draw out a people to Himself. He is doing it now. Christ Jesus is *as much* a match for the world in the *nineteenth* century as ever—*now*, as when in the persons of the Martyrs of the Amphitheatre and Coliseum at Rome, He confounded the

Consuls and Prefects. Jesus Christ, the long-looked-for Reformer has come—has come at last! The promise made to our first parents in the Garden of Eden is fulfilled. The work, for which the Jewish nation was kept together, is done. Israel is scattered throughout the world, an *unwilling witness* to the historical reality and claims of Christ. Is there *any* nation like the Jews upon the face of the globe, scattered, but still unique as a people, and never amalgamated with those, amongst whom their lot is cast? The Jew is a witness, an historical witness, to the claims of Jesus Christ, and wherever he goes he carries That Blood on his hands, of which his forefathers said ' His Blood be upon us and upon our children.'

" The Land of Judah, now, is the Church of Jesus, the company of all those who know Him Whom they have believed, the company, of saved believers made 'whiter than snow' in the Blood of the Lamb. Our Salvation *was finished* when from the Cross, on Calvary, His life's work accomplished, the Saviour said, 'It is *finished!*' He says it, and I *believe* His Word, because *He* says so. It is finished, and it has nothing to do with us or our feelings. We have only to accept it, and then it is CHRIST that *keeps* the Believer, and not the Believer himself. He is then one of *the* Church against which the Gates of Hell shall ne'er prevail. All that know Jesus as their own Saviour, are ready to shake hands with one another, irrespective of sect, as brethren in ' Christ.'

"Then, to come nearer home, the Believer's heart is a little land of Judah, in which the music of Jerusalem, once started, shall never cease below till, in sweeter strains, it echoes up above in the Heavenly Jerusalem, in the unveiled presence of the King. Jesus is the wall between the Believer and Hell, sin, or judgment, and a strong wall, indeed, He is—one that in the fiercest storm can never shake or fail."

The service concluded with the hymn, "All hail the power of Jesu's name," which was most heartily sung by the attentive congregation.

This was but a flying visit from the Father, for almost before it was generally known he was in the town, he had preached and gone—gone but to return with greater zeal and renewed strength for a ten-days' Mission in September. But in spite of his short visit this time, the Rector of S. John's Church sent to ask him to preach for them, or if he was engaged, to "send one of his accompanying monks."

The Bishop now found himself placed in an awkward position, having allowed the Father to preach without asking for any "credentials," as his Lordship of the neighbouring diocese of Massachusetts had just closed the doors of the Episcopal Churches against him. The consequence was that at Bishop Clarke's desire the Father cabled to England to the Bishop of Bath and Wells, for a certificate of his ordination, which, on receipt, was duly forwarded to his lordship through the Rector of S. George's, and declared as fully satisfying the American canons.

In the meantime, two letters had been received from the good rector on the subject of making known the Bishop's feelings. In the first, on August 8th, he wrote: "The action of the Bishop of Mass. has placed me in such a position, that to obey the canons, and protect the Bishop, I had to see him, and act under advice. I was unable to see him until late yesterday. He is exceedingly kind, and says: 'Write your friend Father Ignatius, that his not being able to present his ordination papers, need not be any obstacle if he will *cable* to his Bishop, to send a letter stating he is a deacon of good standing in his diocese; but we must obey the laws of the Church. Then I shall be *glad* to have him officiate and preach in my diocese.'"

In the second letter, on August 13th, the Rector wrote: "I am glad to hear you have cabled for copy of the ordination. They will meet all the canonical requirements, and Bishop Clarke tells me, that will be all that is needful. . . . The papers you so kindly sent me with the remarks upon your work, I shall send to the 'Standard of the Cross,' which had an article lately upon you and your work,* and the *Bishop said* it *should* be answered. . . . I read your

---

*Now in my possession.

letter and reply to the Bishop (Paddock, of Massachusetts), and his letter to you, to Bishop Clarke, and he was greatly delighted with what you wrote." Now I want my readers to compare the Bishop's welcome here to the Father, with his subsequent action, found at the close of this chapter.

Newport and Saratoga are the Brighton and Scarborough of America, where the votaries and devotees of fashion gather summer after summer from all parts of the States and Canada, spending their days and nights in one unceasing whirl of gaiety and frivolity—garden parties, picnics, dinners, balls, and moonlight drives or sails in endless profusion, each one vieing to out-do the other in originality and magnificence. Though called "The Cottage City," the elaborate and stately mansions, of wood, are anything but cottages. Here, all the queens of American society and fashion, with their numerous trains of attendants and followers, gather annually, giving up their precious days and hours, which pass so swiftly by for ever, to the empty pleasures and frivolities of the world.

The meet of the Coaching Club had come, and the Newport season was fast drawing to a close, when the Father suddenly appeared, as a second John the Baptist in their midst, and proclaimed a halt, pointing them out the way of salvation, and preaching repentance and the forgiveness of sins. Very distasteful this must have been to some, fresh from the dance or the theatre, to be reminded that ere long, one day, they must die, and to be asked whether they knew for whence they were bound—hurrying on, day after day, *nearer* and *nearer* heaven *or* hell. They were on the road to one *or* the other (for there was no third or middle place), and they *knew* which. Others there were, who had been *forced* by ambitious worldly parents into the ceaseless whirl of society's vain pleasures, and who were sick and heartily tired of them. To the souls of such as these, the message of the gospel of God's love, came as a sweet, refreshing shower.

It was on August 31st that the Father commenced his Ten Days' Mission, with the Bishop's blessing, in S. George's Church, choosing as his evening subjects: "Jesus and the Man of Business," "Jesus and the Man of Wealth," "Jesus and the Religious Man," "Jesus and the Man with the Unclean Spirit," "Jesus Christ and the Nineteenth Century," "Jesus, and the Woman taken in Adultery."

The first sermon on the Sunday morning was on "Jonah's Mission to Nineveh," while in the afternoon and evening respectively, "Jesus weeping over Jerusalem," and "God's love for the World," formed the subjects of most eloquent and soul-stirring discourses from the strange monk. The concluding sermons, on Sunday, September 7th, were on "The Great Promise Fulfilled," "No Oil," and "Jesus at Bethany, or the Results of the Mission."

I think the following quotations from Boston papers will show a little, the great work, the monk—erratic though he might be deemed—from across the water, was enabled by the Spirit of God to do for the salvation of immortal souls, in worldly, pleasure-seeking Newport. From " *The Newport Observer,*" September 13th, I have culled the following : " Last Sunday, September 7th, Father Ignatius concluded an Eight Days' Mission in S. George's Church, Newport. In the morning the church was filled by a very fashionable congregation, and additional seats had to be supplied from the adjoining schools to accommodate the ' cottagers.' . . . Among the congregation was a very venerable-looking Bishop, who, we are told, sent most affectionate and sympathetic messages to the monk, hoping he would come and preach ' Christ Crucified' in his own diocese. In the evening the service began at 7.45, but long before that time the church was packed by a great crowd of people. Then the street became crowded, and the people positively stood in crowds round the whole church, listening at the windows. Still the people streamed towards the church, and large numbers of carriages attempted in vain, to deposit their contents at the church doors, and had to drive away, finding the crowd so great. The Rector of S. George's read the evening service in a most impressive and devotional manner, and his full voice reached the ears of the whole of the crowded congregation. The choir was crowded with men and boys in surplices, as well as the officiating clergy."

"*The Falmouth Local*" of September 12th copied from "*The Boston Herald*" a report, from which I have clipped the following:

"He made a pathetic and powerful appeal at the close, and his dramatic attitude, eloquence, polished diction and manners, together with his earnestness, held his audience spellbound. Many were moved to tears, and it was apparent, that the man, with shaved head and coarse sandals, was very near to the people, and that *even* in *giddy* Newport, he had made a wonderful impression. Such a scene, as was witnessed here to-night, could not be placed in cold type, before the readers of the *Herald*. The night was hot, but the audience remained almost motionless for one hour and a-half. He is an able orator, but he appears wholly unconscious of his ability to electrify his hearers, and his modesty and sunny countenance will *never* be forgotten. His pen picture of Mary Magdalene is deserving of attention, and, were it spread broadcast, would result in much good."

The following account from "*The Boston Sunday Herald*," September 14th, is rather more detailed:

"I have just returned from Newport, and would like to lay before your readers a brief *resumé* of the great work accomplished there by Father Ignatius.

"The Welsh Monk's visit was ended when I left, and he has returned again to the cottage at Falmouth. Although his visit was coterminous with the gayest part of the season, S. George's Church was well attended on every week-day.

"Last Sunday the multitudes that filled the church and grounds around it, and the streets in front of it, proved that a growing and very extraordinary enthusiasm had been aroused. Far larger numbers failed to gain admission to the church than those who did find room.

"The seats were literally packed, and all the spaces available for additional benches were supplied from the schools next the church. The aisles were thronged throughout the services by standing crowds, who seemed callous alike of heat and fatigue.

"The crush round the church doors was immense, the large porches and ante-chambers choked with throngs of people. Round the church windows, listening congregations remained the whole of the long services. The street was full of carriages and people, and numbers of teams full of would-be church-goers, not being able to get to the church doors, drove away.

"I hear that Father Ignatius has had ample reason to be satisfied with the results of his week's work, and doubtless believing, as he does, that 'the Holy Ghost is the only force for bringing home the gospel to men's hearts,' he is comforted by the reflection that the 'power of God' has been working in S. George's Church, Newport, despite the strong grip with which the 'world, the flesh, and the devil, have been holding so many captive in 'the city of fashion by the sea.'

"It is said that many persons have been deeply affected; for instance, a man who was a professed infidel was seen weeping in the church, and he who had sneered contemptuously at the 'Man of Nazareth' and His claims, left S. George's owning His power, and subdued by His love.

"One man sent Father Ignatius word: 'Tell him I'd sooner hear him than Beecher, and if he will come to New York and open a great tabernacle he will make his fortune in no time.'

"Another man in the street exclaimed aloud: 'Never heard anything like it in my life—I shall never forget it.'

"The men were deeply affected, even to tears—well-known men of the world many of them were.

"I heard of one young lady, engaged the next evening for a ball, who entirely refused ever to go to a dance again, and so resolving to act upon her resolution at once, although her family were indignant at her determination.

"On the last Sunday morning the subject dealt with, was: 'Jesus Christ as the great primeval promise of God to a restless and hungering humanity.'

"The subject was treated historically, pictorially, and practically.

"The afternoon text was from Matt. xxv. : 'No oil.' The great want of the religion and profession in the 19th century, and of the preaching in the churches, too, was the 'oil,' the presence and power of the Holy Ghost.

"Of course, incidentally, the 'coming of the bridegroom at midnight,' the second advent of Christ, when things were blackest and darkest, was largely dwelt upon.

"In the evening the sensation was immense during the sermon on 'Jesus at Bethany'—the dead Lazarus sitting alive at His side, the wandering Magdalene, restored to her home in Bethany again, sitting at his feet. And then the picture reproduced in S. George's Church that night—then and there—and the application came upon the crowd, already strained to a high pitch of nervous tension, with overwhelming force. There now in their midst was the *same* Jesus; there now, were men till lately 'dead in trespasses and sin,' dead intellectually and morally to all things spiritual, pure, eternal—now through the power of the Holy Ghost enjoying the Gospel supper at the side of Jesus, set free in the life of His salvation.

"And were there no Magdalens there as well, wooed and won home again to purity and God, by the voice of Jesus in the Gospel, by the almighty touch of His spirit of power?

"Yes, yes, indeed, there were, for the gospel wrought its work of love in human lives to-day, with the selfsame power as of yore, bringing pardon, cleansing, gladness, rest and peace to the sinful, tired hearts of weary, sinful men.

"Tears were falling from many eyes, and a stillness rested on the thronged church that was solemn indeed.

"Father Ignatius, however, after kneeling some time in silent prayer, left the church for the vestry, attended by the brother who accompanied him. After his three extempore orations in one day, he was no doubt physically much exhausted.

"He promised to begin a Mission in Boston at Horticultural Hall the first week in November. It would have been conducted in a church, as at Newport, only the Bishop of Massachusetts, unlike other bishops in the State, opposes Father Ignatius on the ground that he has revived monasticism in the Church of England.

" The Bishop of Rhode Island was perfectly content that the Monk should preach at St. George's, and other Bishops in America have invited him to preach in their dioceses, sending him beforehand their blessing and goodwill, while Bishop Paddock places him under the severest ban—excluding him unheard from the pulpits of Massachusetts."

No sooner was his work concluded at Newport, than the Father received a most urgent invitation from the Rector of S. Mark's, Warren, R.I.

It was not until two months after* the Father's work was done in Newport, and he had departed for good to other fields, that Bishop Clarke, instigated by the Bishop of Massachusetts, revoked the licence he had *never* given him—though rather late in the day, as all his work in the diocese was done—publishing the inhibition in the chief papers, without communicating in any way with the Father, or giving any reasons till asked for closing the churches of the diocese against him. On the Father writing to enquire the cause, His Lordship replied in part as follows :—

"After I was informed that you had been preaching in Newport without my consent or knowledge, I said to Dr. Gilliat that I must have evidence of your being in regular orders, before you should officiate again, and when this evidence was obtained by telegraph, I consented *verbally* to your fulfilling the engagement made, for a Mission in S. George's Chapel. Your correspondence with Bishop Paddock, which I heard in part, gave me no such comprehension . . . . of the most extraordinary statements of miracles contained in your published orations."†

---

* 24th November.

† It was commonly reported in Boston that Dr. Clarke was himself both a believer in the miraculous as well as the Spiritualistic and had more than once to friends related his own experiences.

This occurring as it did, in the midst of the Boston Mission, and the stir caused by the action of the Bishop of Massachusetts with regard to the Father, added to the excitement, and the papers all over the country teemed with paragraphs as to what had happened, and surmises as to how the next Bishop, whose diocese the Father might visit, would treat him. Whilst in Newport both Bishop Whipple of Minnesota and Bishop Leonard of Ohio had attended the Father's sermons at S. George's, and sent him kind messages of welcome if he should visit either of their respective dioceses. Soon after returning to Falmouth, the Rector of S. John's, Providence, and also one from Bridport, Connecticut, wrote begging for services.

CHAPTER VI.

CANADA—MAGOG—QUEBEC.

IT was on the 1st of October that the Rev. Father and Brother David once more sallied forth from Falmouth to do work for Jesus, and sound the Gospel tocsin in another portion of the New World. This time, with the blessing of the grand old Welsh Bishop of Quebec,* the Father had arranged to hold a mission in St. Luke's Church, Magog, beneath the British flag of our most gracious Queen's Canadian dominions. The letter containing the invitation to hold the Mission runs—" You will have a most hearty welcome from all, even those not belonging to the Church. Methodists, Advents, and Baptists, all say ' Oh ! do get the Father here, he will do untold good amongst our boys." *En route* they spent a few hours at Plymouth, in New Hampshire, a most beautiful spot, which must not be confused with the celebrated Plymouth in Massachusetts. Here they were most kindly received at the Episcopal College.

But now we must proceed with the Father on his journey to Magog, that little manufacturing town so prettily situated on the shores of Memphis Magog

---

* Dr. Williams, R.I.P., 1892.

Lake, at the foot of Mount Orford, the highest mountain in Canada, and hemmed in by mountains. The Welsh Monk's Mission here was to last but three days, commencing on Sunday, October 5th, when the morning subject was "The Mission of the Church of Jesus to the World;" in the afternoon, "The World by Wisdom knew not God;" and that of the evening sermon, "The Sound of the Abundance of Rain." On Monday afternoon he had promised to speak on "What is a Christian?" and in the evening about "Jesus Christ and the Man of Business." Tuesday, in the afternoon, the Father spoke to Christians on "Dear Children of Light," and in the evening, his farewell message of the Gospel, to those who had during the past few days hung with tender, eager longing, in love, upon the words of peace and rest that fell from his lips, was on "Jesus Satisfying the Hungry Multitude." The Mission, which will never, it is said, be forgotten by those who attended it in Magog, closed with an early celebration of the Holy Eucharist on Wednesday morning. Numbers came in from the backwoods and homesteads, as well as from the towns and villages round, to attend the Mission, the Rector having advertised an open house and plain refreshments "for the Love of Jesus" to all attending the services from a distance. At this Mission the true power of Christian love and brotherhood was manifested, the Methodists and Roman Catholics vieing with one another in lending seats and forms to accommodate the crowds that at each service filled the little wooden church to overflowing. Numerous letters of wonderful blessing, pardon and peace found at the services, were received by the Father, and when he left a crowd of grateful souls gathered at the station to bid him God-speed; but the following quotations from " *The Magog News,*" of October 18th, will give a little idea of the Mission:

"Magogian hearts have throbbed and warmed towards Father Ignatius, such as they have never warmed towards any man before. They found an outlet in presenting the Rev. Father with an illuminated address."

" We understand that an illuminated address is to be sent to the Rev. Father Ignatius expressive of the general gratitude felt for the recent mission services, and that a handsome memorial altar-cross is to be placed in the church.

" The great event of the past week was the mission held by the Rev. Father Ignatius. The services lasted three days (Sunday, Monday, and Tuesday) concluding with an early celebration of the Holy Communion on Wednesday. Never was S. Luke's Church so packed; seats had to be crowded in till there was no room for kneeling. The preacher held his hearers spell-bound while with words of fire and love he told of 'Jesus only.' His inspiring presence and heart-moving ministry have brought gladness to many souls and blessings to the community at large. Devout Christians of all denominations have learned in him and his preaching, more than ever before, how real and beautiful is their oneness and common kinship in Jesus. When he left on Thursday evening for Quebec a large number of. friends were at the station to see him off. When he appeared on the rear platform of the train, all hats were instinctively doffed, hearts filled with emotion and eyes with tears. Just a few more words, parting words of the blessed hope, and then, as the train moved off, there burst forth from all, as with spontaneous impulse, the strains of a heart-felt doxology."

"The Rev. Father Ignatius produced a profound impression in Quebec last week. His eloquence, his earnestness, and his deep convictions, have an overpowering influence on his auditors." The following is from "*The Montreal Witness*" of Nov. 1st:

"An impressive Mission has recently been held at Magog by the Rev. Father Ignatius. The prejudices awakened by the ecclesiasticism of his garb were entirely dispelled, as it became evident that the man's whole being was one enthusiastic devotion to 'Jesus only.'

"People of all denominations crowded the church, and by a marvellous power he won upon the hearts of all. The sublime grandeur and earnest simplicity of his eloquence, the felt spirituality of his presence, and the heart-melting power of his singing, made an impression upon the community that can never die.

"The Rev. Father, though firm in his principles of Apostolic Order, is in glowing touch with devout Christians of all denominations, from the Church of Rome on the one hand to the Salvation Army on the other. He is, indeed, a walking *eirenicon*, a remarkable exemplification of his Church's comprehensiveness, and a living embodiment of her capacity for Christian unity. Before returning to Falmouth, Mass., for rest, prior to his great Boston Mission at the beginning of next month, he made a flying visit to Quebec, where he was the guest of the Lord Bishop of the Diocese. He preached on the Sunday evening that I was there, at S. Matthew's Church."

The Rector and other friends accompanied the Father on his journey to Quebec, stopping *en route* for a night at Lenoxville, where the Bishop's Theological College was. Here the Rector of the place, whose heart was touched by a hymn the Father sang, came and invited the whole party to stay at the Rectory.

Whilst in the village the Father called on the Roman Catholic priest and Methodist minister, who, by their reception of him, proved their right to the title of Christians. In the evening Professor Watkins, from the Theological College, visited the Father at his hotel, bringing with him a whole bevy of students, begging him to address them, which he did from Acts xxvi. 17, 18, showing them what their Mission was to be, *if* they were Christ's messengers to a sinful, weary world. The next morning, on asking for the hotel bill for his party of five, the Father found there was none, Professor Watkins having paid it, with the generosity of a true Cymro.

Thence the Father's journey was resumed to Quebec, and it was whilst on this visit, through the dominion of Canada, that he visited Beauport,* the old village of the well-known "Pastor Chiniquy," of Protestant notoriety, and made inquiries as to how and why he left. Arrived at Quebec, that handsome city on the magnificent river S. Lawrence, the Bishop at once sent and invited him to stay at his house, where the Monk spent a most enjoyable visit.

Whilst here, at the request of their Superior, who introduced him as "a very eminent English doctor," the Father spoke to the students of the Seminary of the Christian Brothers; and, in response to a request made to the Cardinal Archbishop, was to have visited his Eminence, had his health allowed it. The Dean and Canon in residence of the English Cathedral called on the Father, and had he been able to prolong his stay in the ancient historical city, he would, in all probability, have preached in the Cathedral on the following Sunday, many having expressed a wish that he should do so. On the Sunday, October 13th, the Father preached at the large English Parish Church of S. Matthew, of which the Bishop's son was the

---

* This Settlement was begun, in 1634, when the French Jesuits first landed in Canada, by Sieur Giffard.

Rector; and was it not a strange coincidence that on this occasion the Bishop, Rector, Curate, and Preacher were all Welshmen, and the beautiful altar had been erected in memory of another Welshman?

In the morning the Father had attended the Early Communion at S. Matthew's, and whilst walking back was struck with the religious and Sabbath, God-fearing aspect of the city, and the crowds coming out of the French Catholic Churches. The following report of the Father's sermon at S. Matthew's Church is from " *The Quebec Morning Chronicle* " of Oct. 14th, 1890:

" The Rev. Father Ignatius, of the Protestant Order of S. Benedict of Wales, who is at present in town, is the guest of the Lord Bishop of Quebec, and, in company with his Lordship, paid a visit yesterday to Lorette.* The distinguished visitor will leave town to-morrow.

" His sermon in S. Matthew's Church on Sunday night was a very able and magnificent effort, and was listened to with earnest interest and attention by the large and devout congregation that thronged the sacred edifice. Evening prayer and lessons having been respectively sung and read by the Rev. J. Kemp, the Rev. Lennox Williams, and the Rev. Canon Von Iffland, the preacher, who appears to be far past middle age, and who wears the tonsure and a monk's cowl and gown, ascended the pulpit, and, before

---

* A Settlement of the Huron Indians.

giving out his text, offered up an earnest and devout extempore prayer that God's spirit would fill the place that night, and not permit His Word to return unto Him void.

"The sermon was from the text: 'Jesus said unto them, I am the Way, the Truth, and the Life; no man cometh unto the Father but by Me.'

"The deep earnestness of the preacher's manner produced a solemn effect upon the congregation, and many who had misapprehended the character and manners of the man from his exterior circumstances, and presumed methods and associations, were amazed, and marvelled at the deep spirituality of his preaching and the purely evangelistic character of his utterances and teachings. His manner, particularly in the closing part of his sermon, was that of the earnest evangelist and missioner.

"'As we came to the House of God this evening,' he said, in commencing his sermon, and in accents of the purest English and most melodious clearness, 'how beautiful were the heavens, and how bright and splendid the celestial bodies! How magnificent is the kingdom of God in nature! How transcendently grand is our Father-God! How often must you have been startled by the beauty of the heavens as you watched the sun setting in crimson glory in the west, or gazed upon the stars and listened to the music of their silent songs, which sing aloud the grandeur of our God!'

"From such flights of eloquence, the preacher descended to contemplate in burning words the heart throbbings that characterize our world of woe, and particularly 'those vast conglomerations of festering humanity that we call cities.' Why, he cried, was the world a home of tears—a tabernacle of discord? Because while mighty worlds obey our God, there is a disobedience in our little sphere to the King of Kings. The very atmosphere is charged with the powers of Hell, for Satan is the Prince of the powers of this world.

"With that wondrous power that great orators possess over their hearers, the preacher conducted the congregation that hung upon his every word, over a brief history of the race in the early period of its existence, and pointed out the feeling of unrest indicated by historians of every time, from Herodotus to our own day, as pervading the human kind—yearning for something better—a desire for peace and rest. Zoroaster, Aristotle, Plato—all the greatest intellects and philosophers of ancient times wrestled with the unknown to discover and to teach, but failed to show the way—which was, indeed, to be found only in Him who employed the words of our text. Others, again, who struggled to know, asked with Pilate, 'What is truth?' Then followed the enquiry—What is true life? The answer to these enquiries was furnished in the words of 'the Desire of all nations'—'I am the Way, the Truth, and the Life.'

"The reverend gentleman in vivid colours briefly sketched the Nativity of Christ, showing that God's ways are not our ways, and asked, suppose that we had been called into God's counsels in regard to the redemption of the world, should we have advised the means by which it was actually accomplished? Christ, argued the preacher, being the only way, it is to Him, and in His own appointed way alone, that we must come, and that as lost sinners, too. He warned his hearers against self-righteousness, and told them they must come, *because they are so bad*, and not because they are so good. It was delightful to him, he said, as a stranger, to visit beautiful Quebec, and still more so to witness the devout Sabbath observance and church-going of all its people—English Church people, French Church people, Methodists and all other kinds. But he pointed out that all this church thronging might be to no purpose. It was not this that saved lost sinners. It was not belonging to this Church or that Church, to this sect or that sect, it was not even the receiving of the Sacraments, it was not trying to be as good as we could of ourselves. It was necessary for all alike, no matter to what church they belonged, to come to Christ as poor, lost sinners, for all had sinned and come short of the glory of God. It would not do to be as good as we could and trust to Jesus to make up the rest. He must be the *Way*, the *Truth*, and the *Life*. Not only the Finisher, but the Author and Finisher, too, of our faith. He concluded with a passionate appeal to all who had not yet done so to come to Christ as lost sinners, and urged those who knew the preciousness of His salvation to redouble their efforts and their prayers for the salvation of others. Happy those, he cried, who could truthfully say, as they so often sung :—

> I heard the Voice of Jesus say,
> 'Come unto me and rest;
> Lay down, thou weary one, lay down
> Thy head upon My Breast.'
> I came to Jesus *as I was*,
> Weary, and worn, and sad ;
> I *found* in Him a resting place,
> And He *has* made me glad.

"'I should like,' he added, ' if not too much trouble to the organist and choir, to have that hymn sung after the sermon.' The request was, of course, acceded to, and the large congregation dispersed, satisfied that they had listened to a sermon by one of the world's greatest living preachers.

" By many who heard the Rev. Father Ignatius last Sunday, considerable disappointment is expressed that his stay here is to be so short, and that he is not to remain and conduct any special series of services in Quebec."

How it must have reminded many of the tales of the Middle Ages, once more to see a fully tonsured and habited Benedictine Monk walking through the streets of Quebec with her Anglican Bishop, as they wended their way to the Church of S. Matthew this evening, where the Monk was to proclaim the Glad News of the

Gospel of Christ, with the Shepherd of the Souls of the Diocese in the front seats at his feet.

Amongst other places visited by the Father on this Canadian tour were the magnificent Falls of Montmorency, so many feet higher (though with not nearly such a huge body of water) than Niagara, and the Indian Settlement at Lorette, where the Bishop had recently been holding a confirmation, and where the Welsh Monk made several small purchases of Indian manufactures.

One Canadian countryman who listened to the Father preaching at S. Luke's, Magog, was afterwards heard to remark: "I don't care how much he crosses himself. Let him cross himself as much as ever he likes, so long as he can preach like that." A clergyman from a neighbouring parish brought a number of his choir over on purpose to attend the Mission.

On the Father's return to Falmouth, the Rector of S. Luke's wrote: "At the services here on Sunday you were in the thoughts and hearts of all of us, and my address could not be otherwise than upon you and the blessed providence that had brought you amongst us, and we offered up a united and hearty thanksgiving to God for the blessings of this *memorable* Mission. . . . The congregation were very much affected all through the discourse and concluding prayers. I have been away from home most all the time since the Mission but all that I have met belonging to the Parish feel that a blessing has come upon the community."

---

* The Rev. R. C. Tambs.

CHAPTER VII.

BOSTON.

MANY and various were the conjectures, as to what reception the Benedictine Monk would meet with, and what his success would be here, in this decidedly English town. By some it was predicted, that if he succeeded here, he must fail in New York, or *vice versa*, as the towns were rivals. Some thought the autocratic action of the Bishop of the Diocese would influence many Episcopalians from giving him a hearing, whilst others declared it would help to draw larger crowds, and be the means of making the Father and his Mission better known than it could have been otherwise. So it proved; for the crowds that, day after day, throughout the month of November, listened to the Father, far exceeded the accommodation the large Horticultural Hall was able to provide.

The same kind American lady, to whose heart the Word of God had come with such power on board "the Trave" as to provide the strange Welsh visitors with roof and shelter all the summer, in the form of a lovely cottage by the sea, had again taken rooms for our whole party, and defrayed the cost in one of the largest hotels of "the Back Bay."* Those who

---
* Hotel Huntington.

were blessed by the Spirit of God at this Mission in finding perfect peace, true rest, eternal life, and joy unspeakable in Jesus, are in a great degree indebted to her for thus providing for the Welsh Evangelist and his party.

It was just before the feast of All Saints that we arrived in the city, invigorated and refreshed from our summer retreat on the Sand Dunes of Cape Cod. Our time was short and precious, for we had only two days before the Mission began, and Boston was to put forth the first American edition of our well-known "Llanthony Monastery Mission Hymns."* On All Saints' Day it was our privilege to attend a most reverent celebration of the Sweet Sacrament of the Altar, at the American Catholic Church of "The Advent," where the Sarum Sequence of Colours had been recently adopted. This, the old Church of Father Grafton (now Bishop of Fond du Lac), who once assisted in carrying the Blessed Sacrament in a procession of the Host from our monastery at Elm Hill through the streets of Norwich, was the first to welcome the Father.

Having seen the Welsh Evangelist Monk at the service, the Rector came straight off to call on him, and to beg him, if the Bishop consented, to give them an early "quiet day" at this beautiful Church. He told the Father, how he had always been interested in him and his work, and wanted to see him;

---

* These are obtainable from The Benedictine Monks of Llanthony Abbey—Words only 2¼d. With music 2/6.

in fact, how he himself once wished to join our order as a monk. Through the kindness of this priest we were granted the privilege of a private celebration of the Holy Eucharist every Sunday morning in our hotel, he himself coming straight off from his own church to celebrate for us ; whereas, during the week, I enjoyed the early celebrations at the Advent, and the daily sharp brisk walk on a frosty morning through the picturesque Commonwealth Avenue and lovely gardens there and back. I have a letter before me now from this kind friend, in which he writes : " Please tell Father Ignatius that I am exceedingly sorry that I have been unable to go to hear any of his orations this past week, but I have received very good accounts of them from some of my people who were privileged to attend. I look forward with great pleasure to being with you to-morrow morning. Please give my love to Father Ignatius, and tell him I deem it a very great privilege to celebrate for him." But to return now to what we did on All Saints' Day.

At eleven we attended the morning service at Trinity Church, as, having heard so much of Boston's great man and America's King of Preachers, the late Dr. Philips Brooks,[*] we were all most anxious to hear him. The church was not half full, but the congregation was made up of the *elite* and learned of the city. The service was very plain, but the singing not congregational. The sermon—how shall I describe it ?—the rapid utterance of the preacher, the words

---

[*] Obiit. January, 1893.

all seeming to tumble out of his mouth one after another, without any difference in tone or change of voice, in headlong speed, making it very difficult at first to keep up, follow, or understand him. Not once did he appear to be at a loss for words in which to frame his thoughts, but his sermon throughout was rich in the mysteries of eloquence and cultured learning; and, although the subject was "All Saints," neither Jesus Christ or the Holy Ghost were once alluded to. One was left to conclude that a saint was a person who had raised himself above his fellows, and that we all might, and ought to be the same. There was no *Christian* teaching of any kind; it was an eloquent moral Buddhistic oration.

In the evening the Father decided to go and hear him again, when he was to give his address to communicants in the chapel at the side of the church. The subject was "Christ, and the Woman of Samaria," in which discourse there was no dogmatic teaching of any kind. It was curious, here in Boston, away from the shores of England, to find many a friend from the old country, some even from our own town of Abergavenny, who knew the monastery and the surrounding country quite well.

The advertised services on the Mission bill were, the first Sunday: Morning, "The One Fold and the One Shepherd;" afternoon, "The Franchise of the People;" evening, "The Mission of Christianity to the World." On week-day afternoons the Father spoke to Christians for the strengthening and refreshing of their souls on " What is a Christian ? " " Jesus Only," as " The Christian's Righteousness," " The Christian's Strength," " The Christian's Food," " The Christian's Example," " The Christian's Rest ; " while of an evening the loving invitation of the Gospel Message was proclaimed to all, the subjects being the same as at Newport, with two exceptions : " Jesus, and the Woman of Pleasure ; " " Jesus, and the Woman of Sorrow," being ' substituted for " Jesus and the Religious Man," " Jesus, Crucified, and The Nineteenth Century." The concluding sermons of the Mission Week, on Sunday, November 9th, were on : " Let them be Merry and Joyful," " The Spies from the Promised Land," and in the evening, " I have found my Sheep that was Lost."

By many it was expected that if the Father personally called on the Bishop, matters would be smoothed, and the churches of the Diocese opened to him, as a similar case had occurred some time previously, when Dr. Paddock forbade the Bishop of Minnesota from preaching in Massachusetts on behalf of his Indians. This the Father did during the Mission week on hearing from one of his Lordship's chaplains, Dr. Chambré of Lowell, that Bishop Benj. H. Paddock* would be pleased with a visit from the Welsh Monk—but without any good result; for though he was most affable on other subjects, and cordial in his reception of the Father, he was thoroughly determined on the great object of the Father's call. Thus the

---

* Obiit. March, 1891.

churches of Massachusetts were finally closed against the Message of the Gospel from the Monk's lips, though, as "Veritas" wrote in his letter to "*The Boston Post*" of November 26th: "I have yet to learn that the Father ever spoke of his brethren who differed from him as inculcating the '*worship of a heathen God and a fabled Christ*,' words preached from a pulpit of a church of this Diocese without Episcopal condemnation. The Father never said 'it becomes a matter of indifference whether one believed the Lord Jesus Christ to be the Son of God or only the best of men.' The same clergyman has said it becomes a matter of indifference whether or not the material from which the 'Kosmos' has been evolved be thought of, as co-existent with God or not. When the author of such sentiments ministers in a church of this Diocese without Episcopal condemnation, it is passing strange to condemn Father Ignatius for holding erroneous and strange doctrine."

To quote the words of "*The New York Tribune*," of November 15th: "The Episcopalians of Boston and vicinity appear to be much worked up over the refusal of Bishop Paddock to allow Father Ignatius to preach in any Episcopal Church in Massachusetts." And "*The Boston Traveller*," of November 3rd, comes forth with the following: "Why he does not have a church is by this time well known, as the fact; the Bishop refuses to recognise him because he does not bring what are, in the opinion of the former, proper credentials. It is not enough that Father Ignatius comes as a *Priest* of the Church of England, and, above all, as a preacher of Him whom all the churches take as their example. But Bishop Paddock seems to think, apparently, that something more is wanting. It is to be hoped that the Bishop will see the folly of the step he has taken, and do that which would give great satisfaction to the majority of Episcopalians hereabouts. Several churches, it is understood, are open to Father Ignatius whenever the Bishop will give his consent."

Of course, the Episcopalians were puzzled as to why Bishop Paddock should inhibit the Father, and state that one reason was the lack of credentials to satisfy the American Canon, when Bishop Clarke, of Rhode Island, had already, in sanctioning the Father's ministrations in his diocese, pronounced his certificate from Bath and Wells as fully complying with the Canons of the Church. The Bishop of Quebec had already welcomed the Welsh Monk to his diocese, and their Lordships of Minnesota and Ohio had both sent him their blessings, and promised him a welcome should he ever visit their Dioceses. The Canadian Bishop of Niagara* had also given his full consent and blessing to a mission at St. Matthew's Church, Hamilton, which the Father, through pressure of engagements, was unable to hold. In spite of this, the Bishop of Massachusetts stood firm to the end, in refusing to allow the Monk to preach in any church in

---

* Dr. Chas. Hamilton.

his Diocese, though his acting in this manner did not prevent numbers of Episcopalian clergy, Roman Catholic priests, Protestant ministers, and laity of every and no denomination from filling the Hall to the doors, and often right into the passage, throughout the five weeks of the Father's stay in Boston.

Some quotations from the local press will give a slight idea of how the general public regarded these services :—

In "*The Boston Budget,*" of November 9th, we find : " The traditional hospitality of Boston to ideas has again been exemplified this past week by the throngs of representative people who have crowded Horticultural Hall to hear the noted Evangelist, Father Ignatius. A man of strong and impressive individuality, with a singular mixture of the mediæval monk, the Methodist, Revivalist, the Modern Churchman, and the Catholic devotee, he has held hundreds of listeners in rapt attention, and has made his message a recognized power in the daily forces of life. Notwithstanding the seriousness of his theme, and the beautiful earnestness with which the Father treated it, the close student of these meetings would need to have been more or less human to have repressed a smile at the manner in which the direct simplicity of Father Ignatius penetrated and warmed the chill of Boston reserve. Boston is decorous in her religious observances as in all else ; she would hold it pharisaical to observe religious rites, and the forms of public or private devotion, anywhere save at the right places and seasons, and this fervent Anglican Catholic who bade all who had the love of Jesus in their hearts to testify to it by rising, doubtless surprised a great many Bostonians into standing who could scarcely have conceived themselves in precisely this attitude. The Rev. Father made it a direct issue, and if one were tacitly to deny his faith by keeping his seat, it seemed a species of ignoble cowardice, and the genuineness of feeling triumphed over the habitual Boston reserve."

God was indeed working in the midst of the assemblies, and by the power of His Holy Spirit poured forth in showers of blessing, brightening and re-creating the souls and lives of numbers, as my readers will see before we close this chapter. The Gospel note was sounding far and near. The Monastery Hymns, which tell the love of Jesus, were being bought in numbers and sent to all parts of the States—some even to California. Papers of other cities were beginning to enquire who this strange preacher was, that the Bishop so opposed, and what was the work he was doing.

Before the Father had been a week in Boston the following characteristic paragraph appeared in "*The Pittsburg Times*," November 6th:—

"The Rev. Father Ignatius, Church of England Monk of the Benedictine Order, in this country to advance his peculiar (?) views of Christianity, has captivated Boston by his zeal and eloquence, saying nothing about the novelty of the man and his cause;" and the following is part of a leader on "Father Ignatius's Mission" from "*The Boston Herald,*" November 11th :—

"The English Monk is a great deal worse in his bark than in his bite. Bishop Paddock appears to have been scared by his bark, and to have refused to him the privilege of showing what was in him in the churches of his Diocese. But this did not prevent Father Ignatius from obtaining a hearing in Boston, and his audiences at the Mission held last week in Horticultural Hall were largely composed of Episcopal people, who were determined that this clergyman *should* have a hearing in the city. He has made a very agreeable impression. He had eccentricities enough to draw an audience, but he retained that audience, and increased it by the qualities of genuine Christian manhood, which find a response whenever one man speaks honestly and faithfully to another. He has evidently done a good work in Boston. His simplicity, his earnestness, his genuineness, won him favour, and then won the hearts of those who favoured him. It is not often that a foreigner visits Boston on a religious Mission who makes his way to the confidence of the people more effectively than Father Ignatius has made his way."

The indignation expressed through the Press at the Father's inhibition was very great and general.

"Essex," writing to "*The Boston Transcript,*" November 12th, says:—

" *What* a picture, *what* a mockery, we have before us in a God-fearing priest of the Church, the Anglican Monk, Father Ignatius, presenting himself before the Episcopal Bishop of the Diocese of Massachusetts, and asking him in vain to tell the 'old, old story of Jesus and His love!'" How the great heart of the saintly Bishop Whipple must have ached in astonishment, as he heard the refusal of his brother Bishop. I don't think we can quite grasp the tremendous import of this lesson, if it at all represented the true spirit of the Church in the United States. Every Christian man, be he Unitarian (? Author.—How can *he* be Christian?), Episcopalian, or Roman Catholic, must, if he be a man, feel that the cause of Christ has been insulted. In these days of doubt and unbelief there are too many ready to cry out religion is a hollow mockery, and that Christian ministers are hypocrites at heart, caring only for the comforts and pleasures of this world, and little or nothing for souls for whom Christ died.

"Oh! that we had a thousand such men as Father Ignatius, ready and willing to proclaim the truth as it is in Jesus. But even more self-sacrifice is necessary! The true life of Christianity will never light up again, as in the days of yore, until her priests are willing to deny themselves everything, to go forth without anything, trusting in Him Who is their

Captain, and Who has promised to be with His Church to the end of the world. As a churchman, I cannot refrain from uttering my protest against that uncharitable and unchristian conduct, which this faithful apostle of Jesus has encountered in his effort to save souls, and further the work so near his heart in his native land. He has come to us a God-fearing, Christian priest—our guest, our brother in religion. Every Christian courtesy is his by right, and I do not envy those who dare to interfere with him.

"George Herbert said: 'None shall in hell such pains endure, as those who scoff at God's way of salvation.' But He who is the chief Shepherd, and Bishop of our souls, has declared that 'inasmuch as ye did it *not* unto the *least* of My disciples, ye did it not unto Me.' God bless Father Ignatius in his noble work, and may he find temporal as well as spiritual comfort on his toilsome journey."

Though the Bishop considered it his duty to endeavour to hinder the Father's Mission work in the city, the Lord provided—and when "He is for us, who can be against us"?—with the result that letters of joy, for unutterable blessings received at the services, daily poured in on the Father.

A Baptist minister wrote: " I have attended your Mission here, and have been greatly blessed. I have stayed beyond the date I had set to return to Nova Scotia to attend your excellent services."

A fashionable woman testifies: "May I add my

blessing to that of thousands for the work you are doing, and the strength and comfort you have given my poor tired, struggling soul?"

Another lady: "May I thank you most earnestly for the help and inspiration of your Mission? It has come from a strong realization of our Lord's love and personal presence."

A third, on November 25th, wrote to the Father: "It would not be fair dealing did I not tell you how much of sweetness and light you have brought into my life. I have listened to your words, and in them I have found the response to the longings of my heart. I have believed in Christ always, but it has not been 'Jesus only.' Trial and disappointment, and people—yes, people more than all else—have made my life a moody one. Now, thanks be to God, through His Spirit breathed from you, I can commit *all* my ways unto my Saviour, knowing that He careth to the uttermost. It was this fullness of surrender, the surrender of mind and heart, that I needed to give, that I might obtain the peace and rest and comfort that Jesus alone, and Jesus only, can give. . . . More than all else, more than your words, though they have given me great help, has your life helped me. *Oh! we who attend fashionable churches see so much that is inconsistent—such a different man in the gown and in the week-day coat.*"

These letters of blessing came from all parts of the

city, from all ranks, young and old, business and professional men, members of all sects, Theological students, and even children — all grieving at the Bishop's action, but rejoicing in what the Holy Spirit had done for them at the Horticultural Hall, where the strange Monk so earnestly and lovingly proclaimed the everlasting, boundless love of Jesus.

A *Physician* wrote: "I have followed your mission now for five days, and my heart is full of gratitude that the naked truth has been uttered. If we could have minds thus vitally connected with the Author of Life, there would be no lack of interest in our churches as there now is."

A *Newspaper Reporter* testified: "You have given me the greatest blessing of my life and there are no words to express my gratitude."

In a letter from *The Boston University* I find "The students of the Boston University School of Theology have been greatly instructed and inspired by your services. Could you not so arrange matters as to spend an hour with us one day this week? There are 140 students in the school, all of whom are interested in the matter."

A *Roman Catholic* business man said, "Accept a word of sympathy and of thanksgiving to God the Giver, and to you as the instrument, for the help and comfort of the Holy Spirit, and a true faith and union with Jesus, independent of Church affiliations vouchsafed during your Mission to a Roman Catholic."

A *Child of ten:* "I am a little girl only ten years old, but I want to write you a letter and tell you how I love you. I asked mama if I could write, and she said yes, so I will try and do my best. I love you very much because you are so good, and I feel so bad because the Bishop will not let you speak in our church . . . . I am going to write to the Bishop myself if mama will let me, and beg him to let you preach in our church. Mama has been to hear you a good many times. She took me with her twice. Dear Father, I hope you will not go away for a long time. I wish you would never go."

An *Episcopalian Catholic:* "The time of thanksgiving has indeed come. For the blessed privileges of the past week your people long to give utterance to their deep gratitude. I think the memory of this last week will remain with me to the end of my life with help and comfort. The attitude of the Bishop is a pain and grief to me and hundreds of others.'

I fear I have wearied my kind readers with all these testimonies of blessings. The crowds at the Mission daily increased, and as the Bishop still remained firm, the Father considered it his duty to hire The Meionaon Hall of the Tremont Temple for the afternoon of November 11th, to explain his position in relation to His Lordship. The Bishop had his representative present to make a stenographic report. The notice bills of this address were headed "Father Ignatius and the Bishop of Massachusetts. The Bishop closes the Church Doors in Boston against him. Why?"

As all the Episcopalian pulpits were closed against the Welsh Monk, though many a rector, had they been free to do so, would gladly have opened them to him, the Ministers of almost every other denomination now came forward, assuring him of a welcome if he would accept the use of their churches, or, as they would be called in England, "chapels." Among the very first to call and invite the Welsh Evangelist was the noted, warm-hearted Unitarian Minister of the City, Dr. Edward Everett Hale.

"I have come," he said, "to invite you to preach in my church. If you had not been excluded from the Episcopal churches by the Bishop I would not have sought you out for this purpose. But since you are debarred from the churches of your own faith, I invite you to accept my pulpit in ours." On the Father replying, "Do you, a Unitarian, ask me to speak to you? Will you allow me to preach Christ as GOD, Whose *vicarious* suffering *alone* has redeemed mankind?" the generous, liberal-hearted Dr. Hale at once replied, "You may preach anything you like, you may convert us all if you can." Then the Congregational Minister of the huge Eliot Church at Newton, wrote: "My Dear Brother. After my brief interview with you last Saturday, I took counsel of the Deacons, and of the officers, spiritual and temporal, of this church, and I have the honour and the pleasure of extending to you, with their approval, a cordial invitation to preach in our meeting house at such time as we may arrange by consultation. One fact of which you may not be aware may remove all objections which you raised. Our church, the Eliot Church, belongs to the original Puritan Churches, which were once the Established Churches of New England. *Episcopalians are the dissenters here, not we.* Until a recent date we were the Establishment, as the Presbyterians still are in Scotland. But we never forbid a man to cast out devils, and to preach in the Name of Jesus because they follow not after us. I sincerely hope that our Church, with an auditorium for 2,000 people, bearing the name of John Eliot, the Apostle of the Indians, and in the apostolic succession of the Pilgrims and the Puritans, may have the pleasure of welcoming you in the Name of Jesus, so dear to you and to us."

Here was a predicament for the Father, an ordained minister of the Church of England, to be in. Two such cordial invitations from churches of other denominations had come to him, and yet how could he accept them, when in England they would be looked on as dissenters, and it would be a breach of the English canons for an Anglican clergyman to take part in their worship. Being told that in America the case was different, and that even the " Episcopal

Bishops," as they were called, as well as the clergy, preached for them, the Father decided to ask the advice of two of the representative Episcopalian priests in the city, the renowned Philips Brooks, whose words carried such weight with all sects and classes, and the Rector* of the Church of the Advent. *En passant*, was it not a curious coincidence that the Father, without knowing it, in asking Trinity's popular Rector as to the propriety of preaching in an Unitarian church, should be going for advice to one who was himself the son of a Unitarian minister, and some of whose brothers are even now reported to be ministers of that denomination?

Before the Father had been a week in the city, the question, "Does Philips Brooks approve?" passed from mouth to mouth, and on November 10th, "*The Boston Traveller*" answered the question, when they put forth the following paragraph:

"If any one could have doubted the success of Father Ignatius's Mission, he had but to attend the closing service of last Sunday evening, when the Horticultural Hall was so packed, that even the platform was occupied by as many people, as could be seated there. By many it is claimed, that it was curiosity that drew the greater part of the crowd; but, while this may have been the case during the first few services, it certainly was not the case the remainder of the week, for a very large number of those

---

* The Rev. W. B. Frisby.

who heard him at the first have been regular attendants at every service since.

"Although many Episcopalians have been present, all the other denominations have been largely represented, and not only by laymen, but by clergymen also. One of the most eminent Unitarian divines in this city, has attended several of the afternoon services, as has also a prominent South End Baptist clergyman. The familiar figure of Dr. Philips Brooks was noticed last Thursday evening, an earnest listener of all that was said, standing the whole time, as there was not a seat to be had. He has expressed himself as much pleased with the simplicity and earnestness of the Monk, and at his own service at Trinity Church, on Sunday morning, quoted largely from the Reverend Father. Could the Bishop's consent be had, Dr. Brooks would be very glad to have the Evangelist Monk preach in *his* church."

When the Father wrote to ask his advice with reference to the invitations he had received, the learned doctor was away at the Church Congress in Philadelphia, but replied, assuring him that he did what was right, in going into a Unitarian Church to preach, and did not infringe any canon of the American Church. The same was said by the Catholic priest whom he consulted.

So the Father preached, for the first time in his life, in a sectarian (I use the word in all kindness) place of worship, on November 14th, at Dr. Hale's Unitarian Church. Many a ransomed soul in Boston will write the date of that cold winter's evening in letters of gold, to the end of their lives. " What think ye of Christ ? " was his startling text, from which the Father preached Jesus as Creator God, and Atoning Saviour, to the Unitarians of Boston. For once a large Unitarian congregation, in their own place of worship, heard a bold attack upon their heterodoxy, and a bold defence of the truths of the Godhead, and vicarious Atonement of the Lord Jesus. After service, as the Father was passing through the crowd, a Baptist minister caught his hand, and said : " Thank God for the sermon to-night ; you have put Christ and His fulness before me, in a way I had never realized before."

"*The Boston Globe*" of November 22nd states: "Father Ignatius preached last evening in Eliot Church, Newton, to over two thousand listeners. Every seat, and standing room in the aisles clear to the doors, was occupied. The audience listened with rapt attention throughout the service. A Presbyterian Church was the next to offer its pulpit to the Father, which he accepted for the evening of Thanksgiving Day," preaching on the text, " Upon *this* rock will I build *My* church."

A Roman Catholic priest wrote to a friend : " Tell Father Ignatius that however he may differ from us, he has preached the *whole* Gospel of Jesus Christ, and that is what we all *want*. I put my Mass as early as possible, so as to be at the whole of his Mission services." In a letter to "*The Boston Traveller,*" November 19th, the Rev. Dr. Winslow writes, over his own signature, on "Father Ignatius and the Canons":

"It is fair to express my individual opinion of the Monk's preaching. His pathos, directness, simplicity, earnestness, power of doctrinal statement, searching of the human heart, application of the Gospel, medicine to heal broken spirits and wounded hearts, are one and all wonderfully strong by nature and training. In these conventional and materialistic days it is refreshing and captivating to hear the voice of a S. John crying in the wilderness, tempered, too, with the sympathy of a loving S. John. This monk seems to combine the bold earnestness of the Baptist with the affections of Christ's dearest disciple. I forget the cowl and the gown when such a man speaks, and I now remember only the good that he has wrought in the name of Jesus. May he not speak some week-days in our churches? Perhaps our Bishop may yet say yea."

After the Welsh Monk's Mission week was over, as is usual wherever he goes, he gave special orations in answer to the question, "Why are you a Monk?" and on "The Spiritual Meanings of Catholic Ceremonies,"*

---

* *Vide* "The Glorious Church; or, Five Addresses on Catholic Ceremonies," by Father Ignatius, obtainable at Llanthony Abbey, 2s., free.

on Tuesday, November 18th. Next day his subjects were a reply to the question : " Why do you belong to the Episcopal Church ? " and an oration on " Materialism and the Supernatural ; " whilst the two concluding ones of the series were " Fashionable Christianity," and " Our Life and Work at Llanthony Abbey," all of which were very well attended, and most attentively listened to.

It was at this time, that Millet's magnificent picture, " L'Angelus," was creating such a *stir* in Boston, that the Father was asked to preach on it, which he made the subject of his last address in that beautiful city, "the Hub of the Universe," " the Cradle of Liberty," the city of aristocracy and learning, the city of hospitality, and historical fame. But previous to this, the Welsh Monk and his party of friends *had* visited "The Verestehagin Exhibition," and gazed with feelings of reverential awe on the *great* picture.

So overcome was the Father, as he sat gazing thereon, that, suddenly rising and turning to the assembled crowd, he remarked, that he did not know, if it was customary to speak in such a place, but he would like, however, to say a few words about the picture, and what "the Angelus" was, and what it commemorated. He dwelt upon the faith of the peasants which the picture pourtrays. Out of it all he drew a picture (so says " *The Boston Traveller,*" November 15th), which was most grand and impressive, and for the time being, an air of solemnity pervaded the entire place. It was *undoubtedly* the *finest* description this famous picture has ever had, as viewed from a religious standpoint, and the people departed, feeling that they more fully understood the "Angelus" than would be possible under any other conditions. A lady who was standing close by, remarked that she had come a *long* way to see the "Angelus," but from the Father's beautiful description, she felt she had received more than her money's worth.

The following is "*The Boston Morning Advertiser's*" report of the Father's sermon thereon, preached November 30th: " In Horticultural Hall last evening, Father Ignatius preached his last sermon before leaving Boston, upon ' The Story of L'Angelus.' The hall was crowded to suffocation, all standing room being taken, the platform packed as tight as it would hold, and hundreds were even turned away for lack of room. Father Ignatius said :—

"'It seems as if this "L'Angelus" possessed the same power of fascination to you, that it did to the people of England. Thousands have flocked here to see and admire it. Your newspapers have been full of its wonderful charm and beauty. Why is it? It is a remarkably *small* picture, but it is one *full* of the most exquisite naturalness joined to a most intense spirituality. It is a picture, in which you can almost see the hand of a loving God stretched out from heaven and touching earth. In its skill it *speaks* powerfully of the love of God *for* man. But the picture is familiar to you all. On the faces of those weary labourers, children of the soil, you can see, that at the tones of the bell from the distant steeple, their faces have caught the light, and love, and liberty of heaven. Amid their toil and weariness, they have caught the rest that comes *only* to the people of God; amid the lowliness of their state they have caught the glory, of the sons and daughters of heaven. "L'Angelus" is only a picture of human life, with all its drudgery and discontent, touched and softened by the story of the love of God, as told in the peals of the distant bell. It is an illustration of that wondrous thing, Christian faith.

" ' Young people, you who are in " the glory of life," as yet, *you* have not entered the weariness of life's disappointments. It is the morning hour of your existence, and if in this morning hour you could catch the note of "the Angelus," it would prepare you for your life's work. It will ennoble and raise you to a higher phase of existence than the world can teach you to occupy. Catch the peal of " the Angelus" bell in the early morning hour, and go to work with Jesus Christ at your side. It will be a life of sunshine for you and others. It will make your life *worth* living. It will make your life a noble and satisfied one, *every* day of which will be a blessing to you.

"'But "the Angelus" bell rings again at noon, calling upon all men to pause in the hurry-skurry of their work. At mid-day, directly as "L'Angelus" rings, all toil and labour ceases. "L'Angelus" calls a halt in the rush of life. There are many of us here to-night who are in the midst of their life's work. If you would but catch that spirit of liberty, harmony, and peace which Jesus Christ brings to the soul, how different would the rest of your short life be from that portion that has gone before. Will you catch the notes of that sweet "Angelus" bell to-night? It would be a good thing to hear " the Angelus " bell ring in Boston. It would brighten many a weary soul with its sweet significant peals. I do not see why if Roman Catholics do a good thing others should not do it also.

" ' At last evening has come. The peasants in the picture have been waiting for "the Angelus" to ring. At last the notes ring out sharp and clear from the distant steeple, and the two clasp their hands and bow in adoration. There are many here whose life is fast approaching completion. Will you be able to bow your head, and catch the sound of "the Angelus" bells? God grant it! But do not some of you elder brethren seriously think how near death is approaching you? What is it to you now, what discoveries are made in science? What is it to you, whether your politician gains his coveted honour or no? You are about to lay aside all the interests of *this* life, for the evening has come. If you have *not* accepted Jesus Christ, in this evening hour, when the shadows of life are lengthening across your path, pause and catch the tone of " the Angelus," I beseech you, brethren.'

" After his address, Father Ignatius said, he desired heartily to thank the people of Boston, for their attendance and liberality, during his mission in this city."

Before leaving the city, at a private exhibition of the phonograph, the Father left a verse of his popular mission hymn, "O, King of Beauty," sung by himself and Brother David, registered on one blank, and a few words on another—to those who would, in the far distant future, listen to his words and voice through this means, when he was dead and buried—words that might help tired, weary souls into the Peace of Christ that passeth knowledge. Since leaving Boston, we have already heard of the joy and blessing they have proved to one soul.

A few days before the Father's departure from Boston, the Bishop, who had refused to make public his reasons for inhibiting him before, now took up some six columns in "*The Boston Post*," explaining them. To these the Father replied the next day. As this was just before the Father's Advent Mission in New York, and he had, only a day or so previously, received Bishop Potter's licence to occupy the Episcopal pulpits of that Diocese, the Father now returned the licence to the Bishop, sending him also the whole of his correspondence with Bishop Paddock, so that there should be no misunderstanding, in case Dr. Potter, after reading Dr. Paddock's attack, might wish to withdraw *his* permission. When the time came, for the Father to say farewell to the city, where he had been first welcomed and opposed on American shores, many were the wishes expressed that he would return for another Mission in the spring. This he promised to do, if it were possible.

A few more newspaper opinions of the Father personally, as well as his preaching, and I must really conclude this chapter. Right away to distant Chicago his fame had reached, and " *The Chicago Inter - Ocean* " of November 8th contained the following :—

" The figure of Father Ignatius should have an ecclesiastical background. It suggests the altar lights, the white-robed processional choir, the cloistered and stately beauty of a great cathedral, yet so *marvellous* is his power that one forgets the bare hall, and is lost in the fire and eloquence of his message. He preaches the gospel of love, of miracle, of supernaturalism, of strict Evangelical doctrine. He emphasizes the vicacarious atonement, and preaches the transforming powers of belief. Yesterday, after a passage in which he described the righteousness that God expected from man, how He would have holiness, how He demanded perfection, and the hearers were brought to a profound realization of how beautiful the ideal, and alas ! how impossible, the reverend Father suddenly paused, and in a sweet, thrilling, penetrating whisper—at once as soft and sweet as an Æolian harp—said : ' But *all this* is God's gift to man.' The indescribable force of this, I cannot hope to pourtray. The vast audience was so still, one could have heard a pin drop. The climax was as telling, as that made by Marc Antony, in his oration over the dead body of Cæsar."

"*The Boston Herald*" of November 9th says in part: "And the audience—the 500 or 600 who gathered, in spite of Saturday-night attractions—listened as if their lives depended upon it. There were young and old, some who seemed to be rich and some who seemed to be poor, but when Father Ignatius's voice fell to a whisper, they all seemed to hold their breath, so that the whisper could be heard in the remotest corner of the hall. They were evidently from different churches, as, when prayer was offered, some stood up, some kneeled, and others bowed their heads. . . . Leaving the hall, the people wore sober faces, and some wet eyes were to be seen. They showed that seeds of interest had at least been sown by the words of the eloquent monk."

As a proof of the excitement the Bishop and Monk's position created amongst the Bostonian clergy, let me tell you, at a large meeting of them, held in "The Episcopal Church Rooms" one Monday morning, when forty were present—*three*—who had drawn up a letter of sympathy to the Bishop, and had shown it to his Lordship *first* for his approval, for the clergy to sign—were unable to obtain their signatures, and the meeting advised the laying of the letter on the table.

The following letter from an Episcopalian will be,

I think, a very fitting conclusion to this chapter, and then, in the next, we shall have a most interesting time to describe, under the Bishop's licence in New York :—

"My dear Sir,—Will you permit me to enclose a very small donation toward your work, as you may see fit to apply it. I heard you read the service—*that* was all, yesterday morning. I had not time to hear you preach. I *never* heard the prayers or scriptures so read. It was a ministry of grace to my soul. Myself born a Baptist, and now a very moderate Episcopalian, you can imagine when a Monk simply reading the prayers brought me nearer to Jesus, how careful I shall strive to be hereafter that I do not let any non-essential differences either of doctrine or dress shut up my heart against any servant of God. Respectfully I will add that, while I may never be able to thoroughly sympathize with you in some ideas which I understand you devoutedly hold, I beg the privilege of telling you that you are a Christian whose shoes latchet I am not worthy to unloose—did you wear shoes.

" May I also ask you, if not too pressed for time in your holy work, as soon after the receipt of this note as convenient, to personally offer a prayer for me individually to Jesus, that He will strengthen me to lead a pure, true life, in word, thought, and deed, for His sake ? If you can find time to thus pray once for me, it will greatly bless and help me. Do not, I pray, burden yourself with any reply.

"I remain, faithfully and sincerely yours,

"———"

Just before leaving the city "*The Boston Herald*" published a most interesting visit to "Llanthony Abbey,"* which I had hoped to have included in an Appendix, but which we have since had reprinted in pamphlet form, as No. 1 of the new series of "Llanthony Tracts."

Two years and more have now passed away since the Father's Mission in the City, and time has wrought many changes in Boston. Both Dr. Paddock and Dr. Philips Brooks have passed within the veil; Fr. Hall, the Broad Church priest of S. John the Evangelist, has been recalled by his Superior; Dr. Everett Hale has moved to other fields of labour—but in the hearts of many the memory of that great Mission, and the burning words of Love from the lips of the Monk Evangelist which transformed their lives, still live as bright and vivid as though they occurred but yesterday.

---

* This may be had, 2½d. post free, from the Secretary, " Llanthony Abbey, Abergavenny.

CHAPTER VIII.

First New York Mission.

"The Monk of Llanthony."
"Vox clamantis in deserto."

" We bid him welcome in the name of One
He serves, That One who 'pleased not Himself.'
A scoffing age looks on, half awe, half jeers,
Disdainful of that mystery called Faith,
With pitying smile for such childlike soul
As follows lovingly in blood-stained prints
Of weary Feet that walked by Galilee
Long years ago. A Churchman sternly frowns,
And draws aside his lawn, lest it should chance
To be defiled by touch of monkish serge,
Breathing anathemas on cowl and beads
'Twixt prayers to Him who lives alone,
And to whose piercing gaze we may assume
Sandals—or mitre—matter not a jot
So that the wearer sees his soul is garbed
In robe of charity that thinks no ill.
Oh! brave, strong soul, enshrined in holy peace,
Nor praise, nor blame, thy spirit's calm can shake !
I think of thee as highest mountain peak,
Snow-crowned and awful in God's solitude,
Around whose base the winds and tempests rage,
And misty vapours float, but cannot fret;
For past the realm of storms its lofty head
Is lifted in the peace of Heaven's own blue!"

A. B. ALDRICH.

Boston Budget, December 7th, 1890.

ON Friday evening, December 5th, the Father, having been granted the freedom of the diocese by Bishop H. C. Potter, preached his preparatory sermon to the Mission, at the little church of S. Edward the Martyr, (whose rector was the first person to welcome him, when he arrived on the American shores), to an overflowing congregation. " *The New York Press* " says :—

" The building was packed, and many had to seek room on the steps of the altar." Another paper: " The church was crowded, and people were standing along the aisles as far as the chancel, and much interest was centered in the missionary, whose address was an exceedingly able one."

On the following Sunday the Mission *began* at the Cooper Union Hall, but at the very first service the accommodation proved insufficient, hundreds being turned away for want of room; so a larger hall, seating three thousand, had to be procured for the afternoon. Throughout the whole Mission all the seats were filled, and numbers waited patiently day by day on the words of the British monk, as he told the story of the exceeding great love of Jesus. The subject of the first sermon was " The Bride waiting for the Bridegroom," dealing with Our Lord's Second Advent; whilst in the afternoon, " Fashionable Christianity " was the subject dealt with.

To quote the words of " *The New York Tribune*" :— " An Episcopal Clergyman, who has heard Father

Ignatius, says: 'His reading of the service is a wonderful revelation of its power, pathos, and beauty. I have heard, probably, nearly all the great divines of the Anglican and Episcopal Churches read the service, but I confess never before, have I heard any one read it, *as* it is read by this English monk. His tremendous earnestness, the thrilling entreaty of his voice in the prayers, and the profound reality which he gives to every word, left an impression on me which I shall never forget. I had always thought that our liturgy was a beautiful classic; but I now realise what a poor and inadequate use is made of it by our clergy, many of whom simply mumble it, without giving any clear idea of its meaning."

Whilst "*The Philadelphia Press*," of December 11th, has:—" Bishop Potter, Dr. Newton, and Dr. Hall regard him as a sincere, though eccentric worker, and they believe that his Mission will do good."

So, with the Bishop's sanction, and the full consent of the two respective rectors, in whose parishes the halls were situated, the Mission commenced. Preaching at "The Chickering Hall," on the Sunday evening, when the vast auditorium was packed to its utmost capacity, in the course of his sermon the Father said: " What is this world? A very little, tiny planet in our solar system. If the *world* is tiny, what must we be? Yet He that takes care of a little bird will take care of us, insignificant as we are, compared to the universe. Do I hear some one say, 'If God is good, why does

He allow all the evil and suffering which exists on earth?' Evil exists, because we are not automata. We are free agents, and if we choose to ill-use our freedom, God permits us. Yet He loves man, although thus ill-using His freedom—perhaps *because* of it. I do not think, you would love the world, if you were in God's place. I wouldn't; I would hate it. We are a little rebel planet, and consequently a planet of pain; yet God has *freely* given us His Son to save the *vilest* sinners."—*Philadelphia Ledger*, December 13th.

Throughout the week the Father preached daily at four and eight o'clock:—On Tuesday, and Wednesday nights, at the Church of S. Michael, 99th Street, on "The Pool of Bethesda," and "Jesus and the 5,000 Hungry Men"; whilst on Thursday evening, the sermon at "The Church of the Holy Redeemer," was on "Jacob's Ladder." "The Christian as a Sinner, a Saint, a Stranger, a Priest, a Soldier, a Prince," were his afternoon subjects "For Christians." Three Bishops, (one of whom, Bishop Talbot, of Wyoming and Idaho, came to the waiting-room to give him his blessing), the Archdeacon of New York,* Mr. Ira Sankey, Dr. Talmage, Dr. McGlynn, and many of the principal diocesan clergy, sat at the monk's feet, drinking in the message of God's great love for man, throughout the week.

Another quotation of "*The New York Tribune*":—
"Father Ignatius spoke yesterday afternoon, to what would, *if* there had been accommodation for them,

---

* The Rev. Dr. A. Mackay-Smith.

have been the largest crowd that has come together to hear him, during his visit to this city. It was *impossible* to get a seat in the Upper Hall of "The Cooper Union" after half-past three, and before four o'clock people were going away, unable even to get near enough to the doors of the meeting-room, to have a chance of hearing the Father's voice."

On the Tuesday, Wednesday, and Thursday evenings of the Mission week—being unable to procure a hall—the Welsh monk preached in the Episcopal Churches of S. Michael's and "the Holy Redeemer" to large congregations, and in the vestries of those very Churches received invitations to preach also in those of Holy Trinity, Madison Avenue, and "The Church of the Incarnation." Throughout the week, day after day, columns in the daily papers were given up to reports and discussions of the sermons, and it was before long *very* evident, that the monk's presence in New York, was making a great stir. Invitations to preach in churches of all denominations began to flow in. On Saturday evening *no* service was held; but next day, the closing services of the Mission week took place in the large hall of the Cooper Union, morning and afternoon, and the Chickering Hall in the evening, as the large Cooper Union was already taken by Father McGlynn, for a sermon on "The Revival of the Gospel in our Midst: or the Mission of Father Ignatius," in a report of which next morning a daily paper says:—"For nearly two hours last evening, the Rev. Dr. McGlynn discussed Father

Ignatius and his Mission, in ' The Cooper Union.' His praise was unstinted. 'Receiving the Sacraments of the Catholic Church,' Dr. McGlynn said, 'was not of the least benefit to *any* man, unless he experienced in himself true repentance. It is high time that Father Ignatius, and hundreds of others like him, should go forth and appeal to the essential religion of *all* men. God speed Father Ignatius! There is great need to preach to men regardless of creeds.' "

The Mission over, on the Tuesday, Wednesday and Thursday following, the Father delivered four orations, on " Why I am a Monk," " An Episcopalian," " The Gospel Meaning of Catholic Ceremonies," and " Materialism and the Supernatural," which were well attended, and reported in the papers; especially the one on " The Monk," and the best report of that appeared in a *Baptist* newspaper. After this oration, the Welsh Monk was cross-questioned by members of the congregation with the result of eliciting some characteristic and amusing answers, of which the following is a specimen: *Q*. " Does Monasticism accord with the Prayer of Jesus, ' I pray not that Thou shouldest take them out of the world'?" *A*. " My dear sir, is our monastery in the moon, then?" At the oration on " Catholic Ceremonies," the Father announced that an American Congregational lady of Boston, had endowed Llanthony Abbey Church, with the best incense, and olive oil, for the sanctuary lamps, during her lifetime. On Thursday night, the Father preached on "Jesus Weeping over Jerusalem," at "The

Church of the Intercession," his sermon being meanwhile interpreted by Dr. Gallaudet, to a company of deaf mutes who formed part of the congregation. On the Friday, at mid-day, the Monk preached at "The Old John Street Church," to "men only," on "Idlers in the Market Place," when the Church was packed, as it had never been before, with the business men of the city, bankers, jewellers, brokers and merchants, who, one and all, listened with rapt attention to the sermon, at the close of which a regular rush was made to speak to, bless, and thank the Monk, as he left the Church. Ministers and members of all denominations were present, and the Rector of S. Andrew's Church, Haarlem,* then and there, placed his new huge Church at the Father's disposal, which he accepted for the evening of New Year's Day. Of this service, *" The New York Commercial Advertiser "* says :—" The congregation joined heartily in the singing, while Father Ignatius kept time to the music like an orchestra director, and beamed on everybody. His presence was perceptibly inspiring. Old business men, who had been accustomed to attending the daily services at the John Street Church, threw more fervour into their voices than usual, while newcomers looked about for hymn-books, and joined in the chorus, which some of them had evidently heard for the first time. There was plenty of discord, but it was of a kind which is said to become most perfect harmony in heaven."

---

* The Rev. G. R. Van De Water.

The next Sunday the Father was asked to preach in the large Episcopal Church of S. George's, Stuyvesant Square ; but having already taken halls, promised to stop an extra week on purpose, and to preach to " men only " on " Purity," on Sunday evening, January 4th. This Sunday, however, he preached in the Cooper Union, morning and afternoon, and in the Chickering Hall in the evening to an *immense* congregation, on " Is the Messianic Idea a Myth ? " This sermon was well reported verbatim in the next morning's *Tribune*.*

After resting on the Monday, the Monk went on Tuesday afternoon to preach at " The New York Magdalene Home," on which sermon " *The New York Sun*," amongst other papers, had the following remarks :— " At no time, has Father Ignatius preached to so small a congregation, and at no time has he proved so eloquent and impressive in his most characteristic way. While he prayed or preached, not only the inmates of the institution, but the few outsiders who were admitted through favour, wept undisguisedly.

"When giving out the hymn, ' How sweet the Name of Jesus sounds,' he said : ' Isn't it beautiful, dear children, to think that Jesus Christ is now in the midst of us, and that we are now singing in His very ears?' After announcing his text, ' There is no difference, for all have sinned,' he said, ' Just realise what God says here ; that the very best of us are sinners

---

* This it is hoped shortly will be published in pamphlet form by " The Monks of Llanthony."

—you and I, the very best people in New York, as well as the very worst, are sinners. I come as a sinner, to speak to you as sinners. But I come also as a messenger of God, who has been washed in the Blood of the Lamb, and can therefore announce His blessing to you, *not*, because I am better than you are, but *because* I have *found* blessing and pardon and peace *in* Jesus. The world has cast you off, dear sisters. Those who you believed loved you, have cast you out, to be trampled into the mire of sin. Your very mother will have no more to do with you, because you have brought shame on the good name of your father, but Jesus, all the more *because* you have sinned, stands with His arms *open* to receive you, *ever* ready to forgive. "Though your sins be as scarlet, they shall be *whiter* than snow."' In the course of his address, the Father said, that had his hearers never sinned as they had, they would never have become inmates of 'the Home,' so that if it became the means of their finding grace, they were better off, than if they had never so sinned. He made all kneel while they sang, 'Just as I am, without one plea,' and as he repeated impressively each verse before singing, the tears, which had flowed steadily through his sermon, flowed faster than ever. Each Magdalene shook hands with him, and he blessed them when the service was over."

The next day being Christmas Eve, the Father visited the Children's Hospital; to speak at their Christmas Tree, of which "*The New York Sun*" reported as follows:—"At no time has Father Ignatius manifested more his many-sidedness, than in his address yesterday to the children in ' the Hospital, for the relief of the ruptured and crippled.' It was not so much, perhaps, what he said that was so striking, as was the *manner* in which he talked to the little sufferers ; his whole figure exhaled sympathy, and his voice had a pathos, which, if it did not affect his babyish auditors, went to the hearts of the children of larger growth, in the shape of friends of the institution who were present. Some of the children being unable even to sit, reclined in perambulators while they listened to the Monk, and not one of the 200, but was manifestly crippled in one way or another. Their faces, however, all wore an eager and happy look, as they gazed on an enormous Christmas tree bowed down with toys, and glorious with wax tapers and spangles. Around the tree were piled packages of things, too large to be suspended. After carol singing by the expectant little ones, Father Ignatius spoke in part as follows : ' This is the night of the children's feast, because it is the night on which God became a little child. And you children, without knowing it, preach to us even, what Jesus taught, when from a child he had grown to be a man : " Except ye become as little children, ye shall in no wise enter the Kingdom of Heaven." We have got to become like you to get to Heaven, and you are not to grow up like us—that is, you must never be grown up people in the sight of God, but must always remain little children in His eyes. If you do, you will see Jesus, who was once a child, as you are, and who loves little children. It is to His love, you owe the pleasant home you have here, and the kind nurses who take care of you. For it was Jesus, who put it into the hearts of people to build this hospital, and by the hands of His servants, Jesus dresses you in the morning, and puts you to bed at night. Don't forget in after years, what the monk from England told you : That all that has been done for you, has been done under the "influence of Christianity." Now, can you say those long words?' 'Influence of Christianity,' repeated the children, in shrill chorus. 'And what do they mean?' 'Love of Jesus,' answered the quicker-witted, who were not a few. 'And how long will Jesus love you?' 'For ever and ever.' 'Is it cruel of Jesus to let you be so lame?' 'No,' chorussed the children. 'Couldn't He make you get up and walk, if He chose?' 'Yes.' 'It is *because* He loves you, that He lets you suffer, for has He not made suffering beautiful, by suffering Himself? What was He called? A man of sorrows'— 'And acquainted with grief,' chorussed the children, completing the sentence. 'You shall be happier and better in all eternity, for having been crippled here on earth. And be happy to-morrow, the day God became a little child, and make Jesus happy by enjoying yourselves.' Father Ignatius blessed his young hearers, and kissed several of them." "*The New York Tribune*" says in its report :—"It is because He loves you, that He lets you suffer. While you are here on earth, He is getting you ready, for your home in

Heaven. He does for each of us, what He believes is best for us. He believes it is best for you to be cripples. You are working out His great purpose. That little girl over in the corner, is teaching Christianity better, than anyone could preach it. If the love of Jesus makes you little darlings tender and gentle and bright, *that* love makes you a company of preachers. I have been preaching to many people in this city; but to-day, by you, I have had a sermon preached to me. I thank God, that I have had an opportunity, of hearing *such* a sermon. I would like very much to kiss you all, but as there are too many of you, I will kiss one boy and one girl, and let them pass the kisses along."

On Christmas Day, after attending Early Communion at S. Ann's Church,* the Father preached, according to a long standing promise, at the midday Mass at S. Edward the Martyr's Church (where full Catholic ritual is in practice) on " The Desire of all Nations." Owing to certain remarks on " The Real Presence," in the sermon, a great stir was made in the newspapers, and columns appeared headed "The Ignatius Doctrine," "The Ignatius Creed." " *The New York Commercial Advertiser* " even sent their reporter to interview the Bishop of the Diocese thereon, the result of which interview they printed as follows :—
" Bishop Henry C. Potter was asked this morning whether the Father's words conflicted in any way with the established Faith of the Church. The Bishop

* Eighteenth Street, Fifth Avenue.

smiled quietly on hearing the question, and stated that he had read the published accounts of the Father's Christmas sermon, and that he saw no heretical utterances contained in them. The assertion of his belief in the *Real Presence in the Host*, qualified as it was by stating his unbelief in the doctrines of Transubstantiation and Consubstantiation, was entirely within the Church Creed, and *was no more than any Episcopal clergyman should believe.*"

On the next Sunday, two services were held in the Cooper Union, and in the evening in the Chickering Hall, the subjects being, respectively, " The Blessed Virgin Mary, or the Christmas Mother," " The Death of the Old Year," and " The Birthday of Jesus." At all these services, the Christmas Carol of the Monks of Llanthony was used.

> Ah me ! for the icy wind
> That sighs through the stable drear ;
> Ah me ! for the Infant's wail
> Ah me! for that Mother dear.
>   Hush ! Jesus is born to-night
>   Songs sweep the sky ;
>   Hush! Jesus is wailing now,
>   Feeble His cry.*

On Tuesday, at midday, the Father again preached to the business men of the city at " The Fulton Street Noonday Prayer Meeting " on " Ye are not in the flesh, but in the Spirit; if so be, the Spirit of God be in

---

*Words and Music, 2½d., are obtainable from Llanthony Abbey.

you," &c. Of this meeting *"The New York Press"* says:
—" The Fulton Street Mission was crowded to the
doors at noon yesterday, with an audience of business
men, who had gathered there to hear Father Ignatius
preach. His address was attentively listened to, and
quite a number sought the Monk after service, and
heartily shook his hand."

Another paper says :—" The chapel was crowded
with bankers, clerks, and jewellers. They heard a most
powerful sermon, and many were moved to tears." The
next night being New Year's Eve, the Father occupied
the pulpit of a fashionable Baptist Church in Madison
Avenue (whose pastor, Dr. Bridgeman, has since left
that community on account of his *disbelief in Eternal
punishment*, but on doing so, was almost immediately
confirmed into the Episcopal Church); whilst on New
Year's Night itself, he preached at the magnificent
new Church of Saint Andrew's, Haarlem, to a large
congregation, on: " Because Thou hast been my helper,
therefore under the shadow of Thy wings will I
rejoice." After the sermon the Rector, the Rev. Dr.
Van de Water, said : " Whatever offerings you give to-
night will, I have no doubt, be put to good use by
Father Ignatius—I believe in connection with his
monastery. I don't know very much about this
Reverend Brother in Christ, or about his monastery,
or his work, or about his relations with the Bishop—
that is a *large* subject; but I know this, that he has
preached to us this night, the glorious Gospel of the

Lord Jesus Christ, and as this church has received the same, in His Name I desire to say to you: 'If we have sown to you spiritual things, is it a great matter if we shall reap your worldly things?' &c."—*Haarlem Reporter*. Next day at 3 P.M. the Father preached again to the city men at Old John Street on "The Rich Man and Lazarus."

On the following Sunday, as he had promised to remain in New York, in order to preach in the evening to "men only," at S. George's, the Welsh Monk held services of his own, in the morning and afternoon at the Cooper Union Hall, and at the special request of some Church people, he, in the afternoon, for the first time since he has been in America, recited the Church Litany. The day was very bleak and cold, snow both lying and falling thickly, but in spite of it, S. George's huge church was packed in the evening, with an immense crowd of men, who had gathered to hear the Monk. It is estimated that there must have been at least two thousand present.

After a night's rest, on the Monday morning, by special invitation, the Father addressed a meeting of three or four hundred Methodist ministers from all parts, in the Public Library* in Fifth Avenue, and throughout his address fervent "Amens" and "Glory be to God" arose from all parts of the room. After the meeting, numbers from all directions came forward, to offer their chapels to the Monk. Next day being the Feast of the Epiphany, the Father left New York by an

---
* The Methodist Book Society Building.

early train for Yonkers-on-Hudson, where he preached, after the morning service at S. John's Church, on Ephes. iii., and in the evening at the Temperance Hall on "Arise, shine, Jerusalem," returning to New York by the ten P.M. train, after a most enjoyable day had been spent at S. John's Rectory, where the greatest kindness was displayed by the good rector* and his wife. On the Thursday, for the first time in his life, the Father addressed a coloured congregation—an event ever to be remembered, owing to the peculiar custom of the audience of shouting out, wriggling, jumping, and shrieking " as the spirit moved them." Friday evening, in the Cooper Union Hall, the Father held a meeting for those who had been blessed at the Mission, and related the story of his own life, the hall being quite full.

There were no services on Saturday, or Sunday morning. In the afternoon, the Monk drove over to Brooklyn, where he preached afternoon and evening to a large congregation (considering the heavy rain) in "the Academy of Music," stopping between the services at an hotel, where some kind Christian New York friends had hired private rooms. It was remarked, especially in the next morning's papers, that, despite the dreadful weather, numbers of people followed the Father over the river from New York and Haarlem. On Tuesday, the Father left New Jersey by the three o'clock train for East Orange, where he had promised to preach in the evening, at the Harrison Street Skat-

* The Rev. Dr. A. B. Carver.

ing Rink on behalf of the building fund of Christ Church, which had been burnt down, for which object tickets for seats had been sold at 50 and 25 cents, during the past week, in all the drug stores of Orange, Newark, and Roseville, there being 3,000 seats, and no free admission. The Bishop of Newark had been interviewed, and sent the Father his blessing, welcoming him to Orange. This fine venerable Father in Christ, when he knew the Father had arrived in Orange, sent for him to his house, where he gave him a special blessing, and was most genial and kind. A peculiar state of affairs this—the Bishop of Long Island inhibiting him, while the Bishop of the next diocese sends for him, and gives him his special blessing! The subject of the sermon was "Jesus weeping over Jerusalem," of which the following is a portion of the report from "*The Orange Journal*," January 17th, 1891:—"Upwards of 1,800 people, Episcopalians, Presbyterians, Baptists, Methodists, Roman Catholics, Swedenborgians, Revivalists, men of all creeds, and men of no creeds, habitual church goers, and those who never bend the knee within hallowed walls, old and young, rich and poor, all standing side by side, singing the hymn 'Rock of Ages,' accompanied on a small harmonium, which stood on a rudely-constructed platform, by a saintly monk, clad in the garb of the Order of St. Benedict. It was a remarkable gathering, an impressive service, the like of which was never before seen in the Oranges. There was no pomp, no ceremonial, no gorgeous ritual, no trained voices, no great organ pealing forth its majestic notes; yet the service was magnificent withal—magnificent in its simplicity and solemnity. In many respects it was a primitive sight, and it was indeed a new, if not a strange, experience in this, the last decade of the nineteenth century, for ministers and laymen of several denominations to sit at the feet of a Benedictine Monk, listening to the impassioned eloquence and fervid exhortations addressed to his hearers in the name of the Great Master. And now the service begins. The Monk slowly ascends the platform and engages in silent prayer. With faultless enunciation and beautiful emphasis, and in tones so clear and distinct that they can be heard all over the hall, he reads the lines of the hymn above mentioned, and then sits down to play and lead the melody. The great audience sings heartily, and with marked effect, and at the close Father Ignatius again kneels, and with hands uplifted and a voice which at times betrays emotion, delivers an eloquent extemporaneous prayer. The Evangelist then rises, and introduces his subject by announcing his text. He wastes no time in introductory sentences, but plunges into his subject matter, and for forty minutes holds the close attention of his congregation, by one of the most masterly discourses ever heard in the Oranges, in which tender pathos, deep earnestness, strong conviction, subtle reasoning, and charming imagery play their respective parts. Jesus is his theme, and throughout, the eloquent Monk never mentions HIS NAME without impressive emphasis and touching reverence.

"Whatever his qualities, one is forced irresistibly to the conclusion that Father Ignatius is a faithful follower of the Christ he preaches, and will continue his labours, despite the inhibitions of *proud* and *haughty bishops*, or the prejudices of a *few bigoted priests* and their *misguided zealots*.

" On Wednesday evening, for the first time since leaving the old Welsh hills of home, the Father addressed a Welsh congregation on "Mor o gan yw Cymru i gyd," taking for his text, " Os anghofiaf di O Jerusalem." Welsh advertisements were inserted in all the daily papers, and the hymns and prayers were in the language of the Cymry. It is an interesting fact to note that there are three Welsh Chapels, and some eight thousand Welsh speaking people in New York and Brooklyn alone. A gentleman from S. David's Society called on the Tuesday morning, to know if they might give a public dinner in the Father's honour.

The following is a report of the service from "*Columbia*" of the following week, *Columbia* being a Welsh paper published in Kansas :—

"Father Ignatius, a descendant of an illustrious family of Welsh lineage, the Druidic monk, now on a preaching tour in this country, is one of the greatest preachers.

"Had it been better known, doubtless the little Welsh

Chapel in East 11th Street would have been crowded when Father Ignatius, of Llanthony Abbey, South Wales (who was the selected orator for two days at the grand National Eisteddfod at Aberhonddu in 1889) preached on "Mor o gan yw Cymru i gyd," Wednesday night, January 14th. This monk, from St. David's own valley of the Honddu, was admitted a Druid (as Dewi-Honddu) by the Archdruid Clwydfardd, at Aberhonddu, then, and in the following October stood up and spoke for the rights of 'The Welsh Church' at the English Church Congress held at Cardiff, before the Archbishop of Canterbury and the assembled Prelates of the English Church, by the permission of the Bishop of Llandaff.†

"The sermon, by the Druidic monk from the ancient hills and valleys of Wales, having only been arranged on the Monday previous, there were but two days to make it known amongst the 8,000 'Cymraeg' speaking Welshmen in New York and Brooklyn. Nevertheless, Welsh advertisements were inserted in the daily New York papers, which succeeded in drawing together a congregation of 150 genuine Cymry and keeping out the Saxons and Americans.

"It is interesting to note that Father Ignatius has been striving to revive the Welsh tongue in his own valley, and we heard only last June that he had three services in Welsh every week-day, and four on Sundays, at his Abbey Church, which is dedicated to 'St. David, Apostle by the Grace of God to the Cymry.'

---
* The Welsh name of Brecon.   † The Right Rev. Dr. Lewis.

J

"After a Welsh hymn and a prayer in the Cymric tongue by the Monk, he announced his text in the national language, 'Os anghofiaf di Jerusalem, anghofied fy neheulaw ganu,'* from Psalm lxxxviii-5, at the same time stating, that he was sorry he was not sufficiently conversant with the Welsh language to attempt to preach 'yn Gymraeg.'† It was a national, as well as a religious address. In vivid colors of imagination, the Monk drew a picture of a patriot in a strange land and his love for his native country. He showed them the grandeur of the Welsh tongue ; their ancient religion ; how the gospel of Christ was brought to them by their own ancestors, Bran the Blessed, and his daughter Eurgain, who learned it, whilst prisoners in Rome with their King Caradoc,‡ in all probability from the lips of St. Paul himself.

"In the very times of the apostles themselves there is found a record in the Menology of the Greek church of Aristobulus (Arwystli) being ordained as bishop for the church in ancient Britain. That the Welsh tongue was far older than the Saxon or any other, the preacher declared. *It* was the language of the *soul*, whilst *Saxon* is the language of *money-making*. Though English histories would lead one to believe the Druids to be a set of harsh and cruel men, it was the ancient Druids of the Cymry, as the Triads of the Welsh proclaim, that prepared the way for the gospel of

---
* "If I forget thee, O Jerusalem, let my right hand forget her cunning."
† 'In Welsh.'   ‡ Caractacus.

Christ and by their sign for God /|\ taught the doctrine of 'the Three *in* One.' Here in this humble home in a strange land, a little band of Welshmen can worship God in their own tongue.

"In England the Queen is thoroughly Welsh, for she sits on the throne of the British Empire as the descendant of Owen Tudor.

"Though century after century had tried to blot out of existence and to persecute even their very language, *yet* there were the Cymry who still spoke the tongue of their heroes, their Druids, their bards, their martyrs, and their saints, whose names still cling to many a hamlet, many a vale, as Merthyr Tydfil, Dewi Brefi, Llangollen and St. Asaph testify. It was their *own* apostle David, who withstood the heretic Pelagius, in the fifth century, midst their queenly mountains. Wales was *indeed* a country to be proud of—dear little Wales, who had suffered so much at the hands of her neighbour, Lloegr.* In her, the light of the Gospel had *never* gone out. To the Welsh Calvinistic Methodists under the saintly Charles of Bala, the noble Rowlands of Llangeitho and Howell Harris of Trevecca, the revival of a spiritual religion and the establishment of the grand Sunday school system is due. God raised them up when the English element (and English bishops) in the Welsh church had *almost* driven out the National one. Then there was no 'Ein Tad' taught there; there was no 'Gogoniant ir

---
* England.

Tad, ac ir Mab, ac ir Yspryd Glan' rising to God in the temples, amidst the hills and vales of Wales. But when the great revival arose at the hands of Charles of Bala and his companions, then spiritual life sprang up once more in the midst of your mountains and glens,—then the great Sunday school movement sprang up, and brought into life true spiritual religion among the ancient people of Cymru. The Cymry always *were* a religious people. Let them always *remain* so, and let the thought of their Fatherland and their grand ancestry, stir them up to prove to their neighbours their love, first for their God and His honor and glory, and then for the land of their fathers. So let that land so richly named 'Mor o gan yw Cymru i gyd' on earth, be but a preparation and sweet foretaste of the 'Mor o gan' in the New Jerusalem above.

"When life's voyage here is o'er
The eternal years shall dawn,
On the everlasting shore,
In the golden rays of morn.

"After the sermon and a hymn in Welsh, the Monk announced that a collection would be taken towards the support of services 'yn Gymraeg' in New York. This was followed by another hymn and 'Gras Ein Harglwydd,'* &c.

"As the Druidic Monk left the chapel many were the kind greetings in Welsh that saluted him, and more than one expressed a wish that he would come again."

---

* 'The grace of our Lord Jesus Christ,' etc.

On Thursday evening, he spoke again at the "Coloured" Church; and on Friday night, the Father gave an address at the Cooper Union on "The Foundation of Llanthony Abbey."

The next was the Father's last Sunday in New York, and the morning and afternoon services were held at "The Lenox Lyceum," Madison Avenue, and without any free admission. The subjects were—in the morning, "The Macquaery Case"; and in the afternoon, "Revivalism amongst the Upper Classes." In the evening, the sermon was on "The God of Peace," in the small Cooper Union. At these three services the receipts were $1,300. This day, all the New York papers had columns about the Father, especially "*The New York World,*" which contained a long illustrated able article on Llanthony Abbey. A few days previously "*The New York Sun*" had published a long and full account of "The Llanthony Visions."* It was during this Mission in New York, that the Welsh Monk received most pressing invitations to preach at S. Paul's, Edgewater; Church of the Ascension, New Brighton; Christ Church, Elizabeth; S. John's, Jersey City; and Christ Church, Tyler, Texas; but, owing to his stay in America being now limited, he was obliged with regret to be unable to accept them. Just before leaving the City the Rector of Trinity Church, San Francisco,† telegraphed to "try and secure the Father's

---
* This "The Llanthony Monks" hope shortly to publish in cheap pamphlet form.

† The Rev. J. Sanders Reed, for whose brother the Father had

services for a week's mission in his church, promising to pay *all* expenses and to give the Father the offertories."

His work in New York over, the Father left, in good spirits and wonderful health, on the Monday night, January 19th, 1890, for a three months' rest in beautiful Florida ; and as a closing proof of the great work of the New York Mission, I think the following letter from a Presbyterian minister* to " *The New York Herald,*" of Sunday, January 18th, is a fair testimony, as coming from a Christian of another communion :—

To the Editor of " *The New York Herald.*"

" There is a beautiful combination of scholarship and deep spirituality in the Evangelist Monk of the Church of England, which the various and varied audiences he has been addressing during the past month have not failed to perceive and gratefully and cordially appreciate. He is as perfectly at home in the Greek of the original Scriptures, and quotes it as fluently and familiarly, as any professor of Old Oxford. What floods of light he has thrown upon many difficult passages of the sacred text, not only by his concise and accurate knowledge as an exegete, but by his enchanting manner, of transporting his hearers to the scenes, and describing the circumstances of their

recently preached at " The Church of The Intercession," New York.

* The Rev. John Boyd, who subsequently proved himself a true and most faithful worker and self-denying promoter of the Father's work for souls, and a friend whose fidelity to " the Cause " will ever be remembered with gratitude.

original utterance, and making his expositions so clear and distinct that the ordinary mind, as well as that of the trained student, rejoiced with joy and gladness.

"Father Ignatius is not only a thoroughly educated clergyman, but, better still, he is a man of deep and fervent spirituality, and speaks *from* the heart *to* the heart. Seldom, if ever, has the writer heard a minister of the Gospel, either in this country or Europe, address his hearers with such an exact knowledge of Scripture, combined with a melting sweetness and tenderness of voice, manner, and every other grace calculated to win men to the Saviour. The prayers, also, of this servant of God are models of adoration, reverence, high faith, and hope in the Holy Trinity. His language, when addressing God, seems absolutely inspired. His heart is filled with deep emotion, and his face is illumined with the light and blessedness of Heaven!

"The audiences are made up of the cream of all the churches—Episcopalians, Presbyterians, Methodists, and Baptists. Even the Plymouth Brethren, who are such hair-splitters, and who seldom deign to listen to any one, however gifted, outside their own denomination—they, too, were among the vast throngs, with eyes and ears wide open, drinking in with avidity celestial draughts of the beautifully-stated Gospel by one, who is at the very antipodes of all *their* notions of church truth and government. It cannot be sneeringly said that his audiences are all women—though of noble Christian women there have been not a few—ladies of the highest culture and refinement, intelligent students of the Word of God, whose presence would adorn any society or any church. Such women have been present at all of Father Ignatius' meetings, but the majority have been ministers of the Gospel from different denominations—lawyers, physicians, bankers, merchants, and many others—men of thought and earnest purpose. The sermons of this English divine are sometimes topical, at other times expository, and always logical. His wealth of illustration is remarkable, especially in the line of history, ancient and classical, with which he is so familiar that his congregations are often charmed and surprised at the ease with which he can quote Greek and Roman names, and incidents to illustrate his subject. His aim *from first to last* is to *glorify* the Saviour, and so lift Him up in His sacrificial work that men may *find* salvation and eternal life. The result of this faithful preaching has been the conversion of many to the Lord Jesus Christ, and the restoration of not a few lapsed ones, including a once distinguished minister of the Gospel to the paths of holiness and truth. The writer has been profoundly impressed by the whole character and style of this Welsh Monk—his remarkable conversion to God at the age of twenty-nine; his distinct call of God to the ministry; his holy consecration; his strange unworldliness, in that he gave up the world and all its advantages and emoluments, that he might follow his Master and be a co-worker with Him in saving souls ; his true heart, refinement, and intellectual superiority, uniting all that is sweet and tender in a true woman, with the power and strength of a great and good man.

" No wonder that little children run to him and love him, that grown people throng his meetings, listen with rapt attention to his preachings, and request his prayers for themselves and for their friends. His face beams with sympathy and love to and for *all* mankind, and young and old alike feel the spirit of the Saviour when they come near him.

" The splendid rhetoric, the graceful and polished delivery, the easy and most natural movements of the accomplished Christian gentleman robed in flowing garments, his heart and eye kindled with holy love, joy and zeal, his face shining oftentimes with transfiguring light—is it any wonder that every heart was melted, and every eye filled with refreshing tears? ' Take him all in all we may not look upon his like again.' God bless the noble Monk who has brought much blessing to our city, and may His power rest upon every such man, whether arrayed in the spotless surplice of the Churchman, the solemn black of the Presbyterian, or the peculiar garb of the Benedictine, who uses the courage of his sanctified convictions, in preaching to religious as well as to irreligious sinners the Gospel of the *once* Slain, *now* Risen, Glorified and *Coming* Son of God, Whose truth and empire will flourish despite the frowns of the great ones of this earth, and Whose true ministers have no need to fear the sneers or threats of adversaries from any quarter."

During this Mission, when there was an abundant outpouring of blessing to many who heard him, a wish was expressed by numbers, that he would leave behind some link, by which they might, though parted, feel connected with him in his work and the Monastery, and by which those "young in the Faith" might strengthen, and be a blessing to one another. Thus "The Bond of the Holy Spirit" was inaugurated and the first meeting held whilst the Father was in Florida. Its members now number about 100 from all denominations, who meet once a month for spiritual converse, praise, and prayer. A list of members' names and addresses is occasionally printed privately and sent to every member, in order that each, rich or poor, high or low, may know one another. Station and wealth are *lost* and *buried* in the Love and Brotherhood of Jesus. By having branches of the "The Bond" in various towns, and each member possessing the names and addresses of all the other members, what a comfort and help in many cases it will be to a young Christian, to know at once where to find friends in a strange city, ready and glad, by the ties of brotherhood and love, to advise and help him as far as lies in their power. Only "Saints of God," with their robes washed *whiter than* snow in the Blood of Jesus, those who have been born anew of the Spirit, or as prodigals have come home to their Father's house, are eligible.

What a work for Jesus these, one and all, *might* do in many a poor parish. How many a bed of suffering and pain, how many a home of misery and sin they might brighten with rays of their own new-found joy in Jesus. I know of one new-born in Christ (in one of the largest cities in the States*), who, though not a member of "The Bond," yet spends daily, many an hour in the wards of " The Children's Hospital," shedding rays of love and happiness around her, *wherever* she goes. When she enters the ward, the children hold out their arms and cry out with joy; the nurses welcome her, and even the parents, who come to visit their sick and suffering little darlings, derive comfort and blessing from her example. Several clergymen and ministers are already members of '· The Bond " in New York. They have a Chaplain, Secretary, and Treasurer; and ladies and gentlemen, young and old, who *know* Jesus as their *Personal* Saviour, are welcome as members to it.

Whilst in New York, the Father received the following most interesting letters and pressing invitation to visit Minneapolis, Minnesota, but his engagements did not permit of his accepting it. The first letter, dated December 10th, is as follows :—" Nearly twenty years ago I used to avail myself of every opportunity to attend the services at the Church of S. Edmund, King and Martyr, in Lombard Street, London, when you were ministering on Fridays. It was the means

---

* Chicago.

by which my soul was touched, and I was brought back into the Fold of the Holy Catholic Church from whence I had strayed in my boyhood under the influence of my respected, holy but misguided father. Since then, I was led to offer my life to the Ministry and I am now here as Rector of a Church in this City. *First*, I wish to thank you and bless you for having come into my life with 'the Power of the Spirit,' and respectfully and humbly to pray the Almighty Father to continue and increase the glorious work for which you have so nobly and so firmly lived. *Secondly*, to ask if it will be *possible* for you to come to this city, even for a few days' services? This City has a population of 168,000—is full of Churches—but it is the hot-bed of Sectarianism. I think the *Non*-conformist places of worship here, are the most luxurious of any sectarian temples I know of in any other city—that is, generally speaking. If you can come, I am sure it would be the means of greatly furthering our Holy Mother Church. I don't think *any* of our churches would be *large enough* for the public services—but if you can entertain the idea—I pray you do so; and, if you will communicate with me, naming all the requirements that are necessary in such matters, I will at once gather the clergy, &c., together here and we will make the arrangements." The following is a portion of the second letter, dated January 6th, in reply to one from me for the Rev. Father:—"On Sunday last, I took the opportunity of placing your letter in the

hands of Bishop Gilbert (the assistant bishop of this Diocese; Bishop Whipple is now absent in Europe). It was also my happy privilege to tell Bishop Gilbert with what blessed memory I look back some seventeen years when I had the happiness of being present at several of your ministrations in the Churches of S. Edmund, King and Martyr and S. Ethelburga's* in London. The Bishop was much interested and touched, and said *he* should be deeply glad if you could spare us some days or week, or as it would be practicable for you, to hold a series of services in this City. I followed this up by laying the matter before the Rector of the largest church in this City. He enters into the desire to send you an earnest invitation, most enthusiastically, and he will be only too happy to treat with you in the matter, and I shall be passing glad to be his lieutenant in all the necessary preparations. . . . This city and S. Paul are regular church-going cities—but nauseated with a surfeit of 'religious?' oratory of the indefinite and agnostic stamp having a 'name to live,' but in reality *terribly dead*. The place is ripe for an awakening. Pray come over and help us ! .
. . Of course all expenses, connected with a visit to us, will be cheerfully and gratefully covered, and if there are any requirements connected with your errand to this country, they will receive the warm attention of a kind-hearted people."

---

* Bishopsgate.

CHAPTER IX.

Green Cove Springs, Florida.

"Have you been to the Sunny South?
 The Land of 'the Rising Sun?'*
Where the balmy air of Summer,
 May be found when in North it's done—
Where the sunshine is dancing ever,
 On the silvery waves of the stream,
O'ershadowed by tall palmettoes,
 Through which orange and lemon gleam—
Where flowers of the greatest beauty,
 Unseen in the Northern land;
And the choicest ferns and foliage,
 May be gathered on every hand—
Where the live oak, and the guava,
 The pomegranate and datepalm grow,
The banana and royal shaddock—
 Where the cold winds never blow—
Where 'tis *one perpetual summer*,
 When the lands in the North are bound
With the ice and snow of winter,
 And the air rings with the sleigh bell's sound—
Where birds of the gayest plumage,
 Like jewels flash in the sun,
As they thread their way thro' the forests,
 Sweet songsters many a one."

W. M. D.

Steaming away from the snow-clad lands and frost-bound streams of the North, a two days' journey finds

---

* So called from the great Seminole chief, Osceola, which in English signifies "The Rising Sun," a device that he always wore round his neck.

one in "the *sunny* South," 'midst the bright green of spring,—in Florida, the Land of "The Rising Sun," where Osceola, the Great Seminole Chief, whose noble name and deeds, figure in the pages of Indian history, both lived and died. After the close of the war, but a few were left in The Great Cypress and the Everglades of Lake Okeechobee, of that great tribe of which *he* was the hero, and to try to conquer and extinguish the Seminoles cost the United States Government $24,000,000. Though it cost them *that to try*, they failed, and the Seminole Indians are once more increasing in numbers, and are as independent as ever. How strange it seems, to be *one* day in the land of ice and snow, of rugs and coats and furs, and in *two* days to find oneself sitting out on a piazza all day long, even *complaining of the heat;* yet so it is in this summer land, where the pineapple and orange grow, the lemon and banana, the date palm and the cocoanut, the sugar cane and rice. Here one finds ladies and children, rambling through the beautiful woodland glades in cotton and white dresses. Everyone and everything apparently wearing the garb of summer, and uniting to praise their Almighty Maker, for the beauties with which He has clothed nature, and the soft, balmy air of Florida in winter.

"Beautiful vistas continually open out upon the river, as you stroll through S. David's Path, and the eye reaches over the blue expanse of water to the distant shore, meeting occasionally along the horizon with a flock of white curlews, grey herons or mallard ducks, —above, the lofty branches of the live oak, the magnolia and the cypress. Long festoons of grey Spanish moss hang suspended from ten thousand forest trees, waving gracefully in the gentle breeze. Sitting upon an old log in these primeval woods, one is able to drink in the air with inexpressible delight. Beautiful it is to see ripe golden oranges, half hidden by the dark, glossy green of the old leaf, hanging on the trees. Mocking birds are singing in the branches, whilst *all* living things, seem basking in the sunlight out of doors."*

Such is the little spot on the banks of the magnificent S. John's River, where Father Ignatius first stopped to rest after his hard Mission work in New York. The name is Green Cove Springs, so called after a warm sulphur spring there, " where the water boils up from a large fissure some 20 feet below the surface, at the rate of 3,000 gallons per minute. Clear as a diamond, the effect is most beautiful at noonday, when the sun shines directly into the spring and objects can be seen at the bottom tinted with prismatic hues. Here, whilst severe snowstorms are taking place in New York, you can go and bathe in the open air with an accompanying chorus of mocking birds in the surrounding trees." But I must again revert to the lovely walk known as S. David's, through Borden Park, along the shores of the S. John's River, and the following quotation from

---

* " *Where to go in Florida,*" by Daniel F. Tyler.

a guide book* is not in the least overdrawn :—" It is nearly two miles in length, and winds through the forest along the banks of the S. John's to Governor's Creek. No picture from the camera can ever give more than a *faint* idea of this romantic spot. It is arched and embowered on each side by lofty magnolias, live oaks, cypress, wild azalea, Indian pipe stem, briar wood, and gum tree, and the ground is carpeted with acres of palmetto shrub. Intertwined in the branches are thousands of vines, wild grape, gourd, morning glory, trumpet vine and yellow jasmine. . . . Every tint of verdure delights the eye, from the delicate feathery cypress leaf to the dark glossy green of the magnolia grandiflora. Every now and then you pause in delight, to look back into the forest, through and along great cathedral aisles, or into some woodland bower, overarched with vines and Spanish moss. In the afternoon the rays of the declining sun glance through the varnished leaves and hanging moss, producing the most beautiful effects; while at night, when the full moon is overhead, it darts its silvery beams through the forest, whilst the singing of tree frogs, here so plentiful by the rivers, break the evening stillness with their discordant music." The Hotel S. Clair, where the Father stopped (located right on the banks of the S. John's River, which is five miles wide and the abode of countless alligators), is at the commencement of this path, while at its end

---

* "*The Tourist's Guide to Florida*," by Henry Lee.

K

is the famed Governor's Creek, famed on account of its water being like a French plate mirror, where the smallest leaf upon a lofty branch, or the tiny twig at the top of the highest tree, is perfectly mirrored in the stream beneath. All the colours of the sky and the passing clouds, all the neutral tints upon the trunks of the trees, the fungi, lichens, and mosses of the forest, the overhanging branches and flowering shrubs, the clustering vines along the shore, every bird that sings upon the outspread branches, all the lily pads, every visible thing upon and above the water, is daguerreotyped in perfection. No picture could be more minute, more exquisite. Where the trees are cut away in the forest, and the view opens back into the country, the land seems to be reflected in the water for half a mile from the shore. There is a pretty little wooden Episcopal Church (without a clergyman) at Green Cove, rather dilapidated-looking outside, but very pretty inside, with stained-glass windows. It is dedicated to S. Mary, and stands on the banks of the river near S. David's Path. The church was built in 1878 *by* tourists and *for* tourists, and is only kept open from January to May. There are also Roman Catholic, Methodist, Baptist, and Presbyterian places of worship, the latter being only a small cottage thrown into one room. All the houses in the village are of wood. The place is very quiet, and it is perfectly easy to walk about, or roam through the woods for hours without seeing anyone. Bears, catamounts, and rattlesnakes are occasionally found on the outskirts.

The village streets, with avenues of orange trees bearing fruit, and live oaks, are very quaint and pretty, the roads being of a silvery white sand; the little wooden houses and coloured people, the ox wagons and mule carts driven by blacks in becoming costumes, add to the picturesqueness of the scene. The Father was indeed able to rest and enjoy himself here in the soft air of summer, and when coming in contact with anyone (black or white) in his walks, met with the most respectful and cordial reception. The first caller upon him in Green Cove Springs was the Roman Catholic priest.* Already the Welsh Monk, who of late had sounded the Gospel trumpet so loudly in New York, was beginning to get much better, and was now far stronger in health than he ever was in England. Owing to the urgent request and wish of certain residents in Green Cove Springs the Father addressed them on Sunday, Feb. 1st, in the dining-room of his hotel, which had been purposely cleared for the occasion, there being no proper hall in the village— some of the huts the blacks live in being miserable little wooden places (shanties) without windows, and in appearance most resembling pigsties, quite unfit for any human being to live in. Long before the time appointed for the Father's services, the congregation began to gather from all parts, some arriving on foot, others in conveyances, some in a steamer which had come over purposely from Orange Park. There were

---

* The Rev. Father Peythieu.

numbers who had come from all parts of the neighbourhood, some for miles around. Old men and women, young maidens, youths and children, helped to make up the congregation, and old inhabitants of Green Cove Springs stated afterwards, it was the largest congregation they had ever seen got together in the village. The Episcopal clergyman* who was taking temporary duty at Green Cove was there, he having postponed his own Evensong, or, as he announced it, "Vespers," at the Parish Church, indefinitely until after the Father's service, that he might attend. The subject of the sermon was "Jesus Christ the Living Bread." Before and after the sermon, "Rock of Ages" and "Just as I am" were respectively sung without accompaniment, the Father leading the singing. Numerous were the expressions of thankfulness afterwards for the sermon, after which many of the congregation went straight over to "Vespers" at S. Mary's Parish Church, in the course of which service, the clergyman thanked God for the Father's sermon he had heard, which was the true old Gospel story, and stated he was sure the Bishop could not know what the Father was preaching, but that he should go next day, and in a personal interview, seek permission for the Father to preach the following Sunday in the Parish Church, or if not, if the Father would preach again at the Hotel, he would give up his own service. Though only accustomed to Communion

---

*The Rev. Mr. Schermerhorn, of Tarrytown, N.Y.

after Morning Prayer once a month, he most kindly offered to have an eight o'clock celebration in the church for the Father and his party the next Sunday. The following is a report of the sermon from " *The Spring,*"* Feb. 7th.

" Jesus said : ' I am the Bread of Life ; he that cometh to Me shall never hunger, he that believeth in Me shall never thirst.'—S. John vi. 35.

"In this assembly there are two classes of people : those who have come to and believed in Jesus, and those who have *not*. Those who *have* believed in and have come to Jesus do *not* ' hunger ' and ' thirst,' for they are *satisfied* with Jesus. These are Christians. You can easily tell if you are a Christian, *i.e.*, one who has come to and who has believed in Jesus, for, as Jesus says, you ' never hunger ' and ' never thirst.'

"When our Lord Jesus spoke these wonderful words, He spoke words that no mere man would dare to speak, unless he were mad. But He was God ; and when He spoke them, He looked away into the ages that were coming, in which His Holy Gospel should be preached throughout the whole world in the power of the Holy Ghost. He saw the vast multitudes of tired, weary, sinful mortals coming to Him in a simple faith, and finding in Him pardon and peace, righteousness and eternal life. Yes, there are longings, hungerings, and thirstings of soul that make the life of man peaceless and wretched. Neither the world, money, nor intellect can fill the aching void or rest

---
* The Local Paper published weekly.

the tired spirit. Religion itself can not really satisfy the soul. I was religious myself as a child, as a youth, as a young man ; but my religion gave me no certainty of salvation, no real peace with God. I was hungry for pardon of sin. I knew I was guilty before God. I hungered for righteousness. I thirsted for peace and rest. I craved to know for certain whether I should and could be saved. I did all I could to win salvation, to gain peace; but I had no assurance of the one or possession of the other. I read texts such as these, but knew nothing of their meaning and power.

"Perhaps some of you are now what I was then; you have *never* known what it is to come to and believe in Jesus, and so you are hungering and thirsting *still*, while we who *have* come to and believe in Jesus can *never* hunger and *never* thirst.

" O, most dear brethren, I want to help you now to come, to believe; and while I am speaking to the unsaved, will those here present who are saved lift up their hearts in prayer to Jesus, who is in the midst of us, that I may speak His word in the power of the Holy Ghost and in its great simplicity. Let us remember, all of us, saved and unsaved alike, that the Holy Ghost *alone* can bring the soul of the sinner to Jesus and His salvation, and I can only preach Jesus to you this afternoon effectually, by the immediate anointing of the Holy Spirit. 'You shall receive power when the Holy Ghost is come upon you' are our Lord's words to His people. But there is still further the promise that the Holy Ghost shall be given to those that ask for it in Jesus' name. The Holy Spirit, then, we have prayed for, and His holy breath is upon us now, and by this power alone can the word I am speaking be brought home to heart.

"Now, unsaved soul, you know that you are not a rested, satisfied, peaceful being. Some here are getting old; grey hair is telling that life's summer tide has passed away; for your life's day has neared to eventide; your pulses are slackening: your blood is chilling now; the world has lost much of its charms for you; the joys and loves of this short earthly life have one by one passed from your heart and out of your existence. You are getting lonely now, but you must become more lonely still. Quite alone you must die; and you are unsatisfied. Your life, as far as eternity is concerned, has been a wasted one: no treasure laid up in heaven; very little, perhaps nothing, done really for God. His House, His Word, His Sabbaths neglected: and each Sabbath you have neglected His sanctuary, you have spent in publicly ignoring God's Being, God's Claim, God's Majesty, To neglect the House of God is to act like an atheist.

"Well, this is how some of us treat God. Others —excellent, moral men—pride themselves upon their uprightness, and, as highly good men, they regularly attend church, read the Bible, and even frequent the Holy Sacraments; but they have *never* realised that they are sinners, they have *never* felt their need of Jesus, and so they have *never* 'come to' Jesus. These, too, are unsaved. The word of God declares 'there is no difference, for all have sinned.' To all such, I say without flinching : 'You are not satisfied, you are not saved.' Jesus says, 'He that cometh to Me shall never hunger,' and He invites you now this moment. 'Come unto Me: I will give you rest: him that cometh, I will in no wise cast out.'

" Some are asking : 'O, tell us, what this "coming" means, and we will come now! We feel our need of Jesus, we are realising His great love, His willingness to receive us, how on the cross He finished the salvation of all who will come to Him! Tell us how we may come, and so never hunger any more!' He tells us Himself that coming to Him is simply a motion of the soul, the heart, the will—it is to ' believe on ' Him, to ' trust ' Him, to take Him at His word.

" Now, as a poor, lost sinner, close thine eyes to all about thee. Jesus is here. He is at thy side. Look up into His face—trust Him as thy very own Saviour —trust all His promises—trust His work, His finished work, upon the cross raised for thee—trust Him who says : 'I will never leave you; you shall have eternal life ! you shall never perish ; none shall pluck you out of My hand.' Ah! your face is glowing with joy, poor sinner! You are trusting Jesus, His work, His word !

"Now—what is Jesus to thee ? He is pardon,

peace, life, righteousness, all—yea, all in all—to thee ; and thou art come, and hast believed, and thou art satisfied. And now you will live with Jesus at your side ; and you will live for His glory, and His light in you shall so shine before men that they shall see your good works and glorify your Father which is in Heaven. Your religion will now be one of gratitude and love, and showing forth your precious Saviour's praise. For His dear sake, you will love and do good to all. You shall be light-bringers and peace-makers among weary and tired men, witnessing for Jesus in a sorrow-laden, dark and dying world, proving in your lives that Jesus *is* the Living Bread that came down from Heaven, and he that cometh to Jesus shall never hunger, he that believeth on Him shall never thirst."

Up to this last Sunday, though there was no Episcopal clergyman at Green Cove Springs, and the churchwardens had telegraphed to Bishop Weed for permission for the Father to officiate in the little Church, his Lordship refused. Consequently the service was read by a layman in ordinary clothes, who was also the bell-ringer, organist, and choir ! The Bishop knew that by preventing the Father officiating, this would be the alternative, yet he *preferred* it. Though as yet but a week in Florida, invitations began to pour in upon the Father, notable amongst which being an invitation to the public annual dinner of " The New England Society in Florida," and to speak at the same. Also an invitation to give one or more addresses in the Exhibition building at "The Florida Sub-Tropical Exposition"* held during January, February, and March every year at Jacksonville and Ocala alternately. On the Saturday in this week the Father received a letter from the Railway Company at S. Augustine, saying, that as they had heard he wanted to preach there, they offered him their large open waiting room, and would run extra and special trains if he decided to come, but the Opera House being already engaged, he was unable to accept this offer. The Minister of the African Church at Green Cove, next sent round to ask the Father to address his large coloured congregation, which he did on the Sunday evening from the text, "One Mediator between God and Man." It was not long before the Father received an invitation also from the Baptist Church; so the Ministers belonging to Green Cove, of all denominations—Episcopalian, Roman Catholic, Baptist and Methodist — one and all united to welcome the Father in their common tie of brotherhood in the Lord Jesus.

---

* The invitation was worded as follows:—"Rev. and Dear Sir,—Understanding that you purpose visiting Florida soon, I desire to write you at once in regard to having one or more lectures delivered at the Exposition Building by you. Your fame has extended here, and thousands have read of the good you have accomplished, and many inspiring words given by you, published in *The New York Press*. I trust most sincerely that, if you visit Florida we will be able to have you with us t the Exposition for whatever time will suit your convenience. With *highest* regards, I remain, etc., The Secretary."

On a fine, warm, sunny day, wonderful and strange was it to northern eyes from a colder clime to watch the chameleons on the Palmetto trees, one minute brown, the next the most dazzling green, changing colour in the sun, the rich colours of the sub-tropical butterflies, and the gorgeous plumage of the birds, especially the American Blue Bird and Scarlet Virginian Nightingale. Cut the dead parts of the Banana trees down, and you can almost watch the trees growing, for they grow a couple of inches in a single day.

The Guide Book states that Green Cove Springs is built on the site of an old camp of the Seminole Indians, and that where we can now walk in security and gaze in wonder at the beautiful architecture of nature, not long ago might be seen the tepees and camp fire of the Indians, with knots of their squaws and papooses around ; and where now the musical notes of the birds, alone break the stilly silence of the woods, once there re-echoed the war-whoop of the Seminole, once their bark canoes alone threaded the maze of lily pads on Governor's Creek. The Guide Book also states, that in S. David's Path there still remains a tree overhanging the river, that the Indians used as a look out, and used to climb to scan the approach by water as well as the far distant horizon for those whose errand should not be one of peace.

"Then the warriors, in their glory,
  Through the virgin forest roamed,
And 'neath the live oaks, old and hoary,
  They passed, with locks uncombed,
And an eye that mocked at capture,
  And scorned a prisoner's chain—
Will they thrill, with a hunter's rapture,
  In the olden haunts again ?
Ah ! no ; for civilization
  Has banished each swarthy face,
And now the Seminole nation,
  Is a half-forgotten race.

" The guava and lime are growing,
  Where once they slaughtered the deer,
And engine-whistles are blowing,
  Where the war-whoop smote the ear.
The orange its fruit produces,
  Where the Indian wigwam stood,
And offers us golden juices,
  Instead of an enemy's blood.
The Sabbath bells are ringing
  O'er hammock and tangled brake,
And we hear the children singing,
  By the shore of the woodland lake."—*Anon.**

---

* From " *Life and Adventures in South Florida*," by Andrew Canova.

CHAPTER X.

S. AUGUSTINE.

LENT SERVICES—THE TOWN—VISIT TO NORTH AND SOUTH BEACHES.

LEAVING Green Cove Springs on the day after Ash Wednesday, the Father went to S. Augustine, the American Brighton of the South, where all the *elite* of the States and members of " *the four hundred* " gather in the winter, when a ceaseless round of gaiety and pleasure goes on. Having promised to preach six Lenten Sermons in the old historical city, the Father hoped to induce many by the Grace of the Holy Spirit to give up the sour crab-apples of the world, for the ripe, luscious peaches of the Kingdom of Heaven. The shop windows on the Plazza being adorned with tickets " Lent Dresses," " Lent Food," &c., and remembering that a New York Paper last autumn, whilst he was preaching at Newport, R.I., stated, that though they had no time to think of religion *then*, they hoped " to be angels in Lent," also having heard it was the fashion of the Upper Classes to be religious and attend churches during " The Forty Days "—all this caused the Father to decide to give them these services. But to return to the journey from Green Cove Springs. It being a lovely summer morning, all went from the hotel to the wharf to see him off, when the Father started down the S. John's River on a steamer for Palatka, *en route* for S. Augustine. Most interesting and delightful was this part of the journey, passing flock after flock of wild duck on the river, who would let the steamer get quite close to them before they started up with a whirr. The scenery along the banks was most varied ; orange groves with balls of golden yellow, half hidden amongst the pale green leaves, and huge live oaks festooned with the grey Spanish moss, and crowned with huge clumps of mistletoe and tall palmettoes, passed in panoramic view before the eye of the traveller. Arrived at Palatka, there not being any train on to S. Augustine at once, it was necessary to find a resting place until the next one at five, so the Putman House was chosen at which to rest awhile. Whilst there, a lady who was a perfect stranger to the Father, offered him a carriage for a drive, but having visited one of the Curiosity Museums to examine the living and dead productions of Florida, he decided not to go. Here we saw the first real appearance of tropical plants and foliage in Florida, the streets being planted with tall palmettoes.

At five the journey was resumed to S. Augustine, the train having to cross the S. John's river to get there. Queer, indeed, was the crossing, as, though some three miles wide, there was no bridge ; only trestles, with two lines running parallel for the train to run on, no side rails, no floor, only these two lines on trestles, and the river shining clearly through underneath. The journey ended, no one was sorry to rest at the nice quiet house of a kind Welsh woman from Pentre Foelas, in the quaint little old Spanish lane designated Marine Street, with its windows overlooking the Matanzas river running between S. Augustine and the Island of S. Anastasia, while right away in the distance could be seen the breaking of the waves on the seashore, swept by the Atlantic Ocean.

Next day, the Soldiers' Cemetery, past S. Francis' Barracks was visited, and the three-stone Pyramids,— under which many soldiers who perished in the Seminole war are buried, and near which is a shaft erected to the memory of Major Dade and his command, who were massacred by Osceola and the Seminoles at the commencement of the war,—were inspected with interest. A few words respecting S. Francis' Barracks will not be inappropriate here. They stand on the site of the old Franciscan Convent, from which many a noble friar, in the time of early Spanish rule, went forth into the unknown wilderness of the Everglades, to a certain martyrdom at the hands of the Indians. Florida owes more to the Franciscans than any other body, for they it was, who throughout her length and breadth, spread forth the Gospel of Christ to the savages. The first members of the Order arrived in 1592, and the Convent was only abandoned for religious purposes when the British took possession in 1763, and twenty years after, on the return of the Spaniards, it was converted into Barracks. The old convent walls of coquina (a substance composed of small shells, joined together by some glutinous substance into a hard solid mass, of which quarries may be found on S. Anastasia Island) still remain standing, and are among some of the oldest structures in the City. On passing "The Alicia Hospital,"* the Father was asked in to see the patients, and promised to visit them before leaving the town, which he did the following day, Friday. During his stay in the ancient city, both North Beach and South Beach, with their magnificent stretches of firm fine sand, strewn with rare and exquisite shells, were visited. No sands can be compared to the sands of Florida. The captain of the steamer to South Beach was most kind, and would not allow the Father to pay for any of his party. Here the Father made his acquaintance with "Homesteaders," so common in the wild parts of the States. One of the chief attractions of this Island is the lighthouse, to the top of which the Father climbed and enjoyed the lovely panoramic view for miles round from the summit; the height is 150 feet from the ground; consequently climbing the steep staircase was no small undertaking for the Father. The painting of the tower in spiral bands is peculiar, but readily distinguishable from any other landmark on the coast. When the lantern is lit, it

---

* Close here on the banks and in the bed of the river, at low water, the ground was covered with thousands upon thousands of tiny little crabs, locally designated "Fiddlers," which swarmed as far as the eye could reach, and scuttled off into their holes in the sand at one's approach.

shows a fixed white light, varied by a white flash every three minutes, and can be seen at a distance of nineteen miles. The first Sunday at S. Augustine, after preaching in the morning on "A voice crying in the wilderness," the Rev. Father was compelled by sudden indisposition to give up the afternoon and evening services.

The following is a report of the morning sermon: — "S. John i. 23.—'The voice of one crying in the wilderness.' This is the name the Forerunner of the Son of God Incarnate gave himself, when asked who he was, by messengers from the Church authorities in Jerusalem, thus appropriating to himself the prophecy uttered 700 years before by the Evangelical Prophet. O brethren! how *unlike* man's ways are the ways of God! Had we been called into the counsels of the Most High, should we not have advised a careful college training at the feet of Gamaliel and the noted Nicodemus, 'The Teacher of Israel,' and that John the Baptist should have studied human nature amid the throngs of the great cities? But God willed otherwise. John, who was to prepare the way of the long expected Messiah, 'the Almighty God,' 'the Prince of Peace,' was in the deserts *until* the day of his showing unto Israel.' And when, after a hermit's life among the wilds of Judæa, he was to commence his most wondrous mission, upon what power should he depend, for aid in gathering the people to hear, or when they were gathered how was he, the wild Monk

L

of the wilderness, to address them? Ah, do *we* consider God's ways here, in the matter of 'the forerunner,' unwise and injudicious? what shall we say of His arrangements for His Own Son when He comes to tabernacle among men in human guise for three and thirty years. Born in the dreary stable cave; rejected, wounded, slain; dying a criminal between two thieves, gibbeted on the Shameful Cross! Yet so it is, and as the Crucified Carpenter of Nazareth and Malefactor of Calvary we adore Him. The multitudes thronged to hear the sermons of the Monkish Preacher; priests and scribes from Jerusalem thirty miles away, multitudes from the country around. Tax collectors and their trains of stalwart soldiers from the Roman barracks of Antonia and Tiberias, delicate maidens and stately matrons from the society circles of the almost Romanised cities of Palestine. How strange to the lonely Hermit, to see the gathered throng of beauty and wealth, of pomp and fashion, hanging breathlessly on his simple words and ringing tones. Undaunted by the grandeur of the crowd, he cries, ' The Voice in the Wilderness.' These notes are the burden of his cry. Let *us* listen to ' the Voice of one crying in the Wilderness,' in this solemn hush of the quiet Lenten-tide—let us hear the three-fold cry, ' Repent, the kingdom of Heaven is at hand.' ' Behold the Lamb of God that taketh away the sin of the world.'

" This is ' the voice of one crying in the wilderness.'

Would to God I too might, in the wilderness of this world, cry nightly this same cry. To-day, here in S. Augustine, fashionable society throngs, to rest from the fever of fashion, and the toil of time, during the solemn season of Lent. A local newspaper tells us that although Episcopalians (including Roman Catholics) are resting during Lent, from social pleasures, meaning ball and theatres, the young people of other denominations are arranging several such society gatherings. Is this really so, or is it a libel upon the other denominations—the Presbyterian, the Methodist, the Congregational, and the Baptist? Why! one of the *chiefest* reasons that these Evangelical sects broke away from our Episcopal Church was, that they aimed at *higher* spirituality of life, a *further off* position from the fashion of the world! Can it be *possible* that now they are more worldly and frivolous than the unconverted in our Church are said to be? *What!* a Methodist at a ball! a Congregationalist at a play! a Presbyterian watching with delight the exposures of the ballet! Oh! Wesley and Whitfield, oh! sturdy Puritans, and brave Covenanters of the old times, is this the result of your teachings, your labours, and your pains? While even our worldly Episcopalians and Roman Catholics are resting in outward form of Lenten penitence for their sins and worldliness, your folks are still planning to enjoy the things you cursed with your bitterest anathemas. Surely, if this *be* true, there is terrible and saddest need for a John the

Baptist in this day. 'The Voice of one crying in the Wilderness.' And is not this gay world of fashion and frivolity a wilderness, where peace and rest, content and true liberty of soul can*not* be found? Ah, yes! children of this gay world of pleasure come to us in bitter weariness of spirit, worn out and sick of the hollowness, the disappointments, the slavery, the sins of fashionable life! We preachers in the wilderness of this restless, hungry world, often hear the stories of this 'Society circle,' stories from underneath the surface they pour into *our* ears. Oh! graceful, beautiful women, go on *till* you are found out. We know the shadows of sin that rest over many a stately home. We will not particularise to-day. Yes; this gay world of fashionable society is a very wilderness of desolation to many of the seemingly gayest sons and daughters of Fashion's tyrannous round. As John the Baptist cried in the power of the Holy Ghost, 'Repent,' that is, change your minds, so now I would cry to you, 'Repent, change your minds.' Jesus is now in our midst, the Holy Spirit is breathing upon you, to aid you to receive His Word, to change your mind; you have been living in sin, in pleasure, with your faces turned *away* from God; now 'repent, be converted,' turn round to Jesus, He is *waiting* to welcome you. He has finished the salvation of *all* who will with a simple trust receive Him in His fulness as the Father's gift to their souls, 'Behold! oh, behold! the Lamb of God,' with the eye of faith behold Him now—in all His Fulness, as salvation, righteousness, pardon, life, peace—all thine, the very *instant* you believe. The Holy Ghost is breathing in His seven-fold power upon you, to aid you in beholding the Lamb of God with this divine and simple trust that lays hold of Him *once and for ever*. Then, when you have trusted Him, His own words to you are : 'You shall never perish, none shall pluck you out of My Hand,' 'I will never leave thee, nor forsake thee.' You may go forth rejoicing, you who have thus received Him, saved and satisfied, pardoned and in peace—for we which *have* believed do enter into rest.

"Father Ignatius then appealed to the old and grey-haired, who had well-tried what the world could do for them, to try what Jesus would do now, by accepting Him as the Father's gift. He told many stories of recent conversions in New York and other places to encourage his hearers then and there to accept Christ as a present and perfect Saviour. This is but a very faint outline of the discourse, but gives much of the gist of it. He concluded by saying that when a man received Christ, the Kingdom of God was set up within him, and Jesus reigned in his love, his will, his life, and that the love of Jesus in his heart was the powerful principle within, fulfilling the Law. Thus the Kingdom of Heaven, which was only at hand, was now within us, and a Christian life in the world was spent in a daily manifestation of this beautiful and practical truth."

S. Augustine is the site of the earliest permanent settlement of Europeans, within the present territory of the United States. In the past, at one time or other, Spain, France and England have all fought for, or against it. It was discovered April 3rd, 1512, by Ponce de Leon and is situated on the Atlantic coast of Florida, near the southern extremity of a peninsula formed by the Matanzas and San Sebastian Rivers. Its streets are most narrow, quaint and picturesque, with here and there an old Spanish house still standing; whilst walking down the centre of Treasury Street, you can touch the walls on either side. The population is composed chiefly of Minorcans, though Hindoos and almost all nations of the globe contribute their quota. The varied costumes of the children add to the picturesqueness of the scene. Daily, at sunrise and sunset, the large gun at the Barracks resounds over the ancient city, while thrice a day peals forth the Angelus, from the Spanish Cathedral on the Plaza, overlooking which the Episcopal Church is also built. The Cathedral was built by the Spaniards in 1682, but burnt in 1887, the present edifice having been rebuilt since the fire. On this plaza is also situated the old Slave Market, and this public square was once the Parade Ground where many an historical event has taken place in the annals of S. Augustine. Whilst here, the Father preached unexpectedly one evening, in the grand Memorial Presbyterian Church, and was much pressed to give an address at the Coloured Church.

There being no services during the week, various points of interest in the town and neighbourhood were visited. I would speak first of Fort Marion, on the site where Menendez, the Spanish general, constructed the first fort (built of wood only) in 1565. This fort he named San Juan de Pinos. It was octagonal, mounting 14 brass cannon, but was destroyed in 1586 by Sir Francis Drake. The name was subsequently changed by the Spaniards to San Marco, by the English to S. John, and by the United States to Fort Marion, becoming in time quite a formidable fortress near the old city gates. Both of these latter are built of coquina, and a greater portion of each is still standing. In Fort Marion is still shown the room, where the Indian chiefs Osceola and Coacoochee were confined, and from the window of which they escaped.

One of the great features of the town, to see which many people come hundreds of miles, are its huge and magnificent hotels—the Ponce de Leon, the Alcazar,* and the Cordova, a few words concerning which will doubtless be of interest. Situated on three sides of the Alameda Plaza, which is laid out with asphalte drives, footways, fountains, and parterres of tropical plants, the Ponce de Leon faces 380 feet on the north side, the Alcazar on the south, the Cordova on the east, and the Villa Zorayda on the west. The Ponce de Leon represents the best school of Spanish architecture, and is the result of a conscientious study of

---

* From Al-Kasr, *i.e.*, House of Cæsar.

principles that have made famous the cathedrals, universities, and palaces of classic Spain. Besides facing 380 feet on the Alameda, it faces 520 feet on Cordova and Seville Streets, the main building with its accessory portico surrounding a court 150 feet square, with central fountain and carefully-tended beds of flowers. The Alcazar is also in the Spanish Renaissance style. The Cordova is monolithic, but with heavy battlemented walls and towers, as found in the castles of Moorish Spain. The northern entrance is an adaptation of the Puerto del Sol of Toledo, and the balconies are after those said to have originated in Seville, designed by Michael Angelo, and known as " the kneeling balconies," for the convenience of devotees who desired to kneel during the passage of religious processions.

The Villa Zorayda was the first modern building to be erected after the Moorish style. Over its entrance is an Arabic inscription signifying " There is no conqueror but God," the motto of Mohammed Aben Alahmas, founder of the Alhambra. It is entirely built of coquina. On the Second Sunday in Lent the Father preached three sermons at the Opera House. The subjects were : " Jonah's Mission to Nineveh " in the morning ; " The Temptations of Jesus " in the afternoon ; and " Jesus Christ and Mary Magdalene " in the evening.

CHAPTER XI.

S. James on the Gulf of Mexico.

Punta Gorda—Sailing down Charlotte Harbour —Pine Island.

BEFORE I deal with this quiet, picturesque island, near the mouth of the Caloosahatchie in the Gulf of Mexico, there were a few points, on the journey from S. Augustine, I would notice. Picturesquely tropical beyond imagination, its shores washed by the warm waters of the Gulf, situated five days' post from New York, on the western shore of Florida, 400 miles from Jacksonville (from whence all the stores and provisions are obtained), it is most out of the way, far south of the nearest railroad, and only approachable by a small primitive steamer from Punta Gorda,* where the railway ends. Five hours and a half is the average time taken by the steamer, which starts every morning at seven.

But to return for just a cursory glance at the Father's journey from S. Augustine, which he left at half-past eight on Tuesday morning. It was impos-

---

* Here it was, that we first saw the strange air-plants so frequent in Florida, plants that grow and live without roots, *entirely* on air,

sible to get to S. James, on Pine Island, before half-past twelve next day, owing to the badly-arranged connections on the line. At Palatka, as the train stopped, the Father was surrounded in the railway carriage by a number of people wanting his autograph, and he must have written some dozens or so. As they were perfect strangers who asked him, I gave them all *Welsh* ones! As the train passed fertile tracts, orange groves golden with the ripe fruit, beautiful and picturesque creeks, magnificent stretches of wild and luxurious forests, one could not help thinking what a grand country Florida is, and with land so cheap and *such* a climate, *what* a home for the enterprising emigrant!

Soon after leaving Bartow, a Junction on the Route, the Father spoke to an Arcadian Cowboy (also Editor of a newspaper at Arcadia, a small town we passed), from whom he gathered much information respecting the life of a cowboy and the Seminole Indians. This interesting young man, before getting off the train, distinguished himself by drawing pistols, and wanting to fight when the conductor asked for his extra fare, he having ensconced himself in an arm chair of ' the parlour car.' The moonlight was very clear as the train passed through the region of the lakes, but I shall not attempt to describe its silvery reflections on the water, and the shadows of the trees through which it peeped.

It was ten o'clock and past, before Punta Gorda,

with its immense hotel, was reached, and by the time a cup of tea and refreshment had been procured, the small hours of morning were fast approaching. Here, to our surprise, was a lady as housekeeper, who had sat at the feet of the Father during his Boston Mission. Welcome was the sight of mosquito nets, as this tribe seem to have a *liking* for strangers. After a refreshing night's rest, we embarked next morning at seven on the steamer.* Among our fellow-passengers were a noted playwright, a great tarpon fisher, and a man *en route* for Naples, a small colony 20 miles south of Pine Island,† for a pineapple plantation.

With scarcely a breeze, and a glorious blue sky overhead, safely and comfortably ensconced on the upper deck, the *countless* beauties of Charlotte Harbour were admired. As the day grew on, the sun began to burn more and more, and so much did we suffer from it that by the time the great city of S. James (only nineteen houses) was reached, our faces were like boiled lobsters, and smarting as if on fire. Subsequently we underwent the novel and not very pleasant experience of *peeling*, as we had never done before. As the steamer glided down the harbour, it was indeed *excessively* interesting to watch the countless pelicans and cormorants (continually diving after their prey, all round the boat), and the

---

* "The Alice Howard," of Capt. White's.
† Founded by Miss Rose Cleveland, the sister of President Cleveland.

porpoises sporting in the sun. Sanibel, Captiva, La Costa, and Gasparilla Islands shut in the harbour from the Gulf, and forming a natural barrier or breakwater, ward off the severe Gulf storms. The two great natural water avenues, leading from the Gulf into Charlotte Harbour, are Bocca Grande, on the north between Gasparilla and La Costa Islands, and the main entrance on the south, between Sanibel Island and the mainland. Big Pine Island,* on the southern extremity of which S. James' City is situated, is fourteen miles long, and varying from two to four miles in width.

Steaming down the harbour, the varied and brilliant colours of the water, which is clear as crystal in the glistening rays of the sun, catch the eye. Groups of small islands, where the rookeries of birds of all sorts are, we continually pass, all overgrown with the mangrove scrub. Arriving at last at the S. James' City Wharf, we obtain our first glimpse of the cocoanut palm, for here the avenues are planted, three with the cabbage palmetto, one with the graceful cocoanut palm, another with Florida rubber trees, and one with the royal ponciana. Here we experience *true tropical* weather. Tropical plants and foliage greet us on all sides—bananas, date palms, pineapples, pawpaws, limes, oranges, lemons, mangoes, alligator pears, pomegranate and cotton plant, all seem to flourish

---

* The largest Island in Charlotte Harbour. Contains nearly 25,000 acres, mainly woodland,

around us, and Punta Gorda is the northern limit of the Koonti plant or Indian bread fruit.*

Whilst the shore of the Island is lined with the mangrove trees, Jamaica dogwood, buttonwood, mastic, small oak trees, and several species of the heath family flourish on its soil. Buttonwood makes the very best fuel for a log; set on fire at one end, it will burn to ashes before the fire goes out, and generates an intense heat. Mangrove bark will some day bring a fortune to some 'cute Yankee, who finds a means to extract its red dye. There are several huge Indian shell mounds on the Island, and in some of these excavations have been made, which have brought to light the bones and skulls of Indians of bygone days, now gone to 'the happy hunting grounds.' In some parts of the Island, the interesting and mysterious earthen remains of the canals and mounds of the Aztecs, may be explored. Wild animals and birds of all kinds abound, including the bear, catamount, deer, wild cat, opossum, squirrel, American lion, white headed eagle (one of which Brother David shot and is now stuffed, with other birds shot in the Island, in the Monastery), buzzard, hawk, spoonbill, scarlet and white flamingo, white and blue cranes, silver heron, scarlet ibis, mocking bird, scarlet Virginian nightingale, golden oriole, wild turkey, etc., etc.

The great occupation of everybody, was fishing.

---

* This is a graceful Palm-like plant, whose root is ground and washed, producing a very palatable fine white flour.

Tarpon* fishing was a mania that attracted ladies and gentlemen alike, who would go out in the early hours of the morning, and stay out all day in the hopes of catching one. Nothing else was talked of in the evening at the hotel, which, though full, appeared deserted in the day time. Round the hotel, on a sunny day, numbers of the most exquisite little humming birds used to hover over a particular red shrub. In a garden facing the Father's window were numbers of so-called ravens of beautiful, various metallic hues. Whilst there Brother David several times tried his skill at sheepshead fishing, sheepshead being a fish with teeth just like a sheep. Driving into the interior was uninteresting, as there was very little to see for some distance, but fir trees and palmetto scrub.

The "City" boasted but one large general store and a taxidermist, the latter possessing two tame buzzards, which used to walk about under the trees near his house. Buzzards innumerable, abounded wherever you went. You could see them in groups on the trees, or perched on the chimneys and the housetops. The prettiest sight of all, was to see a flock of white cranes turning over and over in their flight, sparkling like streaks of flashing silver against the blue sky in the sunlight. One day, whilst out hunting, *i.e.*, "gunning," or as we should call it, shooting, Bro. David came across a most picturesque sight—a boy of about

---

* *Megalops thrissoides* or *Atlanticus* has been since 1885 recognised as a game fish.

fifteen dressed entirely in deerskins, the rough side outermost.

As Sunday drew near, and there was no church or chapel in the "City," but only a schoolroom, controlled by the hotel proprietor, where services were held, a wish was expressed that the Father should preach next Sabbath in the morning and evening, and notices to that effect were duly posted on the Wharf, and at the Hotel.

Saturday arrived, and with it the neighbouring clergyman, a homesteader from Sanibel Island, who generally took the service. He had sent a notice to this effect, over to the hotel proprietor early in the week, to be posted on the Wharf, which he had failed to have done The Father had heard nothing about it. Here was a predicament. The clergyman, who had come all those miles to take service, found, as he thought, his notice torn down and the Father's substituted. He stopped at the same hotel, and the proprietor proposed that he should read the service, and the Father preach (as it eventually was), but he declared *he* should hold the service, *and* preach as he had come to do, and would *not* share it with the Father. The people of the hotel declared, that if *he* did *no one* would go to hear him, and most bitter were some of the remarks.

When Sunday morning and church time came, many who had wished to hear the Father, finding he was not to preach, went out shooting.

We went to church (no one else attempting to), and

found the clergyman sitting alone in the empty schoolroom, when the Father, going up to apologise for and explain what had occurred, completely changed the aspect of affairs, and the priest stated if he read the service, he should insist on the Father's preaching, and taking the whole evening service. Brother David was sent back to the hotel to make known what had occurred, and before long, knots of people, and the hotel waggonette began to arrive, soon forming a comfortable congregation. The priest read the service, the Father playing the Venite, Te Deum, Benedictus, and hymns on the harmonium, as well as preaching, which he also did in the evening. Next morning at the wharf, the Father saw the clergyman off for Myers. A couple of days before our leaving for Myers, a sailing vessel (very dirty) was hired for the day, and a most enjoyable sail to Sanibel Island, and a search for the exquisite shells that lie in such quantities on the shores of the Gulf, was undertaken. Whilst on the Island the Father visited the lighthouse, and enjoyed a nice pleasant talk with the people in charge, sailing home to the vast city of nineteen cottages in the evening.

When the Father preached at S. James, two gentleman came over from Punta Rassa on purpose to hear him.

CHAPTER XII.

FORT MYERS.

MISSION IN METHODIST CHURCH—BLESSINGS—CHILDREN
—HOSPITALITY EXPERIENCED.

THE Father's visit, to this most enjoyable and picturesque spot on the Caloosahatchie (or the river of the Caloosa tribe of Indians), is to form the subject of this Chapter. Fort Myers is the most southerly settlement on the Gulf Coast of Florida, with the exception of a growing settlement at Naples, started by the sister of President Cleveland. There are at present but two ways of reaching Fort Myers, both viâ Punta Gorda. The one is to obtain an oxwagon at the station there, and to then drive twenty miles, over stumps and palmetto roots, through a vast pine forest. The other, and a most enjoyable way on a fine bright day, is by the little steamer that runs daily and takes nine hours; the whole route is most fascinating, the varied colours of the waters being unsurpassed. To Naples, access is only to be had by sailing vessels, or an occasional tug steamer.

Now we will leave S. James's City, Pine Island, and I will pioneer your readers to, and through Myers during the stay of the Blackrobed Monks there.

Leaving soon after twelve o'clock, with a bright sky overhead, with many down on the wharf as the boat left, steaming away towards the Gulf, past Sanibel Island (so noted for its wild hogs and deer), watching many a tarpon boat in the distance, Punta Rassa, our first stoppage, was reached. Here, on the wharf, lay two immense freshly-caught tarpon, so fitly named "The Silver King." Before proceeding, a few words respecting the tarpon may be of interest. Imagine a herring-shaped fish, five or six feet long, with brilliant silvery scales the size of half-a-dollar, in shoals of a dozen or twenty, leaping from the blue surface of a summer sea. Sometimes even after they are hooked, ranging as they do up to nearly two hundred pounds in weight, it is hours before the lucky angler is able to land his prize.

On the wharf at Punta Rassa, with its funny looking farmhouse of an hotel, the headquarters of many an expert fisherman, is a most picturesque Spaniard with a coloured handkerchief round his neck and on his head a · large sombrero. From the telegraph office here, the cable runs to Cuba. We are soon off again, and entering a most intricate passage up the Caloosa-hatchie, round the mouth of which islands large and small are scattered. The captain of our steamer, "The Alice Howard," tells us, he has at times seen deer swimming across the river.

At last Myers is reached, a most picturesque little settlement with several humble wharves, on the right-hand side. Among the first things noticeable were the great date palm (planted by Gen. Hancock, 1837), the giant bamboo in the Hendrys garden, the huge cocoanut palms in Major Evans', and the laboratory built by Edison.

On landing, little did anyone think of the great work the Father was come to do there, and that before he should leave, the whole town would be aroused to the sound of the Gospel, and he would carry away with him, the hearts of numbers of its inhabitants ; yet it *was* to be. Myers was dead in trespasses and sin, and Jesus had brought our Father there, on purpose to rouse it to a sense of its need and God's Love. The Father came to rest. Our Lord had work for him to do, and the results, by the outpouring of God's Holy Spirit, were marvellous and undeniable. There was an Episcopal Church there, but no resident clergyman. The priest who generally took duty there once a month, was most anxious that the Father should preach the next Sunday, —the lady into whose charge the church had been put wished it,—the Episcopalian residents desired it, but it was *not* to be. The Bishop had closed all the churches of the Diocese against the Monk, *so* the Methodists received him with open arms, and a Mission, such as had *not* been known in Myers *before*, commenced in the M. E. Church. But I am anticipating, and must go back a little.

One of the first things we did, on arriving in Myers

was to visit the store, where the Indians trade their plumes, skins, hides and manufactures, and to ascertain, if possible, how soon they might be expected to come into the town. Going on a little further, what was the Father's surprise to meet Dr. Hanson, brother to dear old Dr. Hanson who died at Llanthony. We found he lived next door to our hotel, and that the Episcopal Church was in charge of Mrs. Hanson. Arrived at "The Caloosa Hotel,"* a surprise was in store, the whole building being like one large barn partitioned off into rooms, the accommodation and the food most rough, and lack of paint with plain board being conspicuous. The most unpleasant part of the business was, that the mosquito curtains, or bars, as they are called, were nowhere visible. In the evening, as the shades of night drew on, our first visitor was a little boy with bare legs and a big hat. No one stands on ceremony in Myers, or thinks of knocking at the door. It is the custom to open the door and walk straight in, for the town is just like one immense happy family. So this young child walked in. It was too dark to see. The Father had gone out. The first thing I heard was— "I want to see Father Ignatius. He's been mighty kind to my uncle." The information he imparted to me was most interesting, and from subsequent enquiry his information proved correct. He told me, talking about rattlesnakes, that the Indians knew a root that

---

* This hotel, since we left Myers, has been moved bodily to the other end of the town, and its proprietress is now settled in a pretty little cottage in the grove on the old site.

would cure the bite, but they would not tell the white people for fear they should take it all. The next day, Brother David having gone out shooting, the Father went a walk round the village. First, the day school was visited, just as the children were coming out, but many ran back, to see *what* the father was. The teachers were most agreeably polite, and when the Father enquired the way to the Episcopal Church, volunteers to show the way were not wanting from amongst the children; in fact, throughout the whole of the stay in Myers, there were children willing and eager to show and escort one anywhere. From the Episcopalian, the Roman Catholic Church was visited, a whitewashed building without any chairs or altar, a poor place, not worth seeing. Whilst waiting here for the key, which by-the-bye never came, the Father was offered a chair in a cottage, where he met an old lady of seventy and a little girl of thirteen, both of whom, through his instrumentality, came to Jesus, and found in Him all they needed, before the Father left Myers. The Father asked the child, how it was she was not at school. She replied, " Puppa took me away 'cos the boys kissed me so; he said if I wanted to learn kissing he could teach me." So the Father said, "If little girls were modest and well behaved, I'm sure the boys would respect, instead of troubling them." We afterwards heard that this child had left the Methodist Sunday School to join the Episcopal, in order that she might learn dancing ! Now that she is rejoicing in Jesus, I hope she is back in the Methodist.

Next day, Friday, the day schools were to break up, so the Professor sent up to the Hotel, to ask the Father to address the children before they dispersed for their holidays, which he did, and won for his first convert in Myers, a little boy of ten, who went straight home and told his mother what he'd heard, and how " the Breath of Jesus " had breathed upon him. In the evening a prayer meeting was held in the hotel parlour, where the Father first met the Methodist pastor and his wife, who begged him to hold a prayer meeting in the M. E. Church the next night, which the Father did. Mrs. Frazee, the pastor's wife, had been most anxious to hear the Father, but on account of his dress hesitated whether she was doing right; but now her heart was won. The sun was broiling hot in Myers, often so much that large palmetto sun hats were obliged to be adopted.

On the Saturday morning, with Dr. Hanson as an escort and guide, Major Evans' orange, lemon and lime grove, with trees weighed down with fruit, were visited, and the giant bamboo, 80 feet high, the beetle and cocoanut palms, the latter with numbers of nuts, were admired. The Major, an old Welshman, was most hospitable, and attended most, if not all, of the Father's sermons, manifestly seeking Jesus. Here, at Major Evans', we met a gentleman with a 'Kodak' Camera, who for weeks had been taking quantities of different photographs, but all on the same plate. In the afternoon, towards sunset, as the

Father started for a walk through the woods, two children escorted us to Billy Bowlegs' Creek, named after the Great Seminole chief.

Next morning, Sunday, the Father preached at the morning service to a large congregation at the Methodist Episcopal Church. In the afternoon, he addressed the Sunday Schools, the entire Episcopal School for once, joining in a body with that of the Methodists in their church. There was unity between the two Sunday Schools, as the Father spoke to them from a hymn they had been singing on " Gathering at the Crystal Sea." When the Father asked all those who had accepted Jesus, and had any right to gather *there*, to stand up, only one child stood up, and he, the Father's convert of the previous Friday, jumped up like a shot before them all. The scene was very touching, to see the children come sobbing to the altar rail for salvation, boys and girls—young and old—responding to the invitation, to come forward and be prayed for. After the Sunday School meeting, the Father visited a murderer and the other prisoners in the jail, where God allowed him to sow seed, that now we hear has brought forth fruit. The Marshal of the town with a carriage, came to take him to the jail. In the evening, the Monk Evangelist once more proclaimed to an increasing congregation 'the Old, Old Story' of the Saviour's Love for white men and Indians alike. The ordinary collection for Church Expenses was taken before the sermon, but after the Father's special appeal for better treatment of the Indians, instead of the cowardly treatment certain men in Myers had subjected them to, another collection was taken on behalf of the Seminoles, to get them Scripture reading matter and Bible pictures. This offertory, which amounted to about thirty-seven dollars, was collected by the Father and myself, those who had not the money with them, giving written promises for various amounts on slips of paper, with which we supplied them. All these promises were redeemed next day. After the sermon, the Pastor announced that the services would be continued next day at 10 and 8, and so they were, the Father preaching daily until Thursday morning, when he left Myers; but I wish only to deal now with his last service. Morning after morning, night after night, to see so many sitting at the Monk's feet, numbers of children coming quite alone, and drinking in with avidity the words of Life and Love, that fell from the Preacher's lips, was a striking spectacle, though that on the last night, after the sermon, to hear which many had come miles, was *more* so. To hear this sermon, I know of two people—one a lady—who rode nine miles alone into the town, and had to get back to school by nine next morning, and two young men who walked in six miles.

On the last night the church was full, and amongst the congregation were a number of cowboys who had just come into town, and one of whom was heard to remark : " This man's not afraid to speak out what he thinks." Several shook hands with the Father, and just as we were leaving the church a child came up, with almost tears in her eyes, begging us to return. Standing at the back of the church after service, as sinners sought peace, pardon, and life eternal at the altar rail, was seen a sight never to be forgotten—children, parents, friends, with their arms round one another's necks, and their heads on each other's breasts, sobbing their way home to Jesus, and when they had found Him, weeping for very joy. Children redeemed were pleading with older sinners who were still lost groping in the darkness. One old lady of seventy was found sitting down calmly on the altar rail, ejaculating, " Saved at last, only to think of it, after all these years, I'm saved at last." The common-place matter of fact way, in which she announced her conversion, was amusing.

Throughout the whole of the Father's stay in Myers, there was a constant stream of children's feet up his stairs, with presents of flowers and fruit, fresh milk, and guava jelly. Their gratitude seemed unbounded, and they appeared at a loss, how to do enough for the Father. One boy who had no garden of his own, and was a pilgrim in a strange land, begged a pawpaw, that he might give it to the Father. Delicious guavas of all flavours, lemons, and oranges were brought. Another boy, whose heart our Lord had spoken to through the Father, brought some fish he had caught, which were indeed a treat to the

Monk. The village street was fragrant with orange blossom and limes; the tropical foliage, with the seagrape, mangrove tree (of which you can hardly distinguish the roots from the branches) and the brilliantly coloured flowers, were most picturesque. Strange it was one morning, to see the river streaked with green water-lettuce, floating down to the blue waters of the Mexican Gulf from the mysterious Lake Okechobee. But before I leave the river, I must speak of the scenes thereon at night. The water is most phosphorescent; stir it with a stick, and it is like a patch of fire. Let a fish jump, and behold a display of brilliant water fireworks. Pretty indeed is the torch-light fishing at night, as you see a boat gliding o'er its placid waters, with a lighted torch at bow or stern, casting its lurid glare around. One morning, whilst at breakfast, two boys brought a lovely little fawn they had caught in the woods and wished to sell. One afternoon, the Father went for a row down the river to visit a pineapple plantation, where he found acres upon acres planted with nothing but pineapples. Pomegranates grow and ripen on the trees. Tamarinds flourish. The bread fruit is found, of which the Indians use the root for flour. Strange plants of all sorts are met with in sunny, pretty Myers. The day before the Father left, the Marshal offered, if he would stop over Sunday, to go out himself and fetch some Indians in in two days. So did Mr. Curtis, the Indian agent; but it was too late, and the Father's time to leave had come. Now, in conclusion, I am going to give you a few quotations from " *The Myers Press* " and letters.

From " *The Florida Christian Advocate* " I cull the following :—

"We have just closed a ten days' meeting at Myers with very gracious results — about 25 conversions and reclamations, and 18 additions to the church, while the church has been greatly refreshed and quickened by a deep and pervasive spiritual visitation. 'Father Ignatius,' the Monk of the Church of England, of whom all news readers have doubtless heard, made us a very providential visit, preaching several days and nights in our church with much unction and demonstration of the spirit. How strange that such a man should be objected to by some of the authorities of the Episcopal Church in our country! You forget the Monk at once in the man of God, and the truly Evangelical Minister of Christ. Our church and community have been greatly blessed by his ministry, and we deeply regretted parting with him and his attendants. Long will our people remember him and follow him with their prayers. I have seldom enjoyed a more precious social and religious season.—H. B. FRAZEE, Pastor."

" *The Fort Myers Press* " had the following paragraphs :—

I. "Father Ignatius' visit to Fort Myers will long be remembered by those who had the great pleasure of seeing him and hearing him deliver the Word. He is a man of peculiar force, rarely gifted, and consecrated to God. The effect of his sermons upon believers is like a sweet benediction, while his arguments and power of Christ is convincing to unbelievers. His hearers forget his monastic robe, his sandalled feet, and his shorn head, as he stands before them, in his intense earnestness, feeding them with heavenly manna. He carries them from the Roman palace where dwells the emperor in all his power, to the lowly stall where lies the Christ Child. He leads them by the shores of Galilee, rests them upon the green hill-slopes, and shows them Christ in all His goodness, His glory, His might, majesty, and power, and leaves the message with them. Oh, wonderful message! and wonderfully told by the grand old man!"

II. "Last Sunday, the 22nd, Rev. Father Ignatius was to begin a series of meetings in Washington, and away down here in Fort Myers, there was special prayer offered for him in both churches. It is impossible to estimate the results of his preaching here, for all who sat under the sound of his voice, whether Christian or not, were made to feel that there is a *reality* in the religion of Christ, and that Father Ignatius possesses an influence not born of human intellect alone. . . . The coming of Father Ignatius to Fort Myers was indeed a blessed providence, and long will his earnest, excellent, and evangelical preaching be remembered; while eternity alone can reveal all the good results."

"The Thursday morning of his departure witnessed a very touching and appropriate farewell scene at the wharf, where a goodly number of our people, with our esteemed pastor and his wife, assembled in the early morning to express their adieus, and, as the steamer moved off on the placid waters of the beautiful Caloosahatchie, the hymn, 'God be with you till we meet again, Till we meet, at Jesu's feet, etc.*'" was wafted after him from many voices, expressing the heartfelt sentiments of all, until out of hearing, and followed by a mutual waving of handkerchiefs. Many earnest prayers follow this devoted minister of Christ and his attendants, and the deep regrets of this parting will be equalled by the hearty and joyous welcome that will greet them if they can ever favour us with another visit."

To show the feeling in Myers since the Mission, I am going now to give the following quotations from

---

* God be with you till we meet again!—
By His counsels guide, uphold you,
With His sheep securely fold you;
'Neath His wings securely hide you,
Daily manna still provide you;
When life's perils thick confound you,
Put His loving arms around you;
Keep Love's banner floating o'er you,
Smite death's threatening wave before you;
God be with you till we meet again.

letters received from thence. In one of March 27, Mrs. F. says :—

" The old adage, 'out of sight out of mind,' will not be true, for we shall always remember, even through eternity, the earnest loving ministry of Father Ignatius. The most hardened sinner here, I think, would hardly dare speak the Father's name in disrespect. I heard that someone undertook to say some jesting words to Major E—— of your style of dress. He said, "Stop that, I'll not hear a word of jest about *them*."

Mrs. T——, in a letter of April 15, writes :—
" My children are all sick. When I told them I had a letter from you, they all gathered round me, eager to hear the contents. They will never forget you, and speak of you so often. You all surely left many friends behind in Myers, not only amongst grown-up people, but even the little children."

Such was the work that, by the power of the Holy Spirit, the Father did in Myers. Had the Bishop allowed it, the blessing would have accrued to the Episcopal Church ; but, as it was, the Methodist benefited instead. Almost all the Episcopalians attended the services in the M. E. Church, there being no canon in America preventing an Episcopalian priest or layman taking part in the services and congregations of other denominations.

CHAPTER XIII.

Washington, D. C.

AFTER bidding farewell to beautiful Myers at seven a.m., and touching at S. James City, it was between four and five in the afternoon before we arrived at Punta Gorda. There being no train on for the North, until one o'clock next day, we were obliged to find temporary quarters till then. Hearing a rumour that the Episcopalians were going to give a dance (and this on a Friday in Lent), for the benefit of the Episcopal Church, the Father determined to try and arrange a service for that night, (though there were but three hours left), to denounce it.

Whilst unpacking, the Father sent to inquire into the possibility of holding a service, which was most successfully arranged and well attended. The unpacking done, the Father started out to call on the gentleman who had got up the dance, when he discovered it was not got up after all by an Episcopalian. The gentleman had himself volunteered to give the proceeds to the Church.

At the service in the evening the Father played and led the hymns "Rock of Ages" and "All Hail the Power of Jesu's Name," to the American tunes. Next day, just as we were starting for Green Cove

Springs to rest over Sunday, a gentleman came to the railway car to say there were a lot of letters waiting at the Post Office for our party, which on being fetched, proved over a month old. Once started, our next stoppage was at Bartow, with an hour to wait, where the Father met, and had a nice talk with the Episcopalian parish priest. Again *en route*, our next change was at Lakeland, of two hours, which were to be spent getting dinner at the hotel. During dinner, a waiter brought the Father a note asking him to address the guests before leaving the hotel, which, after dinner, he did in the parlour, where they had assembled, and in which every seat was filled. On going down to the station, we found the train had got off the track, and possibly would not arrive that night, so it was determined to stop the night at the Hotel and go on by the first train in the morning, which was done. We arrived at Green Cove Springs, where Brother David was waiting, about seven in the evening.

Regret was expressed, that this stay of the Father's in the little village on the S. John's river, was to be so brief, and many were the anxious inquiries as to whether there was any chance, of hearing him preach again there. The next day, Sunday, as there was no clergyman in the village, the Episcopalians were without a service in the morning, but a priest from the neighbouring village of Magnolia drove over and took Evensong in the afternoon, which the Father attended, giving a short Bible reading in the evening in the Hotel St. Clair parlour.

The following day the journey to Washington was resumed without adventure, until Savannah was reached, where the floods were out, and all over the railway track. Soon after leaving Jacksonville, we were joined by friends, the same who had been arranging the Washington and Philadelphia Missions. As I know you will be anxious to hear of our passage through the Savannah Floods, I will endeavour to give you as much as I remember. Arriving at Savannah, as the shades of night drew on, we heard that the Savannah River was swollen and almost up to the top of the bridge, so we might not be able to get on that night.

The floods were over the track, but they had sent men on to see if the line in any place had been washed away. Hiss, hiss, hiss, went the engine, every moment in danger of having her fires put out as she ploughed her way through the waters. Water on every side, just the upper parts of the trees visible in the forests as if growing out of water, while the lowlands appeared one vast sea. Thankful, indeed, to Almighty God was everyone to get through it safely.

The next night saw us safely housed at midnight in our Washington lodgings. The remainder of the week was fully occupied in preparation for the Mission, granting interviews to reporters, and sending handbills to the clergy.

On the Friday afternoon a walk was taken down Pennsylvania Avenue, and "The Capitol" visited, its statuary, beautifully frescoed dome and historical pictures admired, and the wonderful whispering stones in the pavement tested, and marvelled at. From the Capitol Terrace, a most beautiful view of the whole city is obtained, with the Monument in the far distance. In that Monument is a Welsh stone brought by Mr. Daniel Jones, of Brooklyn, from Wales, and on which is engraved " Ein iaith, ein gwlad ein genedl."*

On the Saturday morning the Father had a most enjoyable and interesting private interview at "The White House" with President Harrison and all his family, his wife's father, the late Dr. Scott, a dear old Presbyterian clergyman of eighty, included. As the Father spoke to Mrs. Harrison of 'the love of Jesus,' she was visibly moved, and could not restrain her feelings. In talking to the President, the Father related the sufferings and treatment of the Seminole Indians, pleading on their behalf that something might be done for them, to prevent the sale of whisky to them, and to enable them to obtain justice.

Next day, Palm Sunday, the Mission began in " The Masonic Temple," and in the afternoon Mrs. Harrison and Private Secretary Halford were among the interested congregation. The subject of the Sunday sermons were :—In the morning, " Lo, I send you "; in the afternoon, " The Supper at Bethany " ; and in

---

* "Our language, our country, our nation."

the evening, "The Historical and Religious Value of the Procession of the Palm Boughs."

From *The Washington Post* of the next day, I have culled the following report of these services :—
"Father Ignatius' manner is such as would invite one to enter into conversation, and at once become interested in him. He seems to have a magnetic force which excites the curiosity, while an entire absence of any formality or affected dignity makes one feel perfectly at ease, although he may point his finger at you and talk to you alone. His voice is soft and modulated, and all his words were uttered in a clear but quiet tone. His manner is nervous but sincere, and one cannot fail to be impressed with the feeling that—if nothing else—he is earnest and sincere in what he does and says. At times he was dramatic and eloquent, describing in beautiful language the Glory of the Lord. Now he would draw himself up in stately dignity—his smooth shaven face and clear cut features upturned to the heavens, to which he appealed in supplication to Jesus, and then he would lean far forwards over the edge of the platform, and whisper words of exhortation almost into the ears of his hearers; but through it all, in the height of his enthusiasm, he never lost control of himself, to shout in boisterous harangue, as many missionaries are liable to do. His address was of a simple but touching character. He dwelt upon the happiness and joy to be obtained by renouncing the word and clinging to Jesus. People

were led astray from God into the gaieties and so-called pleasures of life, but they were not happy; they could not be contented. Cares weighed heavily on all their shoulders, and sins hardened their consciences with suffering. He was struggling along with a grand object in view, and he intended to accomplish it."

On the previous Friday evening, the Father and Brother David had spoken at Dr. Hammond's revival meeting. Here, at Washington, the natives were granted a treat I know many in the old country would have been glad of. The Father, for the first time out of the Abbey, preached " The Three Hours' Agony of Our Lord on Good Friday," in a public hall. The hall was packed to its utmost capacity, people coming and going all the time. On the table on the platform was a large brass crucifix, with a lighted candle on either side. Away from the sacred cloister, at this most solemn season of the Christian year, to find a daily Mass at S. John's Episcopal Church, and to be able on Holy Thursday to visit our Lord in the Blessed Sacrament on an altar of repose at S. Patrick's, which church was open all night for those who wished to spend the hour of our Lord's Agony in the Garden in His Sacramental Presence, was indeed a comfort. On Easter Day, the concluding services of the Mission were attended by such numbers, that it was found necessary to move into a larger hall, which was packed to overflowing.

In the morning, we made our Easter communion

at Emmanuel Church, afterwards attending the eleven o'clock service at S. John's, admittance to which would have been impossible to obtain on account of the crush, and as all seats were reserved, had it not been that a parishioner who had attended the Mission secured us seats. In the afternoon, amongst the congregation and those who came up after the sermon to thank the Father and express their enjoyment, were the old blind Chaplain of the Congress, and Dr. Scott, the dear old Presbyterian Minister, father of Mrs. Harrison. The clergy of the town were *all* very nice and sympathetic, some begging the Father to stop on, especially the Dean, who called several times and announced the Father's services from the chancel of his own church. Twice, the Rector of the large Roman Catholic University sent his secretary to see the Father, and ask him to go over and visit them, which he was unable to do. On Easter Day, a small altar was fitted up on the platform with crucifix, candles, vases of Eastern or Bermuda and arum lilies, flanked by some palms a lady had kindly lent.

Throughout the mission week, it was indeed distracting to have dancing classes three times a day, thrice a week, though the dancing master, out of respect to the Father, gave them up on Good Friday. The dancers used to listen, and peer through the door cracks; and pleasing it was to see them sometimes drop into the service, and listen to the message of God's love.

Here at the mission were friends from Boston and New York, glad once more to be able to listen to the Father as he opened up to them the Word of God.

From Washington we went to Philadelphia, the mission there commencing on Low Sunday.

CHAPTER XIV.

PHILADELPHIA.

SERVICES—VISIT TO INDIAN SCHOOLS—SIOUX INDIANS.

AT last the Father visited Philadelphia, but so long was he in America before going to "the Quaker City," that some people there, stated they began to wonder if he was ever coming. It was from S. Mark's Episcopal Church, Philadelphia, that the Father received one of the first invitations to preach after his arrival in America, and through the kindness of the Rector and Curate (the latter of whom had been a member of Llanthony) of the Church of the Ascension, a series of sermons had been arranged for the second week in January; but, owing to the Father's continued hard work in New York during December and January, beginning to tell upon his health, the long-looked-for Philadelphia Mission was obliged to be postponed, until after his return from the Sunny South.

With a view to the opening service being in "The Church of the Ascension" the Rector saw the Bishop,[*] who said there would be no difficulty, provided the Father could show the usual credentials; though his Lordship afterwards, in respect for the recently

---

[*] Dr. Ozi W. Whitaker.

deceased Bishop Paddock, of Massachusetts, saw fit to change his mind, and ask for the production of a paper, he knew the Father had not in his possession. So the service at "the Ascension" was unable to be held; but the Rector heralded the Father's coming with a special article in his parish magazine, *The Ascension News*, which was the means of bringing many of his congregation. He, besides, kindly secured apartments which we never occupied (though had to pay for) through losing the address and wandering about looking for the house; and supplied boys from his choir and confirmation class to distribute the Mission handbills. These were printed in black with a red cross on various pale coloured papers. At the head of the handbills (or dodgers as they call them there), stating the Father was to hold an "Easter Revival Mission in Philadelphia;" above the cross, the Druidical sign and Cymric motto, was the text, "Blow the Trumpet in Zion: Sound an Alarm in My Holy Mountain."

Amongst the first callers on the Father were, a lady engaged in Mission work, who had sat at his feet and drank in the words of love and life eternal that fell from his lips at Boston, and the Curate of S. Mark's who celebrated one Ascension Day at Llanthony. This lady took it upon herself to call on the Bishop, who, she states, said "though he could not see his way to licence the Father, having made it a matter of prayer for months, he should not put any obstacle in the Father's way, or to attempt to hinder him in his Mission work;" in fact, from her showing, " he was most kindly disposed towards the Father." S. Mark's being the nearest (Catholic) Episcopal Church, I attended the early Mass there, the first Sunday morning, though nearly succeeded in losing myself.

Coming home, I was greatly impressed with the enormous crowds coming out of the Roman Church of S. John the Evangelist, making the street quite crowded round it. At S. Mark's, we had a very nice quiet celebration (vestments, lights and Catholic Ritual being in vogue there). Seeing three of the parish clergy at the Mission one evening, they told me I should be welcome, whenever I liked to go there to Mass. The opening services of the Mission were held on Low Sunday in " The Musical Fund Hall," the week-day meetings being in " The Industrial Hall.

The Philadelphia Ledger of the following day has the following paragraph :—" Two austere priests— bereft of any hat or cap, and barefooted, except for open sandals, which were but poor protection against the chill air—wended their way yesterday from the Windsor Hotel to Musical Fund Hall, where were gathered a great host of people to hear them. They were Father Ignatius, the Evangelist Monk of the British Church, and his brother in the Faith, Michael, and the truths which were uttered on the platform of the great hall were as strange to the ear of the average church-goer as was their garb to the eye. It was the opening of an Easter Revival Mission, which will continue throughout the week at the Industrial Hall."

The subject of the afternoon address was "The Fashionable world in the Episcopal Church," while that of the evening was "The Church of Christ. What is it?" A white silk banner with the cross and Druidical emblem, the crown of thorns and usual Llanthony mottoes in gold, which had been presented to the Father by a lady at Boston, was used to-day for the first time. In the evening, by special request, the Father in his sermon alluded to the evils of Gloucester, a small country town in the vicinity, where racing, gambling, and all vices reign unchecked. The following are the reports of his remarks from two Philadelphia papers:—

The Philadelphia Press, April 6.

"Father Ignatius stated, he had read in the Sunday Press of the lives that had been ruined, and homes that had been wrecked, by the Gloucester race track and gambling dens, and he found language inadequate to express his horror, at the existence of such a sink-hole for the filthy and bestial element of Philadelphia.

"He was preaching from the text, 'The Church of Jesus; and the Gates of Hell Shall not Prevail Against It.' He had told how 'worldliness and the devil' were creeping into nearly all the churches, when he exclaimed:—

"'Why, the men who take the lead in all the devilries at Gloucester, may belong to some church. If they do, the gates of hell are prevailing against that Church. For such iniquities, as are there permitted to thrive, and drag people down to hell, cannot be countenanced by members of Christ's Church. The very mention of the name of Gloucester, gives every respectable Philadelphian a shiver, so great is the stench that comes from this pit of sin. It is leading the youth of your city to ruin, and you will never have peace of mind, until you wipe away all the evils that exist there. Gloucester, quiet peaceful Gloucester, has been transformed into a riotous place, where the worst forms of Sabbath desecrations are practised, and where all the vices of the devil have full sway. Philadelphia is sending all her filth and her bestial element to Gloucester, and they are unmolested. And all of this, is in defiance of the law! To think that such wholesale lawlessness should be permitted, to continue for months in a Christian community!

"'It is monstrous! It can only be accounted for, by the wholesale bribery and corruption of those in high official places, such as I have seen intimated in your papers. Now, my dear people, you should not rest until you have relieved Gloucester of her deep disgrace, for you share it with her. So long as these contagious and monstrous evils, are permitted to have full play in the little country town so near your shores, your children are not safe from their influences.

" 'I have spoken thus mildly about this matter, because, there is no language strong enough to anathematize the crimes committed in Gloucester, and the men who are responsible for their commission.

" ' You may ask, what business have I to speak about these matters. I answer that I am a man, and that I am a Christian. When my fellow-men are threatened by such a pitfall, as you have at your very doors, I do not shrink from denouncing it, and calling upon Christian people to exterminate it.' "

The Philadelphia Times, April 6.

" The Father took as his text the sixteenth and part of the eighteenth chapter of the Gospel of S. Matthew, being the words of Jesus Christ to S. Peter on His Church. He began by reviewing how the Jews worshipped their God in one little territory, and spoke of the advent of Christ, and Peter's confession that He was the Son of the Living God. The Father said: 'One cannot learn to know Christ by study or investigation, except by communication with His servant. Christ will build His own Church Himself. Each separate stone of Christ's Church, He builds Himself. Other sects may erect temples of worship, and by the eloquence of their pastor may build up a Church, but it will *not* be the Church of Christ.

" ' Concerts in Methodist churches ! Think of that !

he continued, 'and dancing rooms in Catholic churches! Verily the gates of hell have worked into our churches. The *devil* is *more* in our churches than Jesus. Now at Gloucester, the man who sells drinks, or the bookmaker at the race track, may be the warden of an Episcopal or Presbyterian Church If so, I think it is pretty plain proof, that the gates of hell *have* prevailed.

"'Gloucester is a disgrace to humanity. When I think of the devilry that is going on, in that little country town, how our sons and daughters have been, and are being, ruined by wholesale, I enquire where is the law? Is not all this against the law? How can the law be enforced, when the officials are charged with taking bribes?

"'Whenever Gloucester is mentioned, you bow your head in shame. Philadelphia sends her filth to Gloucester, I am told, and Gloucester is degraded by the grossest and vilest deeds. I cannot use language strong enough to anathematize such a diabolical curse to humanity, as is made by the rush and overflow from Philadelphia of cowardly villains into pretty, moral Gloucester.'"*

The subjects during the week were:—Afternoons: What is a Christian?—The Christian's Righteousness,

---

* Gloucester is celebrated for its shad fisheries, and planked shad dinners, which in their season, especially endear the place to epicurean Philadelphians.

—Strength,—Food,—Example,—Rest; while those of the evening were: Jesus at the Pool of Bethesda, Jesus by the Lake of Galilee, Jesus in the Desert Place, Jesus and the Adulteress in the Temple, Jesus and the Brazen Serpent, and "Saturday night, or the Voice of many Waters." Throughout the week the congregations were very varied, Quakers, Baptists, Episcopalian clergy, Methodists, Roman Catholics, all uniting to swell the crowd of listeners to the words of the British Monk. Several ministers offered their chapels to the Father, and more than one Episcopalian minister thanked him for the work he was doing, and wished him success. Night after night, the same faces appeared, no matter what the weather, at the Mission. One afternoon, before the Father arrived, a Quaker lady got up and addressed the congregation, asking them to be more liberal in their alms, and support of the Father, who had done so much for them, by helping defray his expenses. All through the week, afternoon and evening, the Father preached without a single omission, though suffering all the time from a severe attack of influenza, which would have confined an ordinary person to his bed. The last Saturday night, the service was very much interrupted, (in fact at one time the Father thought he would have to give it up) by a dancing class. The Industrial Hall was situated, exactly opposite a large Roman Catholic School, the children of which used to delight in crowding round the door, to see the Monks leave, and to screech at the top of their voices "He's in bare feet," etc., dancing round to look at one's feet, so much so that one was often in danger of tumbling over them.

Amongst those blessed at the Mission, were a poor Roman Catholic man who came to the hotel and brought the Father a dollar out of his hard earnings, the night before we left; and an Episcopalian sexton, who had been at S. Clement's Church for years, and in days gone by, whilst at S. Raphael's, Bristol, had known and heard the Father, but had never come to Christ. Now the Lord called him, and he gave his heart, in full complete surrender to the Saviour, at the Foot of the Cross. One young girl of about seventeen, who came alone to all the services, when the Father sat on the stairs after the last address, to say good-bye, completely broke down, and between her sobs declared, "The Father must not go." On the last Sunday evening, a Welsh minister brought all his Welsh congregation to the service. The same evening, in the front seats, were twenty Indian boys from the Wild West, whose Superintendent had brought them from the Indian School, to hear the Father. Here, at this school, on visiting it we saw full-blooded representatives of the Mohawk, Sioux, Chippewa, Crow, Cheyenne, Winnebago, Iroquois and other well-known warlike tribes of the noble red men of America. Fine fellows, regular Indians they were, with long, black, straight hair, some utterly unable to speak or understand English. During the previous week the Father had visited and addressed all the inmates of the Indian Girls' School and spent a most interesting time at "The Educational Home for Indian Boys," where he heard them play the organ, and sing hymns in their native language,* and ate off the plate with one named William Luther.† Everything there was most clean and comfortable, the whole interior having more the appearance of a gentleman's house than an institution ; a lovely little chapel with stained glass windows, texts of Scripture illuminated hung on the walls, all about the rooms and passages, fine airy dormitories with specklessly white pillows and pillowcases, etc. Two of the boys, being confined to the hospital with typhoid fever, were visited, and the Father prayed with and for them. They seemed perfectly happy with their toys, which some kind friend had given them.

The dining-room was inspected, whilst they were all at dinner ; these young savages were eating in a perfectly

---

* The following is the first verse of the hymn "Nearer my God to Thee," in Sioux, which these Indian boys sang :—
"Mita, Wakantanka
Nikiyena
Kakismayanpi sa
He taku sni
Kici ciun wacin
Mita Wakantanka
Nikiyena."

† He was a boy of 16, of the Wichita tribe, whose Indian name was Doditsseah

civilized manner with knives and forks, and on the Father's remarking on the whiteness of the table linen the superintendent said they gave them clean table cloths and dinner napkins at *every* meal. When the Father, talking to one of the authorities in her private parlour, asked if the boys might come in, she at once replied, " Nothing is *too* good for the boys." After the Mission was over, one morning, through the kindness of a friend, the Father went a long drive up the Wissahickon to Chestnut Hill. Who,—that has visited the Wissahickon and admired the beetling crags and overhanging trees, the brawling rapid stream in its upper course swirling around the boulders that intersperse its bed, with an eddying sweep, making us think of trout,—will ever forget the romantic beauty of its scenery and the happy moments spent at the Hermit's Glen, Lane or Well, or castle building in the air at the Indian Rock, the Lover's Leap, or the Devil's Pool. All these possess their stories, and legendary romance casts its halo every where, throughout this wild and picturesque locality. Had I the space to spare, what countless spots of peaceful rest and beauty, of magnificence and grandeur I could describe to you, along the shores of the picturesque Schuylkill River.

It was at Philadelphia, that the British Monk first preached to the Red Indians of the Sioux tribe in their native dress, just come from the recent battlefields of North Dakota. They had been brought to

Philadelphia for exhibition in Forepaugh's Wild West Show, but through the kindness of Mr. and Mrs. Cooper, the proprietors, the Father was granted a private view before the show opened, and subsequently was photographed by the chief photographer of the town, with the two chiefs, Black Bear and Hoop Hawk,* whom Mr. Cooper sent down with their interpreter to the hotel where the Father was staying.

The following is a paragraph, that appeared next day in the chief Philadelphia papers:—

"Father Ignatius visited the Indians at Forepaugh Park yesterday. . . . On his arrival he was met by Mr. and Mrs. Cooper and Miss Forepaugh, and was introduced to each of the Chiefs. Expressing a desire to address them, Manager Cooper stopped the rehearsals, which were in progress for the opening on Saturday next. Artistes, employés, and Indians gathered about the priest.

"To this extraordinary congregation Father Ignatius talked for almost an hour through the interpreter. Observing that one of the Indian squaws wore a crucifix, he reverently kissed it, and, taking it as a text, he delivered an earnest discourse. Several of the Indians, when he had concluded, thanked him for his kindness, and Black Bear invited him to visit him, when he went back to his home in the far west."

There were, altogether, sixteen Indians (eight chiefs,

---

* These Photographs, by F. Gutekunst (2s. 6d. each), may be obtained from The Secretary, Llanthony Abbey.

five squaws, and three papooses), an interpreter, by name Louis Deon, and a number of cowboys, all dressed in the most picturesque costumes, and the Indians' faces highly painted in red, green, and yellow. On leaving, the Father asked Mrs. Cooper if he might send them each a crucifix and sacred picture, and if she would give them to the braves herself. One of the chiefs asked, if the Father would give him a piece of writing, so in the afternoon the Father wrote him a letter about Jesus, as follows :—

Philadelphia, April 15th, 1891.
Jesus † only
Peace.

" My dear Brother,—

" I am sending you the crosses I promised, with my love, and whenever you all look at them, you will remember all I said to you to-day, about the great Lord Jesus, who came to earth from the great Heaven, and became a man like us, so that He might be able to feel like we do, and feel for us. He died for us, and suffered for our sins, that the great God might forgive us, for His sake. Then He went to Heaven, to get ready a home for those who trust Him, but by His Holy Spirit He still remains with us who trust Him here on earth. In His own words, written by those who heard Him speak, He says to us : 'I will never leave you, nor forsake you.' Trust in Him, dear brother, and it will make you happy, like we are happy, and when you come to die, He will take you to be with Him for ever, in the great bright happy country above. Don't forget *me*, for I love you all so much, and I am your brother in Jesus Christ the son of Wakantanka.

"IGNATIUS, O.S.B.,

" A messenger of love, peace, and salvation from Jesus Christ our Lord."

On the way home, the Father, passing a Catholic Repository, got a crucifix for each of the Indians, a small glass bead rosary for each papoose, and a picture of Our Lady for each squaw. In the photographer's, next day, passing through the shop, the only thing that attracted their notice, and which they wanted to purchase, were some silver medals, (so fond are the Indians of anything bright and shining) which had been granted the photographer at various exhibitions. As they were unable to buy these, the Father gave each chief a silver dollar, which their guide and interpreter said, they would probably make a hole in, and wear round their necks.

The concluding services of the Mission were held in "The Horticultural Hall," attended by large congregations, and it was at the last moment decided, without a single bill or advertisement, to give two orations next day on "The Monk" and "The Episcopal Church." Though with so short a notice, and *no* free seats, the hall was quite full at each oration, and would have continued so, had the Father gone on day by day all the week.

Philadelphia indeed is rich in fine buildings and grand architecture, conspicuous among her finest structures being the magnificent and stupendous City Hall (visible for miles), the Museum of Fine Arts, the Masonic Temple with its fine arched doorway, and several churches. Of the magnificent buildings in the park where the great Centennial Exhibition of 1876 was held, only the Memorial Hall and Horticultural Hall now remain, but their picturesquely grand situation and elaborate design make them worthy of admiration. The green stone, of which so many churches are built, is extremely picturesque and rich looking. In the City are numbers of Welsh, whilst Welsh Colonies and Welsh names surround it on all sides. The villages of Brynmawr, Bala, Cynwyd, Bangor, Llanwellyn, Elwin, Berwyn, S. David's, and Radnor, carry one back in thought to the hills and vales of one's Fatherland, the other side the ocean deep, from which, in days gone by, the founders of these villages came, and in love for which they thus designated them. Two Episcopal churches are dedicated to " Saint David, Apostle by the Grace of God to the Cymry," whilst the parish church of Little Bala, in the County of Montgomery, is under the patronage of S. Asaph. The name of Bala, of Welsh origin, proclaims the large Welsh element amongst the early Quaker settlers.

South of Richmond, at Kensington, where the river front is still called Shackamaxon, after the old name of an Indian village, is the spot where William Penn, in 1682, made his original treaty of peace with the Delaware Indians. Until 1810 the Great Treaty Elm still stood, under which the agreement was signed, but now a small monument of stone, alone marks the historical spot.

In conclusion, let me give you the following amusing quotation from " *The Syracuse Journal*," May 5th:—

" The other day, one of the monks with Father Ignatius was walking on the street in Philadelphia in his sandalled feet, and attracted the notice of two old coloured men, who began to speculate as to whom he might be. At last the elder exclaimed : ' Rastus, I has it ! Dey kain't fool yoh uncle. Look dah at 'is foots. Dat ah gemmen is Mistah Jerry Simpson, de sockless statesman of Kansas.' And they went away happy."

From Philadelphia, the Father went to New York for his second and last revival mission there, and to open a crusade against "Infidelity in the Episcopal Church being openly preached and taught by clergy paid to teach The Truth."

CHAPTER XV.

New York.

SECOND MISSION—INFIDELITY OF THE EPISCOPAL
CHURCH—RECEPTION BY THE WELSH.

SEVERAL gentlemen having come forward after the last sermon in "the Cooper Union" in January, to guarantee expenses and arrange a Mission, if the Father would return, it was the 18th of April when, as "*The New York Herald*" of April 19th put it, "the Rev. Father Ignatius, O.S.B., returned from his Floridian trip yesterday much improved in health. . . . He brings with him a tongue of fire, and he proposes to wield it valiantly against the Rev. Heber Newton, and the Protestant Episcopal Church of this diocese for not turning Dr. Newton out neck and crop, as the Rev. Dr. MacQueary was turned out in the West."*

To leave you to judge for yourselves of the orthodoxy of Dr. Newton, a duly licensed and ordained rector of the Episcopal Church, allow me to give you two or three quotations from his printed sermons, &c. On

---

* He (Mr. MacQueary) has now gone, as he should have done long ago, and honestly joined the Unitarian Church.

Sunday, January 13th, 1889, Dr. Newton uttered the following words in a sermon or discourse of his to the congregation of All Souls', Church, Madison Avenue:— "God the Word was as *truly* incarnate in the person of the Monk Martin Luther *as* in the person of Jesus Christ." In a sermon on "the Resurrection," preached November, 1888, the Rector of All Souls says:— "As to the Resurrection, while many strands of the tale must be pulled out and thrown away, the central strand must not be thrown aside thus lightly. Strip the story of every accretion of legend, and you will touch the core of the matter—the appearance of Jesus from the spirit sphere."

Again, in a type-written sermon of his on "The Incarnation," we find: "There is no need then for the miraculous conception of that Divine Word. Believe it if you feel so drawn, or disbelieve it if you feel thus constrained. In either case, consider it as among the matters which, by the Scriptures and by the Church, are left as things undefined and secondary."

The preacher of these words was brought up to trial for heresy eight years ago in the same diocese, but, the Bishop of the diocese dying, the proceedings fell through, and were never renewed. Only this last Passiontide, he, with Dr. Rainsford, rector of St. George's, got into trouble through inviting ministers of other denominations, even Unitarians, to conduct service on Good Friday in their churches. This Dr.

Rainsford, the popular (with a certain set) rector of St. George's Church, Stuyvesant* Square, is well-known as a dancing clergyman, a theatre-going priest, and a sporting parson. His photograph in tennis costume is on sale in shop windows. Only a short time ago he was had up, and forced to pay the fine for shooting game out of season. And *this* is a priest, appointed rector of a church, and as a guide to young people preparing to take the solemn Confirmation vows of renouncing the world, the flesh, and the *devil*.

"*The New York Sun,*" of January 19th, has the following interesting little paragraph :—"Dr. Rainsford often describes himself as a 'latter day' or 'new school' preacher. His pictures are on sale in the shops where the photographs of celebrities are displayed, and in them Dr. Rainsford may be seen sitting in his study writing, what is presumably a sermon, with his neck encircled by a very lofty Piccadilly collar, and his muscular figure enveloped in a tennis blazer"; whilst "*The New York Town Topics*" of January 22nd has:—"Never make a verbal contract. Dr. Rainsford certainly ought to have

---

* So called from Peter Stuyvesant, the fourth and last Dutch Governor of the Colony formed by Peter Minuit on Manhattan Island (which he bought from the Indians for less than 25 dols.) in 1623. He was a brave man, though intolerant, sending a Quaker to prison and fining a Baptist 1,000 dols.—"*Picturesque Journeys in America,*" by Rev. E. J. Bromfield.

thought of this, for it is not long, since his failure to have a written agreement with a woodcock that it would not turn into a quail after death, caused him no little embarrassment, not to speak of a fine, at the hands of a non-saintly Long Island justice of the peace."

Such are the two beneficed rectors in the Episcopal Church the Father opened a crusade against—the one for teaching infidelity, and the other for worldliness—when he headed his Mission handbills with the note of alarm, "Blow the trumpet in Zion; sound an alarm in My holy mountain." On the Saturday night before the Mission, the Father preached at the Chapel of Holy Trinity, Madison Avenue, which is under the charge of an old schoolfellow of his, the Rev. Dr. Walpole Warren. The subject of the sermons for the first Sunday of the Mission, the services of which were held in the morning and afternoon in the Lenox Lyceum, and in the evening in the Berkeley Lyceum, were:—Morning, "Jonah's Mission to Nineveh"; afternoon, "The Mission of the Little Maid to the Great Syrian General"; and in the evening, "The Doctrine of the Resurrection; or, Infidelity in the Episcopal Church."

Up to this time the Father had not seen any of Dr. Newton's published sermons, but was only acting on hearsay, first aroused when Mr. MacQueary last Fall, during his own trial for heresy, quoted Dr. Newton as a clergyman of like belief to himself. This being the case, the day before the Mission the Father sent the following letter by special messenger to the rector of All Souls':—

New York, April 17th, 1891.

Jesus ✠ only.

Pax.

"My dear Dr. Newton,—

"From a purely secular point of view, it might be said that my writing to you is an unwarranted liberty, and that my making a stand for what is called 'orthodoxy' in a foreign Church is a piece of unmitigated impertinence, and therefore that my doing so would make an apology look ridiculous. But I write to you as a believer in historical Christianity, and as a firmly convinced disciple of the Jesus Christ of the Gospel. In my month's Mission in New York, to begin (D.V.) on Sunday, I hope to combat 'infidelity' within the Episcopal Church.

"The *vox populi*, so very unfair and so very non-divine, declares yourself to be the most influential infidel clergyman in the New York diocese; in fact, that you are so *extreme* an 'infidel' that you make no secret of your unbelief, in the miraculous birth of Jesus from a Virgin, and also of the physical resurrection of His natural or material Body. As you are a public teacher in a Church of which these two mysteries are *de fide* and fundamental *dogmata*, will you tell me if this public and widespread accusation is fair or false? I should think it unchristian and unmanly to attack any man's position in an underhand way.

"Mr. MacQueary has publicly accused you of this 'infidelity'; so have I, but I should be only too glad, if you would give me the power to retract and publicly apologise for the accusation I have made. If you were not a *minister* of the Visible Christian Church, it would be no concern of ours what you believe or disbelieve, and *outside* the pale we can accept as an honest man the gnostic or agnostic unbeliever. The atheist, has as *much* a right to a fair field, as the Christian. But the time has come, I believe with my whole heart, when the disciples of Jesus, I mean those who by the Light of the Spirit of the Eternal Wisdom have received Him as Salvation and Eternal Life, as Pardon, Peace, and Righteousness, should rise as *one* man, and open the Church's portals very widely, and insist upon the infidels going out from the folds of the Visible Church. Surely we have a right to say that from *within* the fortress our *paid* defenders no longer shall undermine our foundation! Dear Dr. Newton, common sense and common honesty must confess that we have right and justice on our side. Designing confederates must no longer plot, from *within* the Union ranks, the ruin of our magnificent Christian Spiritual United States—I mean all those, everywhere, who acknowledge Jesus Christ as God Almighty, *Atoning* Saviour, the Virgin Born of Bethlehem, the Glorious Risen Christ of the Arimathean's *empty* tomb. I write in the greatest haste, having very much to do, and a very large correspondence. If you find yourself unable to give me an answer, 'yes' or 'no,' for no more is needed to the public charge of infidelity, I shall understand that silence is assent to the truth of it, for if you *are* one of His disciples you can grasp my hand in love and gladness, that I, insignificant as I am, resolve publicly 'to contend for the faith once delivered to the saints' and common to Catholic and Protestant Christians alike. I am, dear Dr. Newton, yours most sincerely in Christ,"

"IGNATIUS, O.S.B., Monk."

After perusing this letter and turning it over, reading some passages several times, the only reply he vouchsafed to the bearer was, " Who made Father Ignatius my Father Confessor, or Bishop of this diocese?" and "Is this the way gentlemen treat one another in England?" "If Father Ignatius wishes to know my views, he'd better come to my church and hear me preach."

The battle for the faith was begun, and a hard and trying ordeal it proved. Those who had flocked round the Father at the last mission, hesitated and held aloof, so much did they care for "public opinion." Alone, like the monk Athanasius against the heretic Arius of old, the Father stood, as a valiant soldier for the *truth* of the Gospel of Christ. Instead of crowded halls, he had small congregations—for everyone was against him, and thunderstruck at his courage, in denouncing two of the most popular Episcopal clergy in the city. The papers teemed with columns upon columns. Once it was even rumoured that the Father's licence would be cancelled; but the Bishop, in spite of all, remained silent.

The following appeared in "*The New York Herald*" —" That the clergy are much disturbed over the sensation created in the church, by Father Ignatius's impetuous and original tilt with Dr. Newton, cannot be doubted. A large number of them, it is said, will meet to-day behind closed doors, to discuss what is to be done, and to devise some means of silencing the criticisms of the English Monk upon the Rev. Dr. Newton and other priests of the diocese." This meeting was *never* held. Not only was the Episcopal Church in New York aroused and stirred, as it had never been before, by the Father's denunciation of certain of her clergy, but the whole of America.

"*The Boston Transcript,*" of May 2nd, states :—" A little dog barked at a railway train, but still the train went on. The same thing is taking place to-day. Father Ignatius is the little dog, and the Rev. Dr. Heber Newton the railway train." This time, in spite of the aforesaid prophecy, the " little dog" *managed* to stop the train and bring it to a standstill, as you will see later—causing Dr. Newton to submit to a trial for heresy.

A subsequent number of "*The New York Herald*"

states that " when Dr. Huntington, rector of Grace Church, was told that Dr. Heber Newton had praised the Father's eloquence and efficiency of mission work, he observed, in the words of Sir Walter Scott, ' Of what use is a pail of sweet milk from a cow, if the cow puts her foot in it ? ' "

The organ of the American Episcopal Church is " *The Churchman,*" whose editor, the Rev. Dr. Mallory, *keeper of a large theatre in the city,**** annoyed at the Father's denunciation of worldliness, spread and published abroad the report that the British Monk was "crazy," which elicited the following amusing little paragraph from " *The New York Herald* " :—

" The English Monk, Ignatius, is an interesting figure in the city. It is charged that he is mad, but there is method in his madness. He has been eccentric from boyhood ; but those who have known him best, declare that he has always been earnest and honest. You cannot say that he is—
High and hazy,
Low and lazy,
Broad and crazy.

Rev. Father, what are you ? As a monk you are a Roman Catholic, in orders you are an Episcopalian, in preaching you are a Calvinist, in exhortation a Methodist."

Another paper states later :—" Father Ignatius,

---

* The Madison Square Gardens Theatre.

reinforced by the Rev. Dr. de Costa, has the Rev. Dr. Heber Newton on his toasting fork directly over the coals."

Bishop Potter, of New York, was the first person to incite the Bishop of Ohio the previous year to proceed against another blasphemer—the poor, insignificant rector of Canton, who, in his farewell sermon, confessed to his congregation, that no good had come from his ministry amongst them—the Rev. Howard MacQueary—now put out of the Episcopal Church. " This late Rector of Canton," " *The Milwaukee Sentinel* " of July 13th, 1890, states, " has written a book in which he practically repudiates the dogma of the Immaculate Conception, asserts his disbelief in the literal resurrection of Christ, and refers to the records of miracles as phases of the credulity of the times. Yet he has been asked to deliver an address at the Church Congress which meets in Philadelphia soon, 'and had it not been that Bishop Potter, of New York, refused to attend the Congress, if *he* was allowed to give his address,' *he would*—to judge from the papers— *have been lionized for proclaiming his heretical views.* Since then he has been tried for heresy, and put out, as Heber Newton should be *now*. But ' the Church of America ' is asleep to its danger in the great crisis it is passing through. The faith once delivered to the Saints, seems to-day *not* worth contending for, and instead of heresy being ousted from the fold at all risks, she is *welcomed* and *openly* received into the ranks of the Episcopal clergy."

Dr. Bridgeman who in May, 1891, resigned from the Baptist Communion—as in the columns of the papers he publicly declared—on account of his disbelief in the doctrine of eternal punishment, was *within a month* ordained by Bishop Potter into the Episcopal Church. Dr. Briggs, the Presbyterian heretic, whose trial last spring at Detroit made such a stir, is now reported also to be about to enter our Church's fold as a priest, and the influential eclectic Rector of All Saints', New York, who has been undermining the faith of his congregation for eight or nine years, is still allowed to remain, it being stated that the Bishop was hand-tied in the matter, and could not move, unless the heretic priest was presented to him, for an enquiry into his teaching, by three beneficed clergy.

From "*The Brooklyn Eagle*" of January 20th, I have culled the following interesting paragraphs, showing that Heber Newton's heterodoxical teaching was *not* unknown to Bishop Potter:—"*Since* Bishop Potter persuaded the Rev. Heber Newton to discontinue the lectures and sermons in which the latter had given great offence to orthodox Episcopalians, there has been manifest no intention to discipline the Pastor of All Souls. . . . . There was no pretence, however, that he had experienced any change in his convictions. He did not take back anything he had said. For reasons which did not affect the question of the truth, or falsity of his views expressed by him, he consented, at the request of his ecclesiastical superior, to desist from urging them. But now he urges them stronger than ever, and yet is allowed to remain a recognized beneficed minister in a Christian Church." In his sermon, on "The Nicene Creed," reported in " *The New York Herald* " of April 27th, we read " that under the Nicene Creed he declared emphatically that it was possible to hold *all* the divergent views concerning future punishment, creation, evolution, the Atonement and other doctrinal matters which are at present turning the religious world upside down." And now the new Bishop of Massachusetts, Dr. Philips Brooks, is reported to uphold him in these views.

The Father, after giving several lectures, on the denial of the faith from an episcopal pulpit, wrote to three of the chief rectors of the city—Dr. Morgan Dix, of Trinity Church, Broadway; Dr. Huntington, of Grace Church, Broadway; and Dr. De Costa, of S. John's, Wyndham Place;—quoting several of the blasphemous utterances of Dr. Newton, and the statement of Mr. Savage, the Unitarian minister of Boston, that "*not one in ten* of the Episcopal clergy believe in the Apostles' Creed in its entirety," and asking them if, for the honour of the church and the glory of Jesus Christ, they would present the rector of All Souls to the Bishop for heresy. To this letter Dr. Morgan Dix did not reply at all, so subsequently the Father wrote him the following letter :—

"My Brother in Jesus Christ,—Solemnly, in the Name of Jesus, I implore you no longer by your silence to lead the people of God, in and outside of the Episcopal Church, to suppose that the doctrines of the Incarnation and Resurrection of our Lord Jesus are not worth defending in the Episcopal Church. I adjure you, in the name of God Almighty, to reflect upon the awful responsibility, this prominent position God has placed you in, lays upon your conscience and your soul. Directly you come forward, I will cease to raise my puny voice in this crucial crisis of the American Church. A priest of this city tells me, that the clergy here treat the denial of the cardinal doctrines of Christianity *in* the Church *as a good joke*. Can your silence now be interpreted into a supposition that you, Dr. Morgan Dix, are one of them? God forbid! In the hour of death, when all life's golden opportunities of 'confessing Christ before men' shall have passed for ever away, will you not mourn that in such a time to speak, as this fearful crisis presents, you were silent, and the weight of an awful curse upon your soul. 'Curse ye, Meroz,' said the angel of the Lord; 'curse ye bitterly the inhabitants thereof, because they *came not* to the help of the Lord, even to the help of the Lord against the mighty.'

"Your faithful brother in Jesus,
"IGNATIUS, O.S.B., Monk."

Dr. Huntington, the well-known rector of Grace Church, in a Jesuitical manner, replied that, "while I fully recognise the right of Father Ignatius, and the right of any man, to incite me to the discharge of my duty as a Christian minister, I hold that when a clergyman of the Episcopal Church has reached a stage when he no longer believes, and therefore can no longer honestly teach, the affirmations of the Apostles' Creed, he is in honour bound to relinquish an office with which he was originally entrusted, upon the understanding that he did so believe and teach. But when it comes to determining that, in the case of a particular brother clergyman, such a stage has actually been reached, we must proceed with caution," finally declining to have anything to do with the matter; and this, after the heretic rector of All Souls for eight years had been denying the Christian faith publicly from his pulpit.

Dr. De Costa replied, in part, as follows:—"Hammer away, then, Father Ignatius, and if your own material is not sufficient, there is *plenty* stored up in the diocesan archives. *Compel* the attention, if you can, that was *denied* three American clergymen acting under the highest ecclesiastical advice. Hammer away heartily, I say, and give us the riven Rock. By-and-bye, Father Ignatius, you may, perhaps, be remembered as another 'voice crying in the wilderness.' But to-day, in the estimation of many so-called wise men, you are a 'heresy hunter' and a 'crank.'

With a class of unprincipled men, the hunt for 'heresy hunters' has become a fad. They are thoroughly illiberal and often in league with the basest elements of society, deriving in many instances support from gamblers and speculators. It is not in the nature of things that people of this sort should tolerate a voice like yours. They are identified with a class of men to whom your bare feet, however 'beautiful' they may feel 'upon the mountains' of rugged Wales, form not only a stinging sarcasm and rebuke, but a proletarian menace. Your plain garb even is a reproof to the ecclesiastical sybarite luxuriating in gilded salons and marble halls. Your cause is not popular yet, nevertheless I believe there are presbyters in this city who might make it popular, and who could speak and make themselves heard and speedily cleanse the church of these sad scandals."

The Father then decided to call a Mass meeting of Christians of all denominations, at the Chickering Hall the next Sunday, and so New York was placarded with gigantic bills, headed:—"Bold Repudiation of the Christian Religion *in* the Episcopal Churches!" On this Sunday, the Father being too unwell to undertake the three advertised services, the morning and evening ones at the Metropolitan Opera House had to be given up, but the British monk was able to conduct the "Great Mass Meeting," crowded to the doors in the afternoon.

"*The New York Herald*" of the next day states:—

"When Father Ignatius knelt at his desk to pray, Chickering Hall was *crowded to the doors*. He was greeted by an immense audience, evidently in sympathy with his outspoken policy. Clergymen of all denominations were plentiful in the audience. Ladies and gentlemen, equally prominent as ardent church people and as ornaments to the fashionable world, listened to the monk's fiery utterances with a sympathy that frequently burst into applause. The service commenced with the singing of the Old Hundredth and the recitation of the Apostles' Creed. Father Ignatius let himself loose. He prefaced his scathing denunciations with no apologies. Like the prophet of old, he commanded all those who were on the Lord's side either to join him on the platform, or rise in their places in the auditorium. Several clergymen sprang from their seats and mounted the platform in response to this appeal. Amongst them were Dr. De Costa; a Presbyterian minister; and a man who was rather muddled; but we will deal with him later.

"Dr. De Costa spoke in part as follows :—' I am not here to talk, but simply to aid and comfort Father Ignatius. In a few minutes I must be elsewhere. God bless you, Father Ignatius, and uphold you in your fight for the American Church. This is not a battle of ritual, but a battle of the creeds. Come everyone to the help of the Lord against the might of the world' Before leaving the hall, Dr. De Costa invited the Father to preach at his Church of St. John the Evangelist the following Thursday evening (Ascension Day), which he did twice before leaving the city. Now, the clergy began to be aroused and rally round the standard of the Cross, with the result that finally a petition, signed by twelve of the leading representative clergy of New York, was presented to Bishop Potter, begging that an inquiry might be made into Newton's alleged heretical utterances, which his lordship, in reply, promised *should* be done."

I must not forget to tell you that at the mass meeting, when the Father invited the Christian clergy on to the platform, a man, with brown kid gloves and silk umbrella, jumped up, and, after bowing to the applauding audience, said : " I am a Roman Catholic, and an illiterate Irish peasant. If aught is said against *Parnell*, I want to protest against it." After he had been persuaded to seat himself, the Father turned to the audience, and said : " This gentleman seems to be confused in his mind between our Blessed Lord, Dr. Heber Newton, and Mr. Parnell," upon which, everybody laughed.

In reference to the Father's denunciation of the heretical utterances of Dr. Newton, the following appears in " *The Southern Churchman*," published at Richmond, Virginia, for May 14 :—" No man ever visited the United States who, in a few months, has made himself so very disagreeable as Father Ignatius. High Church, Low Church,

Broad Church, and Romanizers like him not, '*The New York Churchman*' saying he is crazy. It has been a good many years ago, but there was a class of Churchmen in Jerusalem who were very particular—paid their tithes, went to church, prayed, fasted, and full of zeal. There was One who called them hypocrites or play actors, and said they could *not* escape the damnation of hell. *Very* disagreeable did the Lord Christ make Himself to *these*. St. Paul did likewise, not only to Jews, but to heathen ; Savonarola and Luther and Wesley were very disagreeable to their contemporaries. Monk Ignatius finds himself in good company. A very disagreeable man indeed ; cannot let things alone, and they getting on so nicely and quietly in this diocese of New York ; everything so prosperous ; and yet *God* seems to be speaking to New York and us all, *through* this monk. We much prefer quiet ; no one likes to be disagreeable ; but *the truth of God*, is it worth preserving ? Are we *willing* to bear the cross ? "*

"*The Philadelphia Episcopal Recorder*" (which is one of the ultra-Protestant papers of the country, similar to the *Rock* of England in its earlier days) for April,

---

* It hardly seems as if we are, or that it matters *one straw* whether our grand old Christianity is undermined and explained away or not, whilst such men as Heber Newton, Drs. Mallory, Rainsford, Brooks, Bridgeman, Lester of Milwaukee, and others, are *allowed* to remain as licensed Episcopal clergy, to propound their strange and heretical views.

has the following :—" We had the pleasure of again listening to Father Ignatius last Sunday afternoon, and heard nothing to make us take back what we wrote concerning him in our last issue. His extemporaneous prayer was most beautiful and scriptural, his presentation of the Gospel *true* to the word, clear and definite. He defined a Christian to be one who believes in Jesus Christ; not, however, in the Jesus Christ of Strauss or Heber Newton, but in the Jesus Christ of the New Testament. His denunciation of those Episcopalians (which poured forth in a perfect torrent of words) who, as soon as they have finished their Easter Communion, make a break pell-mell for the world, the flesh, and the devil, was something never to be forgotten. His sarcasm, expressed by a burst of laughter, at the thought of a believer in Jesus, having to go for pleasure, to the ball-room, or to the theatre to see one woman put her foot over another woman's head, was decidedly unique, but telling. Father Ignatius is, without doubt, a sensationalist, but somewhat in the same sense as those who long ago were complained of, because they 'turned the world upside down.' The Protestant Episcopal Bishops *may* frown, but the Great Bishop of souls will surely smile, as long as he lifts up, and glorifies His Son."

Next, to the crusade we have just dealt with, the most important and interesting thing in this, the Father's second New York mission, were the great Welsh reception given to him by 1,200 Welshmen of

New York and Brooklyn, and the Welsh monk's sermons, in the midst of the excitement caused by his fearless language, at the Transfiguration Church* and that of St. John the Evangelist. For months before the great night, Mr. Daniel Jones, of Brooklyn, "the Welsh Patriarch of America," and the St. David's Society in New York, were busy organizing the public reception to the Father to be given on a Wednesday in April. The Tabernacle Church in Second Avenue, seating 1,500, was hired, and the Druid Glee Club engaged for the occasion. The Hon. Thomas James, ex-Postmaster General, was called upon to preside, while Judge Noah Davis and the Hon. Ellis Roberts promised to support him. Admission was only obtainable by invitation ticket, distributed previously at the various Welsh churches and chapels, yet a goodly number of Cymri indeed, congregated to meet the Welsh Druidic monk, " Dewi Honddhu," known to the Americans till then, only as Father Ignatius. On entering the church, the first thing to catch the eye to the left of the platform, was the " Ddraig Goch," or Red Dragon of Wales, floating in all its glory. The ushers, &c., each wore a sprig of

---

* Known popularly as "The Little Church round the Corner," on account of the burial of George Holland, an actor, who was refused burial at a fashionable Madison Avenue church, whose rector suggested that there was 'a little church round the corner where they did *that* sort of thing,' to which Mr. Joseph Jefferson replied, 'God bless the little church round the corner.'"—*Appleton's Dictionary of New York*.

oak with the Druidic acorn, whilst the young ladies of the Druid Glee Club on the platform, dressed all in white, carried bouquets of flowers. One of these Druidesses subsequently presented the Father, with a magnificent basket of cut flowers. As he entered, the grand organ struck up " The Men of Harlech," followed by " The Star-Spangled Banner." " The climbing of y Wyddfa," and many a grand old Welsh hymn, were subsequently sung by the choir, the audience throughout being most enthusiastic and patriotic. All doubts, as to the genuineness of their Cymric nationality, were quickly dispelled by their accent and the warm Welsh greetings, they pressed forward and waited in crowds in the streets, to accord the Father, after it was over. The Father, as is usual when addressing his fellow-countrymen, quite carried away his audience, by his eloquent and patriotic address, and subsequently received the following Englyn :—

"I, y Parchedig Dad Ignatius, O.S.B.
pan yn Efrog Newydd, Ebrill, 28ain, 1891."
" Ignatius, gyda egni, Gyfododd
Gofadail uchelfri,
Lle in Tad yn Llanthoni
Porth Ne—perthyna i ni "
" Hyny yw, os Duwioldeb—Ein rhan,
Rhinwedd a Doethineb;
Da i ddyn yw hyn, ac heb
Gwên Ion ni ddaw i, n gwyneb."
Lewys Maldwyn.

This time in New York, our resting or abiding place was very conveniently situated for good churches, and afforded me a most enjoyable early morning walk, to the daily mass at the Church of the Transfiguration, or, for a change, to the grand American Catholic Church of St. Mary the Virgin, where Jesus in His sweet Sacrament dwells Love's Prisoner on the altar. Our rooms too were exactly opposite the hall where the Father held his daily services, so that we were able to watch the people going in. Whilst here, the Father paid a visit one morning, and preached, to the old people of Mr. Mackey's Coloured Home; many of the directors and their friends also gathered right there to hear him. The poor old coloured people were very moved, crying bitterly, and frequently calling out, for mercy and salvation. Before leaving, they begged him to come, and tell them of Jesus, again. Soon after, as our stay in New York was longer than we expected, we were obliged to vacate our lodgings for new tenants, to whom they had been previously let, so, the next Sunday morning I attended the early celebration at St. Anne's, the church of the deaf and dumb. It was whilst in this new abode of ours, that the Father preached at the midday mass at the Transfiguration Church on "The Ascension." In spite of the preaching of the late Dr. Philips Brooks, the popular and *most* eloquent preacher in America, but two streets off, the congregation that gathered to hear the Father, notwithstanding that his sermon was unannounced, was very large. Later, just before leaving New York, he preached twice at St. John's Church, Waverley Place, and once at the Salvation Army

Barracks, besides holding a conversazione for the members of "the Bond of Holy Spirit in the Life of Jesus," to re-organize the committee, &c., before leaving the city. On Ascension Day we attended the early communion, and the Father attended the 11 o'clock mass at the Church of the Transfiguration, whilst Brother David, Sister Annie, and I went to the grand Ascension service, of which we had heard so much, at Trinity Church, Broadway. Admission to this, was only obtainable by ticket; and tickets were very hard to get, as all the chief church clergy and choirs of the city united, to make this *one* service as grand as possible. The music *quite* came up to what we had heard, and the great organ was supplemented by a band. The church was packed with the *élite* of New York and clergy without number. The service, as was but right, proved to be a High celebration of the Holy Eucharist, with its proper accompaniments of lights and vestments, but the latter were only of linen. I was lucky in securing a seat amongst a number of clergy, by the chancel gates. A most eloquent and gospel sermon on the "Old, Old Story" was preached by the rector, Dr. Morgan Dix, though Bishop Potter *was* to have occupied the pulpit. After the service, we met an old brother of Llanthony, now a priest in the city, with whom before leaving the city I took a walk through the Central Park. The happy children without number, who were enjoying themselves on that Saturday afternoon, was a sight never to be forgotten. The whole Park seemed like a great fair, but the holiday-makers were *all children*—the wealthy and the fashionable, the poor and the low, all were there enjoying themselves and basking in the sunshine. Brother Sebastian told me that on a Saturday afternoon, it is a rendezvous for all the children of the city.

Worn out with his hard and exciting mission in New York, the Father was glad indeed to get away and rest in a quiet village among " the Highlands of the Hudson," before proceeding to Chicago.

CHAPTER XVI.

CORNWALL-ON-HUDSON—THE HIGHLANDS OF THE
HUDSON—SERMONS—BEAUTIES OF NATURE.

AFTER his hard and vigorous battle for '*the Truth*,' and the month's mission in New York, it was to the little village of Cornwall, Orange County, New York State, situated at the foot of the majestic Storm King Mountain, amidst all the beauties of the historical " Highlands of The Hudson,"* that the Father retired, to rest and recruit his strength for his Chicago mission.

It was whilst we were here, that the blaspheming heretic, Heber Newton, was presented to the Bishop for trial. It was also from this spot, that the Welsh monk fired his first broadside against Dr. Philips Brooks (the newly chosen Bishop of Massachusetts), in a characteristic letter to "*The New York Herald.*"

We must not anticipate too much, but rather return to the points of interest we passed, on our journey to Cornwall by steamer, one bright sunny afternoon in May.

From the moment we left New York, the beauty and grandeur of the surroundings, the peculiar rock

---

* These " Highlands of The Hudson " reach from Stony Point to Newburgh.

formations, known as "The Palisades," on the New Jersey shore extending for over twenty miles, were impressive to a degree. These Palisades, or vast cliffs, in many places 300 feet high, are an irregular column-like precipice springing from a sloping bank of shale and *débris*, the slope and top of the ridge in many places being covered with a forest. A view of these "Palisades" in winter, hung with countless glistening icicles of all kinds of fantastic shapes and sizes, with the ice-blocked, frozen river at their feet, is, indeed, grand.

The first point of interest passed is Tappan, three miles south, the place where Major André was executed. Soon we reach West Point,* on the western shore, whilst "Garrison" faces it on the east—a place of great natural beauty, and also of immense national and historic interest and importance. West Point is the site of the great New York military academy, and is to the Americans, what Sandhurst, Woolwich, or Aldershot are to us. Next comes Tarrytown, where Major André was arrested, September 23rd, 1780. At West Point, also, is "The Key of the Hudson," being situated as it is, at the narrowest part of the river; and during the American war this was the great stronghold and storehouse. All this is *holy*

---

* It was from here, the only point on the Hudson capable of being so fortified as to prevent the passage of the British fleet, that in the winter of 1778 the *great* chain, weighing between 140 and 150 tons, which was made at Stirling, some 25 miles inland, was stretched across the river.

ground to the Patriotic American, as so many scenes of the Great War for Liberty were enacted in this neighbourhood and all around. Steaming up the river, passing Stony Point, leaving Peekskill on the east, and the grand old "Thunder Mountain" on the west; "Anthony's Nose," another peak, is seen to our right, as we draw nigh to Cornwall. We are now, going through the most picturesque scenery of "The Hudson Highlands," and *well* may the river be called "The American Rhine." Very Swiss are the views. Iona Island with its vineyards, the Sugarloaf Mountain, Fort Independence, Buttermilk Falls, and West Point are soon left behind, and the majestic forest-clad peak of "The Storm King" with its precipitous rugged cliffs and huge boulders on the river side, comes into view. At West Point, the ruins of the old Fort Putnam* on the heights, can be seen, from the river. Bull Hill, Breakneck Hill, Fort Constitution, and other features of the landscape come and go, and we are soon disembarking at the Cornwall landing point.

The first glimpses of the village to be our refuge and resting place for a few weeks, are *indeed* lovely. Lying in a rugged valley is Cornwall, hemmed in by "The Storm King" on the left, and other lofty verdure-clad irregular hills all round, with the broad glistening river at her feet, its opposite bank of

---

* Called after Brigadier-General Putnam, of America War fame, born at Sutton, Mass. 1738. Died 1784.

Q

rugged hills adding to the romantic beauty of the scene. Here, indeed, is a resting place and source of refreshment for any over-worked worn-out brain; the magnificent beauties of Nature in hill and vale, woods, land, river, birds, and flowers, uniting one and all in the bright golden sunshine, in singing the love and praises of their Creator God, Who in His great love and power is visible *wherever* you turn. In the woods, 'midst the tender green of the spring leaves, are countless golden orioles and bright American blue birds, with an occasional brilliant *scarlet* tanager, with its black wings,* all warbling out their happy praises to God. The white locust flower, the delicate fern, the sweet scented lilac, syringa, and laburnum, all are in their profusest blossom. Everything is glad; and joy, happiness and peace reign undisturbedly around. Man *alone* neglects his God, though *he* owes more to Him, than the birds and the flowers of the earth.

Our rooms here at "The Grand View," were found for us by a New York Presbyterian minister,† who accompanied us hither, and we were glad to find that our future landlord was a Welshman. Looking out of our windows, from which we could see for miles up the river, far away o'er the horizon, the Catskill Peaks appeared.

---

* This bird, though the most brilliant scarlet in the spring and summer, turns green in the autumn and winter.

† The Rev. John Boyd.

Away, too, in the distance lay the City of Newburgh, on the west bank, noted for "Washington's Headquarters," and exactly opposite on the east, the town of Fishkill. Throughout our sojourn in this delightful spot, we enjoyed golden sunshine, through the love of Jesus. Yes, the love of Jesus, for He knew how the Father had worked for His glory in New York, so He sent the sunshine and fine weather, to help recruit his strength. Here the sight of the blackholl, deutzia, and lilies of the valley reminded one, indeed, of home, as they dispersed their fragrance in the soft spring air. From the time I first caught sight of it, I had a great ambition to climb "The Storm King," in spite of the report that rattlesnakes abode there; but it was not until we had been in our new home a week, that one glorious May morning, as the sun rose o'er the horizon, and the early dawn was fleeting over the hills, I made this ascent.

The village of Cornwall, about four miles from West Point, situated at the base of "The Storm King," the highest mountain but one, of the Hudson Highland cluster, contains many summer residences on its hill slopes. At this point, the river broadens into a beautiful lake, from which Pollipels Island* lifts its granite mass, crowned with verdure. Here, too,

---

* Here during the American war a *chevaux-de-frise*, composed of massive pikes projected from sunken cribs of stone obstructed the river, whilst the obstruction used at West Point was a boom and chain.

at Cornwall, was a romantic spot named Idlewild, the summer home of the poet Willis.

Mount Taurus, 1,586 feet, bears off the palm for height in the Hudson Mountains, followed by Storm King, 1,529 feet; Breakneck, 1,487 feet, and Cro' Nest, 1,418 feet.

Though the Father came hither to rest, God had work for him to do. No sooner had he entered the Episcopal Chapel of S. John (the very first Sunday), than the Rector* came forward, and begged him to address the congregation, which the Father did, from the text, "It is expedient for you that I go away, for if I go not away, the Comforter will not come unto you," etc. Before giving this address the Rector introduced the Father in these words : "It is our unexpected privilege to have in our midst this afternoon, one whose entire life has been consecrated to, and set apart for, the service of God in a manner it is seldom our lot to meet with, one who, though he has come here to rest from the noise and turmoil of cities, has kindly consented to speak to you this afternoon, at the end of this hymn—the great Welsh Monk, Ignatius."

As was to be expected, directly it was spread abroad that the Father had preached, many in the village wished they had known it beforehand, and it was not long before the Presbyterian Deacon called to

---

* The Rev. P. C. Creveling.

invite the Welsh Monk, and obtained his promise to preach for him, the following Sabbath evening, in the Presbyterian Church. The Rector also called several times. As it will interest many, I have clipped this report from "*The Cornwall Local,*" of May 28 :—

"THE DISCOURSE OF FATHER IGNATIUS. — Father Ignatius delivered a sermon on Sunday evening, which was the most eloquent and powerful appeal we ever listened to. His opening prayer was a marvel of elegant English. During the opening of the service, conducted by Rev. Mr. Barron, the Father listened attentively, and sat with eyes closed part of the time, his face wearing a placid and peaceful smile. He took for his text Luke vii. 11, 13, which is the story of the Lord's calling back to life of the son of the widow of Nain. His description of the miracle was so vivid and powerful as to hold the whole attention of the listener, and one could picture in the mind's eye the scene he so thoroughly described. Words seem to flow from the devout man's lips like water from a gurgling spring. His command of the English language is marvellous. His style of preaching partakes of that of the usual Evangelist. He gets warmed up to his subject at times, and seems to strain every nerve to impress the words upon his hearers' minds, using his hands, head and whole body in making gestures to hold the attention. At other times he sinks his voice almost to a whisper. I wish it was possible to publish the whole sermon of

Sunday evening. It would be a most interesting reading.

"At one time he gave a grand and masterly description of the infinite greatness, glory, power and love of Christ; at another a clear vivid description of the funeral *cortège* bearing the dead man to his grave; then of the multitude of people following Jesus over the hills of Galilee. He told how Christ had commanded the young man to rise—how He had saved him.

"Then, in a burst of tremendous eloquence, he assured the people of the congregation that this *same* Christ was ready and willing to save *them*. It was a grand sermon from beginning to end. We hope he may again preach to our people. The church was crowded to its utmost capacity, and many who would have liked to hear him could not obtain seats. Whatever the 'religious critics' may say of Father Ignatius, we are sure that he is a follower of Christ, a firm believer in the inspiration proceeding from the Holy Ghost, and a man who has faith that he will reach Heaven *because* Christ died on the Cross to save mankind. This is the religion, pure and simple, and he endeavours to live it as well as preach it."

Next day a deputation called from the Military Academy to ask the Father to address the boys, which he did on the Wednesday evening. Then our Presbyterian host wished the Father to baptize two children, which ceremony he performed the following Sunday afternoon in S. John's Episcopal Chapel, when, as the Rector was absent at a funeral, he conducted Evensong, and again addressed them. In the morning we had driven out to the nine o'clock celebration at the Parish Church of Canterbury, between which and Cornwall there are a Roman Catholic, Episcopal, Methodist, and Baptist places of worship. Hence its name of Canterbury, " The City of Churches." The Father could not be inactive when there was work for our Lord and Master to be done. Evening prayers and Bible readings were held most nights, of which the people of the hotel gladly availed themselves. Many an hour the Father spent at the bedside of their sick son, and even the Presbyterian deacon, in his lovely farm up the mountain side, was visited by the Welsh Monk, *directly* he learnt he was ill. The Father so won the hearts of the boys at the Academy, that often one or other used to come and see him, and when one day, on the road to Newburgh, he stayed the carriage to watch them playing baseball, they cheered him.

Oh ! the lovely country walks round Cornwall, the delightful early morning rambles I enjoyed, in spite of the anti-American warning profusely scattered about—" Private grounds ; trespassers will be prosecuted ; no shooting." All round, whichever way you turned, beautiful ravines and woodland glens, great rocks overhanging the roads so prettily, the sweet choruses of innumerable birds, the chestnut and acacia trees in full blossom, greeted the eye; while wood anemones, yellow and red columbines, wild strawberries, and many a lovely wild flower, shining like countless stars, studded the rich undergrowth and moss-grown banks, along which Spring's soft fingers were hard at work. Gas being apparently an unknown luxury in this quiet country village, oil lamps, which in many cases burn all day, are hung all along the country roads. It is all hill and dale, wherever you go, and the views from some of the hills, especially from the top of Storm King, stretch for miles, and are exquisite beyond description on a clear spring morning.

Some time ago, there was a great fire on Storm King, which has in many parts left its traces. Half-way up, almost hidden amongst the trees, are the ruins of "the Artist's Cottage," now all desolate and bare, for the artist has departed, no one knows whither. But the ruins, besides adding to the picturesqueness of the scene, remind the natives how the artist, being unable to find anyone to build for him in such a uniquely picturesque and romantic position, and to which there was no road approach, carried all the boards up on his own back.

My long looked-forward-to ascent of this mountain, with the flag flying at its summit, was made at half-past six on Saturday morning, May 13th; and though the *ascent* was supposed to take two hours, I was home again at nine. Before you can commence the ascent, a walk of a mile is necessary up the delightful mountain road, with the trees meeting across overhead (in many places), to a bathing pond, from whence a bridle-path starts, through the forest, for the summit. Easy at first, it soon becomes necessary to clamber over huge rocks; but on we go. As we reach the first flat ridge, and wend our way, through the tall pine woods, in the miniature cañon, what a scene of beauty and grandeur surrounds us on all sides. But, the summit reached, WHAT a view! As far as your eye will carry you to your right or left, the silvery Hudson glistens in the sun, as it serpentinely flows upon its way through countless hills and forests. A boy, whom I asked how long it would take to get to the top and back, exclaimed, "It'd take *me* a week!" Going back, and meeting a boy I had passed, as I began to ascend, he exclaimed. "You been right up to the top and back? Oh my! you *ain't* been long; take me three hours to get up." Another couple of boys whom I met were carrying a snake they had just killed, for these slippery creatures abound in the woods round there. I myself was destined, before I left Cornwall, to have an adventure with a "rattler."

Have you ever seen, on a clear night, the stars— "God's forget-me-nots"—spangling the sky like silver dust, and the silver moon kissing, as it were, "the Storm King's" crest? It is indeed grand, and calls to mind, that allegory of Munro's, "The Combatants," in which the dark mountains and the distant hills shut out the land of the free, the land of life, of joy, of peace, in the presence of the King—that land so very far off, where we shall *one* day see the King in His Beauty.

A great deal of fruit is grown at Cornwall, vines and cherry trees being especially plentiful. The royal shad and sturgeon abound in the river, though the only fish I ever caught there, were "sunfish," a silvery fish, with a dazzling golden red stomach just like the sun.

One morning, I watched for some time a lovely golden oriole from my window, as it actually *drew* threads of cotton, out of the washing hung out to dry, and carried them off to its nest. I mustn't forget to mention the number of savage dogs round and about Cornwall, which a Presbyterian friend speaks of, as "the unconverted dogs," for he declares the Father *converted* the hotel dog, which at first used to fly at us, but eventually liked to go out walks with us, and became very friendly. Whenever other dogs used to fly at him, he would take to his heels and tear away home, which our friend declared was *another* proof of his conversion, as now he had *given up* fighting!

There being no Episcopal service in Cornwall of a Sunday morning, as the parish church was at Canterbury, a mile and a half away, a most enjoyable walk along the shady country roads, every Sabbath morning we wended our way thither.

A few days before leaving Cornwall, we enjoyed a most pleasant and picturesque drive to Newburgh and Washington's headquarters, and visited the Roman Catholic Cathedral and the Episcopal Church of S. George. A priest of the Cathedral, who came out himself to show us round, was most agreeable and Christianlike in his behaviour. "The Hasbrouck House," or Washington's headquarters, is where General Washington resided from the spring of 1782 to August 18th, 1783, and from whence he issued his orders during the great war for American Independance.

The house is still standing, and daily visited by numbers of people, for on July 4th, 1850, "the property was dedicated and set apart to be for ever a reminder of 'times that tried men's souls,' and to awaken patriotic memories."* This is, indeed, "holy ground" to the patriotic American, where the seeds of their great American liberty were *first* sown. With reverential interest we went through the house (now turned into a National Museum), and saw the room with the seven doors, the old piano of Martha Washington,† her watch, an authenticated lock of

* "*General Orders of Georde Washington,*" by Major E. C. Boynton. Published by Ruttenger and Sons, Newburgh, which are most interesting historical reading.

† Made in London by Astor in 1730, and said once to have been the property of General James Clinton, Commander-in-Chief of the English Army in the American War. It is the oldest piano in America.

Washington's hair, and one of La Fayette's, and considerable furniture that was in use in the time of America's greatest general, as well as the General's armchair and bedroom. Now, on the lawn sloping towards the river, a magnificent arch of Victory, at an enormous cost, has been erected, whilst in the grounds also, may be seen the tomb of the great General's last aide-de-camp, Uzal Knapp.*

We had some weeks previously visited West Point with the Rev. Dr. De Costa, of S. John's, New York, who knew the place well, and had come down to stay a night with us. He took us over the library and gymnasium, after which we wandered about the grounds until five o'clock, when we reboarded the train for home. Whilst at West Point, on passing an

---

* Uzal Knapp was the last member of Washington's Life Guard. He entered the army on the 1st of June, 1777, and was in service from that time until his final discharge by Washington in 1783. He was in the battle at White Plains ; in the skirmish at Ridgefield ; passed through the horrors of Valley Forge ; was one of La Fayette's Corps, and in the action under him at Barren Hill, and in the battle of Monmouth. In 1780 he was detailed, with other soldiers of known fidelity, to form an increase in the Life Guard, and received a Sergeant's commission. Soon after his discharge he took up his residence in New Windsor, Orange county, where he lived to the age of 94 years, honoured and respected by all. His body lies buried under the monument near the flag-staff. The monument was erected by a local military company, the Newburgh Guard, in 1859.—*Catalogue of Manuscripts and Relics at Washington's Headquarters*, by E. M. Ruttenber.

omnibus, we heard a voice shouting out: "Why! it's *Father* Ignatius!" The owner of the voice having stopped the omnibus, proved to be a Russian lady just returning to Russia, who had heard the Father at Washington, and derived great benefit from his preaching.

The following little story, of something that happened at Cornwall, is true:—You must know that in America, in very many instances, when a railway has to cross a river, it does not do so by a bridge, but on trestles, with a few boards here and there across, through which the water is clearly seen. There was just such a place across an arm of the Hudson above Cornwall (round which was the favourite fishing place of the village boys). One day a boy tried to walk across, but he had *not* got half way, before he saw a train coming to meet him. It was impossible to turn and retrace his steps, for it is all one can do, to keep one's balance; death stared him in the face; so he jumped over into the river and got safe to shore, upon which he begged some boys who had witnessed it, not to say a word to anyone, as he did not wish it known. At once he rushed off himself to the newspaper office, and gave a full account of the occurrence (hoping to earn something by it), which duly appeared in the next issue of the local paper.

From this, our quiet resting place among the lovely Highlands of the Hudson (where we had a comfortable and beautifully situated hotel, for some time all to ourselves, on account of our visit being so early in the season) we went to Niagara, to see the Falls, of which we had heard and read so much, before proceeding to Chicago.

CHAPTER XVII.

THE FALLS OF NIAGARA.

AS we were obliged, *en route* for Chicago, to spend a night and some hours of the next day at Niagara,* we selected the hospitable Spencer House as our resting place. Though it was past two on a June morning when we arrived, we found refreshments awaiting us. After a few hours' rest, we were up betimes, and began to think and talk about the far-famed Falls, now so near, and whether there would be time to see them. We learnt they were but five minutes' walk, and that the tramcar to the Suspension Bridge passed our door. In talking the matter over and planning what we should do, one of our party stated *he* thought, as we *were* so near, it would be TOO *vulgar* to visit the foaming cataracts, for *every-*

---

* The name "Niagara" is supposed by many to be a contraction of the Indian word "Oniahgahrah," meaning "thunder of waters"; others think that this mighty cataract derived its name from the "Onghiahrahs," an Indian tribe, who formerly dwelt on the northern bank of the river, and who endeavoured to live at peace with the Huron and Iroquois Indians who were on either side of them. They were a brave, but not warlike tribe, who being in time absorbed or destroyed by their fiercer neighbours, became extinct in the eighteenth century.—*" Niagara Park Illustrated."*

body did that. However, it was decided to take a carriage, and see what we could in the time, and we were soon on our way to Goat Island Bridge. There, we obtained our first view of the American rapids, which descend forty feet in half a mile. Alighting from the carriage we stood on the bridge, and watched them in silent *awe* and *admiration*, the thunder of the Falls filling the air around. No pen can fully describe my impressions, or those of anyone, on viewing for the first time these rushing, foaming waters, tearing along in headlong fury, dashing up clouds and mountains of spray in their wild course. On beholding them one feels, as at the Falls, a *strange* overpowering *fascination*, an inclination to "gaze *on for ever*," and a reluctance to tear oneself away. Having crossed the bridge which spans these rapids, and reached Goat Island, on our left is the Fairy Spring, whilst to our right a path winds through luxuriously wild pine woods, gay with many a spring flower, to Luna Island and Stedman's Bluff, overlooking the American Fall, the river gorge, and the Suspension Bridge. Goat Island is the largest of the Niagara group of islands, and is covered with original forest.

After a view of the American Fall and a descent, across to Luna Island, once more ascending the flight of steps, as we pursue our way, we pass the Biddles Stairs and house. From here, all expeditions start for the Cave of the Winds, *i.e.*, a most exciting passage *under* the American Falls. Here we get a beautiful view of the Canadian or Horseshoe Falls, in which, 'mid a heavy shower of rain, I witnessed half of one of the most *perfect* rainbows I have ever seen. Gazing on these immense and excessively beautiful Falls, carries one's thoughts far away from earth and earthly things, to the Infinite and the Almighty Creator of the Universe.

It is a marvel how any atheist, after beholding these cataracts, can deny or even doubt the *existence* of a God. Passing a little further along the edge of the cliff to Porter's Bluff, we descend by a bridge and stairway to Terrapin Rock, a point upon the very brink of the Horseshoe Fall, from which is obtained the best general view of the Falls from the Island. The next point of interest we find to be "The Three Sisters' Islands," gloriously wild and picturesque, with their lofty pines standing out as they do (though connected with each other by rustic bridges) in the midst of the Canadian Rapids, thus forming most desirable points from which to observe the scenery. Here is the beautiful "Hermit's Cascade," formed by the first Sister Island bridge*

This cascade derives its name from Francis Abbot, the son of an English clergyman, who in 1829 took up his solitary abode on Three Sisters Island and became the "Hermit of the Falls." For two years, he lived alone with his cat and dog, a life of almost total seclusion, beneath a roof, which was the work of his own hands, preparing his own food, and bathing daily, even in severe weather, between Moss and Iris* Islands.

"As with the American Thoreau, a free communion with the spirits of the waters and the woods, was the absorbing delight of his existence. It was his habit to watch the smallest animals, so as to detect their secrets. Birds seemed to recognise him instinctively, and came to him freely, to receive food from his hands. On Goat Island, at all hours of the day and night, he could be seen, wandering through unfrequented paths, to watch the mighty Niagara, from every point of view. Neither the heat of summer, nor the piercing cold of winter, stayed his feet from going, where the cataract

>In deafening sweep,
>Girdled with rainbows, thunders down the steep.

He had worn a beaten path from his cottage to Terrapin Bridge. At that time a single shaft of timber, eight inches square, jutted out ten feet from the bridge over the precipice. On this it was his pleasure to sit, sometimes carelessly on the extreme edge, or grasping it with his hands, suspend himself over the fathomless abyss. To this point he would pass or repass at all hours of the night, apparently undisturbed by the slightest tremor of nerve, certainly without any hesitancy of step."† His favourite

---

*Now known as Goat Island.

†"*Niagara Park Illustrated*," published at 96, Fulton Street, New York.

pursuit was music, and he was very learned in the languages, sciences, and the art of drawing. Though given to writing a great deal, all his compositions were written in Latin, and he destroyed them as soon as finished. With rare skill he played on the flute, violin, and guitar. He was only twenty-eight years old when he was drowned, having been seized with cramp whilst bathing.

From the head of the third Sister, may be seen one continuous cascade, extending as far as the eye can reach, from Goat Island across to the Canada shore, and from which the spray rises in beautiful clouds. This presents a phenomenon that has been termed the "Leaping Rock." The water striking against the rock, rises perpetually in an unbroken column twenty feet or more, producing a brilliant effect.

Charles Dickens,[*] in describing his first impressions of Niagara, writes, " I was in a manner stunned, and unable to comprehend the vastness of the scene. It was not until I came on Table Rock and looked—*great Heaven*! on what a fall of bright green water! that it came upon me in its full might and majesty. *Then*, when I felt how near to my Creator I was standing, the first effect and the enduring one— instant and lasting—of the tremendous spectacle was *peace*. Peace of mind, tranquillity, calm recollections of the dead ; great thoughts of eternal rest and happi-

---

[*] "*American Notes.*"

ness; nothing of gloom or terror. Niagara was at once stamped upon my heart, an image of beauty, to remain there changeless and indelible, until its pulses cease to beat, for ever."

One more quotation, from *Anthony Trollope*, and I have done:—"The greatest charm of a mountain range is the wild feeling that there must be strange unknown worlds in those far off valleys beyond. And so here at Niagara, that converging rush of waters may fall down at once into a hell of rivers, for what the eye can see. It is glorious to watch them in their first curve over the rocks. They come green as a bank of emeralds, but with a fitful flying colour, as though conscious that in one moment more they would be dashed into spray, and rise into air, pale as driven snow. The vapour rises high in the air, and is gathered there, visible always as a permanent white cloud over the cataracts; but the bulk of the spray that fills the lower hollow of that Horseshoe, is like a tumult of snow. . . . . The bend of it rises ever and anon out of that cauldron below, but the cauldron itself will be invisible. It is ever so far down—far as your imagination can sink it. But your eyes will rest full upon the chasm of waters. The shape you will be looking at is that of a Horseshoe, but of a horseshoe miraculously deep from toe to heel, and the depth becomes greater as you watch it. That which at first was only great and beautiful, becomes gigantic and sublime, till the mind is at a loss to find an epithet for its own use. To *realize* Niagara you must sit there till you see *nothing else* than that which you have come to see; you will hear nothing else and think of nothing else. At length you will be at one with the tumbling river before you, you will find yourself among the waters as though you belonged to them. The cool limpid green will run through your veins, and the voice of the cataract will be the expression of your own heart. You will fall as the bright waters fall, rushing down into your new world with no hesitation and no dismay; and you will rise again as the spray rises, bright, beautiful and pure. Then you will flow away in your course to the unconfined distant and eternal ocean."

Everything of interest from, and on, Goat Island having been seen, we started for the Suspension Bridge and Canadian side, where at an Indian store just over the border, we purchased a number of photographs. Then we proceeded to inspect the view of the Falls and Rapids, obtainable from the Victoria Jubilee Park in our own British Dominions. From here, a view of the entire face of the American and Horseshoe Falls, Table Rock at the brink of the latter, Cedar Island, the Rapids, Drive, etc., are to be had. As time flew on and we had to catch an early afternoon train to Chicago, we were compelled reluctantly to hurry back. On recrossing the Suspension Bridge, to go over which we had already paid 25 cents* each,

---

* One shilling.

the Customs House officer stopped the carriage and levied duty on all the photographs, etc., which we had purchased the other side. Though rather a joke, that occasioned a lot of laughter, it was a very unpleasant one, especially as the duty mounted up to nearly as much as the photos, which had been bought not a stone's-throw away. We told the officer, he should have told us what he was going to do, before we crossed the Bridge, and then had he done so, we would not have bought them. There being no time to visit the Rapids and Whirlpool to-day, a speedy return was made to the Hotel, and we were soon *en route* to Chicago.

On our way we passed over the Cantilever Bridge at Niagara—with the Rapids surging and rushing along beneath—into Canada, and did not again get into the States till we crossed the river (the train bodily) in a ferry at Port Huron and reached Detroit.

Shall I attempt to describe some of the beautiful scenery round Dundas and Hamilton, St. Catherine's— and everywhere in Canada? It would be useless, for I feel inadequate to do it justice. At South Bend (I think) as we passed it at seven in the morning, though it was no special saint's day, the bells of four churches appeared to be ringing, and the poor people of the village *flocking* to Mass, with their prayer books in their hands. At length Chicago was reached, and we soon found ourselves in the Dearborn St. Depot, seeking a cab, to take us to the rooms our friends had previously obtained for us in Dearborn Avenue.

Some three weeks later, on returning from the city of the coming "World's Fair," to New York, we again broke our journey at Niagara, arriving there in the middle of an afternoon, and leaving again the next night.

This time we stayed at "The International Hotel," situated on the banks of the rapids themselves; for the proprietor, having heard that Father Ignatius wished to visit the Falls, offered to take *him* free of charge, and all his party half price. Here, consequently, we experienced the greatest kindness. A newly married couple staying at the hotel, hearing of the Father being there, at once sought his blessing on their union, for they stated they had many times heard him in New York and been blessed.

Directly we had arrived and unpacked, we started out for a walk to the Falls, this time through Prospect Park to Prospect Point, a lovely spot at the very edge of the American Fall itself, from which a most beautiful view is obtainable of the Canadian or Horseshoe Falls. Here, by leaning over, you can put your hand in the water of the cataract, as it plunges over the precipice. The rapids are clear as crystal, and apparently but knee deep. The sensation, of standing here at the edge of the Great Fall, is most fascinating and magnetic, like the spell with which the serpent draws its victim within its coils. From here an inclined railway descends the cliff to the river shore.

In the evening, the fountains in the hotel gardens

being illuminated by electric light of various colours, gave a most fairy-like appearance to the scene.

Next morning, up with the lark, I spent a most enjoyable two hours from six (when the gates open) wandering about Goat Island, and gazing once more in wondrous awe and admiration on the Falls, exploring the wildest nooks of the primeval woods and kodaking " the beauty spots."

In the afternoon, hiring a carriage, and the hotel keeper's son kindly coming as guide, we all started for the Whirlpool Rapids and Whirlpool. As these have been so often described far better than I feel able to do, I will leave them. In the morning Bro. David went for a trip on the " Maid of the Mist." This is a small steamer which plies backwards and forwards up to, and right under, the Falls many times a day. Once she shot through *the rapids and whirlpool*, and came out but *slightly* damaged. Niagara does not impress all her beholders similarly; as many do not give themselves time to behold and appreciate her beauties, which by numbers are said to be more magnificent in winter than summer. Thousands flock there to see her icebound, with her vast ice bridge —and the youth of the neighbourhood coasting and toboganning in the moonlight, when

> The hoar frost spangles the waste with flowers,
> Fairer than any where night dews weep.

CHAPTER XVIII.

Chicago.

The City of "The World's Fair"—Crowded Services—Mission Results.

HAVING travelled all night, it was a little past nine, on the third day after we had left Cornwall, that we arrived at Chicago. On reaching our rooms, we found our friends had gone to meet us, but that very quiet and comfortable apartments had been engaged, in a house all to ourselves in the day time, the other occupants being out and away at business. We learnt, there were no servants (or 'helps' as they are called in America) in the house, so that we should have to answer our own front-door bell, and that our meals would be brought in, from over the road, to us. The unpacking done, in the evening we were inundated by an army of newspaper reporters, to know the Father's views, plans for the future, and receptions so far in the States.

Next morning (Saturday) our first callers, whilst we were at breakfast, were the Rector and Curate of the Pioneer Catholic Church of the City—"The Ascension." They had called to welcome the Father to Chicago, and to ask him to preach next day at the

High Mass. Before coming to the "City of the West," the Father had written to her Bishop, asking his wishes, should he be invited to preach in the churches, but as yet had received no answer. In the afternoon another priest, the Welsh Rector from "The Church of the Good Shepherd," called, and also the President and Secretary of the Welsh Cymrodorion Society, who much wished to get up a Welsh meeting for the Father, whilst he was in the City. The Welsh clergyman told us *what* interest the Bishop took in the Welsh, and how he wished they had a church, and also that they had held a great Welsh service in the Cathedral.

This great City of Chicago, burnt by fire in 1871, at a loss of 200,000,000dols., is now one of the largest cities of the world. It is built on the site of Fort Dearborn, a little history concerning which may be of interest. This Fort itself was built in 1803, but evacuated August, 1812, and the stores distributed amongst the Indians. Very soon after, the troops, women, and children were massacred, and the Fort burnt by the Indians. In 1816 it was re-built, but after "the Black Hawk War" it fell into gradual disuse. John Whistler, the richest Indian in the world, who recently died, was born at Fort Dearborn. Here, in Chicago, the very first sermon ever preached, was preached in 1825, by Isaac McCoy to the Indians. There are now over 497 churches in the City, of which the largest number are Roman

Catholic (60), there being but about 21 Episcopal, 46 Methodist Episcopal, 18 Jewish, and 46 Baptist places of worship. Both the Roman Catholics and the Protestant Episcopalians possess a Cathedral, that of our Roman Brethren being dedicated to "The Holy Name of Jesus," whilst our own American Episcopalian one is under the patronage of "SS. Peter and Paul."

On the first Sunday morning after our arrival in the City, the Rev. Father and I started off, to the early Mass at "The Church of the Ascension," which, though we knew it was quite close, we experienced some little difficulty in finding. Nevertheless, arriving there in good time, and finding the service would be in the Chapel, not in the Church at all, we entered and found ourselves in a lovely little "Church,"* seating some 300; railed off at the east end by a Gothic oak screen, surmounted by a crucifix. The altar, which was of white marble, with its crimson lamp, glittering tabernacle, and glorified crucifix, added to the Catholic appearance. What joy it was, once more to enter a church on whose altar, Jesus, in His Sacrament of Love, ever and continually dwells, enshrined in the Tabernacle. How refreshing, again, to feel we had so close to us, and in one of our own churches, a place of perfect rest and peace, a source of calm refreshment and sympathising love, to which one could flee

---

* This Chapel was the temporary Church during the rebuilding of the Church itself after its destruction by fire.

at any hour of the day, to converse face to face with our Saviour, our *ever-changeless* Friend who is Love itself, Perfect Joy and Peace that passeth all understanding, to the soul that has *embraced* the promises, and *taken* God at His Word.

" Here, O my God, I see Thee *Face to Face*,
 Here I may touch and handle things *unseen*,
 Here grasp with firmer hand the Eternal Grace,
 And *all* my weariness upon Thee lean."

Some of my happiest hours in Chicago were spent in this "Holy Place," where, in the very early morning hour, the faithful gathered, to assist at the offering of the Divine Mystery, before going to their daily tasks in the outer world. In this parish, there is *indeed* a work going on for the glory of God, and His Church, through the unceasing and self-denying labours of its good Rector, who appears to have won his way into the hearts of all, little children and grown up people alike, *i.e.* to say, if appearances and testimonies may be taken for anything. Well, on this first Sunday morning, after a sweet and peaceful Communion, on our way home the Father wished to look into the Roman Cathedral which we were obliged to pass, and *what* a sight we beheld. The Mass was just finishing, but the building was packed right out through the very doors, with a silent and reverent congregation of all ages, some kneeling and the back ones standing. And this takes place at *all* times, whereas, in many places, *our* Church and her "Liturgy" are neglected and scantily attended.

Arrived home, (our house was opposite the Cathedral in the parallel street), and breakfast over, as the Father had no Mission Service until the afternoon, Brother David and I prepared to attend the High Mass at " The Ascension."* When we arrived there, the Children's Sung Mass was just finishing. Very soon the Curate came out into the Church and asked me into the vestry. Here, were the choir and clergy in various stages of vesting. On being invited to serve as Sub-deacon, their own having failed them, I remonstrated as to what the Bishop might say on the matter, when I was informed he had *already* notified his clergy, that they were at liberty to invite the Father, to preach in their pulpits, or to take part in their services. Quite a treat it was, once more to enjoy a High Mass with all its accompanying solemn Ritual, though a tonsured

* The new High Altar in the permanent church was given by Mrs. G. H. Wheeler, in memory of Mr. Gilderoy Lord, of Watertown, New York, and is of pure white statuary marble. It is eleven feet in length. The five panels in the front will contain mosaics of great beauty, the work of Salviati at Venice, and in imitation of the mosaics of the High Altar in the celebrated Church of St. Mary, in the Capitol at Cologne. The panels on the face and at the ends of the altar are relieved by columns of Mexican onyx with exquisitely carved capitals of white marble. The Tabernacle is very handsome, and is surmounted by a lofty octagonal spire of Gothic design, of which it forms the base. The Tabernacle, Canopy, and Throne are the most striking features of the altar, and embody in their device and construction the best that artistic skill and workmanship can do.—"*Illustrated Church Bells,*" by Rev. Cory-Thomas, Grand Crossing, Illinois, U.S.A.

Monk serving as a Sub-deacon in full vestments, must have carried the thoughts of many a one back to the Middle Ages.

In the afternoon, the first service of the Mission was held in Kimball Hall, Wabash Avenue. On arriving there a little before four, *what* a sight met the eye. People were already coming away, for the hall and platform, as well as the aisles, were packed as close as they could hold, like herrings in a barrel. Numbers outside were struggling to get in, and the heat was *intense*. Such a sight! On a bright June Sunday afternoon in world-serving Chicago, and all to hear a *Monk* preach! The subject of the sermon was, " The Object of the Mission."

In the evening, at eight, the hall was just as crowded. The Father then preached on "What think ye of Christ ? " and, before leaving the hall that night, the pulpits of seven Methodist Churches were offered him. As one man went down the stairs, apparently quite bewildered, and scratching his head, he was heard to remark, " Well, I never ! I *thought* he was going to preach the Pope's toe, Eternal Damnation, and Hell fire."

Though so far from the shores of Albion, and in a strange city, old friends and former hearers of the fearless monk, now began to make themselves known, and to welcome him to their magnificent city. In the morning, at " The Ascension," we found two gentlemen, who had known and heard the Father in the old days of the riots at St. Edmund's, Lombard

Street, whilst in the afternoon, a gentleman called who had been choir boy in the Father's time, under Father Lowder, at St. George's Mission, Wellclose Square, London. It was soon *very* apparent, that during the Welsh Monk's Revivalistic Mission in Chicago, he would have *no lack* of hearers.

Throughout the week, he preached daily at noon in the heart of the city, at " The First Methodist Church," which had been hired for that purpose, and which seated about 1,200. The subjects were " Jesus Christ and the Man of Business," " Jesus Christ and the Man of Wealth," " Jesus Christ and the Man who was a leper," " Jesus Christ and the Religious Man," " The Rich Man in Hell and *how* he got there." The admission was free, only the front four rows of seats being reserved, for those who *preferred* paying—*not* to hear the Gospel, but for their own comfort and convenience.

Since the days of the riots at St. Edmund's-the-King, Lombard Street, when the monk, in his early days, addressed the bankers and merchants of the City of London, I do not suppose he has ever had such a vast multitude of men of all classes and denominations among his hearers, as this week, day after day, gathered in their dinner hour, in the Methodist Church. "Packed like herrings in a barrel," only faintly describes what the congregations were. Canons, High Church, Low Church, Episcopalian Clergy, Methodist and Baptist Ministers, Bible

Christians, and Presbyterians swelled the daily increasing crowds, that poured into the church, to hear the Welsh Monk. Every seat occupied, the aisles and galleries full, and crowds standing at the back and in the doorways. *Such* was the scene enacted for a week, at the busiest hour of the day, in the church at the Junction of Clark and Washington Streets. The results of the Mission proved, that not only did the people of Chicago gather thus, to hear the Father, but the Spirit of God was indeed present at the services, and that rich showers of blessing descended upon the hearers.

The following few quotations, from daily papers of the city are interesting.

"Business men and clerks, type-writists and shop girls, crowded the auditorium, eager to hear the far-famed monk evangelist, who is travelling about the world."

"Nearly *every* church in the city has been offered to Father Ignatius."

Though Chicago may be spoken of as "the modern Sodom," its inhabitants appeared *eager* to listen to "the old, old story" of the Gospel, and to drink in its Divine truths with avidity. On the Monday of the first noon meeting, the Methodist Ministers, who were holding *their* meeting in the same building, "adjourned, that those present, might attend the noon services of Father Ignatius." Next morning, the President of the

Baptist Ministers' meeting called on the Welsh Monk, to invite him to preach in his chapel. He said, that the Father had numbers of the *best* ministers in the city the previous day at his services. He also stated, that he had announced the Father's mission, in his own chapel, the previous Sabbath. A *Methodist* Minister, after one of the services, said to an attendant of ours, " I *never* want to hear any better Gospel than this."

So far, no letter had been received from the Bishop, but at last it came, having been sent by mistake to Cornwall. Everyone was anxious and eager to learn what line Dr. W. E. McLaren would take, as so many Bishops of the States had opposed the Father, who was now just fresh from his crusade in New York against " Infidelity and Worldliness WITHIN the Episcopal Church." As we have seen, the majority had been against him, *because* of it. It was now unfashionable to stand up for Jesus Christ, and the doctrines of His Divinity and Resurrection, when they were denied by some of the leading clergy of the day. *Public opinion* had taken the place of Jesus Christ. To be singular, and hold old-fashioned truths, had grown unpopular. Yet, Chicago received the British Monk, (who for months had posed as " Champion for the Faith " in America), with open arms. Her noble Christian Bishop *asked* for no " credentials " or recommendations, but "*in the Name of Jesus Christ,*" for the greater glory of God, and the salvation of

s

souls, opened the churches of his diocese to the monastic Evangelist, and wished him *God speed* in his work. The Dean of Cleveland, Ohio, Dr. Y. P. Morgan, which is almost the next diocese, had lately designated the Father as "an irresponsible tramp;" but here, was the Bishop of *the greatest city in the world*, thankful that God had sent him thither, by the grace of the Holy Spirit, to awaken souls, asleep in the lethargy of sin and unbelief. It was even *reported*, that his Lordship stated, HE should have liked the whole Mission to have been held in "the Cathedral." At any rate, the Father *was* asked to conclude the Mission there, which he was unable to do, though he preached there twice to crowded congregations, the first time being on a Sunday morning, and the second on the fourth Wednesday evening in June.

To return to the Mission week itself, and its evening services. Among the first of the Episcopal churches, to be offered the Father was S. Clement's*, though the pulpits of Calvary and S. Mark's were subsequently placed at his disposal. As each successive service seemed to draw a gradually increasing congregation, the Welsh Monk, whose stay in the City was limited, was only able to accept the pulpits of the largest churches and chapels.

On the Tuesday evening he preached on "Jesus and the Sinner of Magdala" at Grace Methodist

---

* The Rev. Canon J. H. Knowles, Rector.

Episcopal Church, La Salle Avenue, to a vast congregation; and on the Friday night, after Solemn Vespers, at "The Ascension," on "The Glorious Church and her Ritual." Being *the* High Church of the town, many were curious to see, in what light the Father regarded their Catholic ceremonies; in fact, one Methodist minister, who lived the other side the city, stated he should be there to see " if the Father will preach the SAME Gospel." And sure enough there he was in the front seats, and many other members of various denominations, who, in all probability, had never smelt so much incense or seen such a display of ritualistic ceremonies *before* in their lives. One poor soul, sitting next a friend of ours, as the procession passed through the chancel gates, with a deep sigh, caught hold of our friend's arm, and exclaimed: "He's *broken* my heart, for he's " (the Rev. Father) "bowed to the altar "! A Methodist, brought to Christ at the Mission, as a result of this service, was baptized, and joined the Church. Throughout the week, daily, at the noon service, a Methodist minister kindly assisted in the taking of tickets and showing people to their seats; whilst another gentleman, to save the Father's strength, gave his services as organist, "for the love of Jesus," and the work the Holy Spirit was *accomplishing* in the place.

Amongst the congregations, were men who had known the Father, whilst boys, at Claydon, Surrey,

England, and also a man who had heard the monk in his early days, when he addressed the Freethinkers in Bradlaugh's Hall of Science, Old Street, City Road, London. This gentleman subsequently wrote as follows:—

.... "I write to inform you that the addresses I have heard you deliver this past week have been very helpful to me, and have benefited me much spiritually, but the crowning appeal was, when I heard you at 'the Central Music Hall' last Sunday evening, the 14th inst., on 'Jesus and the Great Calm.' I went to my room that night with new and better desires, and with more resolutions of purpose and power, than I had experienced for some time. That night, before retiring to rest, I knelt down, contrary to my custom of late, and asked God to help me become the *possessor* of THAT PEACE which 'Jesus' gives, and I can tell you that I now have a measure of peace, strength, and lightheartedness, which has been foreign to me for some time.

"It is my desire that Jesus' life should be manifested in *my* life, and to that end I desire to have constantly in mind the life of Jesus (the life He led). Up to last week I had not seen you for over 20 years. About that time back, or a little more, I was employed then in one of the mercantile houses in Mincing Lane, London, England, and I noticed on some placards the following: 'To-night, at the "Hall of Science," Old Street Road, the Reverend Father

Ignatius will debate with Charles Bradlaugh.' Subject: 'Jesus Christ.' I was somewhat acquainted with Bradlaugh then, and became more so later. I knew that he was a formidable opponent to meet in debate, possessing as he did great command, of himself, (apparently no fear), of withering sarcasm, cutting ridicule, and of venomous and malignant invective. I attended *that* meeting, and that was the only time I have seen you up to the time I saw and heard you in this City last week. I remember *that night* years back—how the Hall was packed, with probably four-fifths of the audience opposed to you in thought—how you *baffled* and *outreasoned* the infidel, and made favourable impressions on many there who were sceptical. I was sadly troubled that way myself, and am, if anything, worse *now* at times; yet, on account of my religious ancestry and training, I suppose I have even now a sufficiently religious tendency in my composition to join heartily in that hymn you closed with last Sunday evening:

'To Him all majesty ascribe,
And crown Him Lord of all.'

... You have been the means, in God's hands, of having caught me again in the Gospel net." ...

Many, indeed, were the letters and cases of blessing during the Mission. A young Jew, who was saved at a noon meeting, came forward after the service, with tears in his eyes, saying: "I *want* to be a Christian." One of the most touching scenes of all was the beautiful salvation and reunion of a husband and wife after one of the evening services. They came forward at the close of the service, to tell the Father how the Lord had come to them, and as the Welsh Monk put his hands on them, to bless them, they fell on one another's shoulders sobbing for joy, whilst the people sang—

"Praise God from Whom all blessings flow."

The night before the Welsh Evangelist left the City, a man walked five miles, after his hard day's work, "to get one more *look* at the Father;" and a young man, who was *now* rejoicing in the newly-found, *unsearchable* riches of Christ, came to tell the Father, that, though he could ill afford it, he felt he *must* go off at once to his family in Pennsylvania, and bring them to a knowledge of that joy and peace he had himself found. But these were only a few cases.

In the midst of the first Mission week, the Father's throat became affected by the Lake air, and, losing the use of his voice, he was obliged to see a doctor, who ordered rest and cessation from preaching. Consequently, though Mr. Moody's large Baptist Church was now offered him, and the date of the Episcopal Cathedral sermons unfixed, the Father was obliged to rest for a week, at the end of which time he again preached daily at noon to the City men, for one more week; and in the evenings—Tuesday, at Moody's Church; Wednesday, the Cathedral; Thursday, Welsh

Presbyterian Church; and Friday, Ada St. M.E. Church, all of which were crowded with attentive audiences.

" *The Chicago Evening Journal* " of June 13th contained the following interesting paragraph :—" Father Ignatius makes, on the whole, a pleasing impression, disappointing agreeably, rather than disagreeably, his hearers. We have heard so much of him that, while we go to hear him with a keen edge of curiosity, we go also, like that Greek voter of old, to cast a ballot against him—well, just because we hear so much about him. But now that we have sat in his audience, and seen him, and heard him, we think him, after all, a pretty clever fellow, a very good Catholic, a surprisingly good Anglican, orthodox enough to be a Presbyterian, scriptural enough to be a Congregationalist, and earnest enough to be a first-class Methodist. He reminds one not a little of the preacher at the City Temple, London. People get the idea, from his criticism of certain prominent divines, that he is a belligerent, and nothing else—a regular fighter.

" But, to tell the truth, his speech and spirit, in closer hearing, impresses you quite differently. He is tender as a lamb toward truth and truth-seekers, though bold as a lion towards error and ITS teachers. He preaches a very practical, every-day gospel, a religion that he wishes to see carried down into the marts of trade. A good deal has been said about his diatribes on money; but, after all, he has a good word to say to the rich man who wishes to live a Christian life. He tells of some who have 'come out' and consecrated their energies and powers, including that of wealth, to the service of the Nazarene, and of the joy that has come into their lives. If religion is worth *anything*, it is worth *living by*. It is not a thing to die by merely, but to live by, so as to make the world better. And this is eminently orthodox."

One who found Jesus at this Mission, has since written: "I cannot help feeling so lonely, for I realize what I have lost, and how much I shall miss the good teacher and kind friend, who has helped me more than I can now know, and more than I can ever express. I do not mean that I have *lost* him, only that for a time I must do without the pleasure of learning from him; but thank God, through his teachings and example, and by the grace of our dear Jesus, and the love of our Holy Father, who is INDEED a comforter, I know that we are *all one* in that Blessed Trinity; that there is really no parting, that means entire separation, and that nothing good is ever lost. I have all the sweet memories of those precious services, and life can *never* be the same again, for with 'Jesus only' as my watchword, I shall live so near to my Saviour that looking at everything by His Spirit, nothing can be common. By His life lived in this world for us, He has for ever glorified and ennobled *our* every-day life, and if we will only let Him, He will lift our lives to such a plane, that to work *for* Him, and *with* Him, will be our *only* wish and JOY UNSPEAKABLE."

On the Father's last Sunday in Chicago, he preached in the afternoon, at "The Kimball Hall," on "Chicago and the World's Fair," and in the evening, at the large "Central Music Hall," on "Magnificent America, Her Past, Present, and Future." At this service, the platform was occupied by a large volunteer choir, organised by a gentleman of the congregation, who had paid for the printing in leaflet form, of two of the Llanthony hymns, with music. After the service, as the monk sat at the door, to say "Good-bye" as the people left, the scene was most touching, some almost breaking down as they came to take their last look at him, who, by the power of the Holy Spirit, had brought them to a *personal* knowledge of Jesus. In the morning the Rev. Father had preached at the High Mass at "The Church of the Ascension," on "The Real Presence," at which, as I had done each Sunday whilst in Chicago, I was privileged to serve as subdeacon. Of the two daily Masses at this church, the half-past six is always better attended than the later one.

During his mission in this great city that is to have "The World's Fair," the Father received a pressing invitation to visit and hold a few services at Racine and Beaver Dam. He was also asked by the Catholic Priest of All Saints', Ravenswood, to occupy the pulpit of his church one Sunday. Even the Swedish Church offered *their* pulpit to the Welsh Monk, and on his attending an Orthodox Synagogue of the Jews one Sabbath, he was received with the greatest kindness, and subsequently invited to address them the following Sabbath in *the very Synagogue itself* on " The Restoration of the Jews to Palestine "; but this was not to be.

The Father's stay in Chicago was limited, and fast drawing to a close; but on his last Monday in the city, the British Monk addressed the Chebrah Chobbe Zion, in Rochester Hall, on " The Restoration of the Jews to their own·land," for which handbills were printed and distributed, in Hebrew as well as English. This was the Father's last address in the city, and many were the hopes expressed, that he would return for another mission during "The World's Fair," in 1893.

Whilst in the city, strange but refreshing it was to see in " The Cathedral Sisterhood " a photograph of our own High Altar (in its early state) which had been given them by the late Bishop De Koven. The set of monastery photographs we had with us, were subsequently sent, there and to the choir of " The Ascension " for exhibition, and greatly admired and enjoyed.

One day at the noon meetings, a poor man who had

not missed a single service, and had derived great blessing, on seeing an Episcopalian Priest cross himself at the Benediction, made the following amusing remark to your humble servant, pointing to the priest : " Beant he a Roman Cartholick ? " and when I asked " why ? " he replied, " Because I seed him a blessing of himself."

The poverty, misery, and vice of some of the back slums of Chicago, which the Father visited, to see for himself how much of what he had been told was true, was appalling,* and far surpassing anything he had ever witnessed, whilst working round Ratcliffe Highway, in London. One gentleman, who gave altogether by gifts at various times, some 200dols. towards the expenses of the Mission, came several times from the country to the services, and to see the Father to try to get saved, as he was in unutterable misery, believing himself predestined to be damned. The last time he came with a carriage, and took the Father a drive along the shore, and through the beautiful Lincoln Park, where the menagerie is, where the brilliant flower beds and statue of the Indians were much admired.

Whilst in Chicago, the first " Children's Day " in the city was celebrated, all the children being taken in procession to the various parks, supplied with

---

* Vide "*Chicago's Dark Places*," published at *The Craig Press*, Chicago, which indeed makes Chicago out a *modern* "Sodom."

amusements, refreshments, and treats of every kind.

On looking into a Unitarian Church, on Dearborn Avenue, we were not a little surprised to find a font, and a communion table prepared for communion. To see the cross towering towards the sky on the gables of Methodist and Congregational Churches was a common sight.

Chicago certainly holds the palm, for elegance and beauty amongst cities of the present day. Her streets, planted with avenues of shady trees, and beautifully kept grass plots between the road and the pavement, the different style of the architecture of every house being scarcely found elsewhere; her magnificent squares, parks and boulevards make her, though as yet but in her babyhood, the greatest city of to-day. Of an evening after the work of the day is done, the people may be seen in knots, sitting on their doorsteps, many of which are spread with various coloured carpets and rugs, adding greatly to the picturesqueness of the scene. Everywhere in this magnificent city, and from everyone, true American kindness and hospitality was experienced, and our visit to Chicago was one NEVER to be forgotten.

CHAPTER XIX.

LAST SERMONS—FAREWELL TO NEW YORK—
HOMEWARD BOUND.

AFTER the Chicago Mission, though arrangements had been made to sail from Montreal to England on July 15, our Lord had other work for the Father to do, and we once more found ourselves *en route* for New York, breaking the journey at Niagara for a day. It was through repeated requests and wishes from friends in that city, and in reply to a telegram, praying that the Father would preach his *last* sermon in America, in the same church where he had preached his *first*, that it was finally and definitely decided to return to New York for a week, before going to Montreal, from whence to sail for home.

When we arrived there, we found our old rooms ready for us, and that arrangements had been made for the Father to preach his farewell sermons in the States, at S. Edward's Church at Mass on the Sunday morning, and at S. John the Evangelist's in the evening. The members of "The Bond" had also hired the Y.M.C.A. Hall in East 23rd Street, and advertised the Father to give a final address on Tuesday, on

"Magnificent America: Her Past, Present, and Future."

It was "the Glorious Fourth," when we reached the city, and from morning to night, the streets echoed and re-echoed with countless Chinese crackers and fireworks of every kind. All the shops were closed, and the streets were gay with the flag of liberty, whilst the people kept high holiday. At night the scene was very pretty, as from the flat roof of our abode, we watched the fireworks and illuminations—the rockets and coloured fires turning the night, as it were, into day. Our kind landlady told us, people had been continually calling, to know if it were really true that the Welsh Monk, to whom they owed so much, was returning to New York to bid farewell to his friends, before recrossing "the Atlantic Ferry."

On the first Sunday morning, I enjoyed a quiet early communion at S. Ann's Church, whilst the Rev. Father attended a later celebration at "the Church of the Ascension." At ten o'clock, the Rector having sent a carriage, we started for S. Edward's, where the Father preached at the Mass on "The Lord is my Shepherd," whilst in the evening, his subject at S. John's was, "To wait for His Son from Heaven." Driving to and from S. Edward's, through "The Central Park," it was very sad, to see the crowds of pleasure-seekers breaking the Sabbath, when they should have been in the Lord's House on His *Own* day. Though, at this time of the year, everyone almost was out of town on account of the heat, and numbers of the churches closed, *ostensibly* for repairs, yet very fair congregations greeted the Father, both morning and evening, and crowds lingered after the services to try and shake hands, and exchange a word with him.

One of the great events of these few days in New York, was the reunion, after many years, of a husband, wife, and children.

On the Father's entering the Hall on the Tuesday evening, it was somewhat disappointing to see that the audience was so small, but comforting to recognise so many *old friends* and faces present. The subject was " Magnificent America," and Lieutenant C. A. L. Totten, Military Professor of Yale University, occupied a seat on the platform. His works, on the Anglo-Israelitish Theory, entitled " Our Race " * had created such a spreading interest and sensation throughout

---

* " The Romance of History ; Lost Israel Found in the Anglo-Saxons." " The Voice of History ; Joshua's Long Day and the Dial of Ahaz." " The Philosophy of History ; Tea, Tephi, Jeremiah's Ward." " The Secret of History ; The King's Daughters—Flight of David's Line." " The Renewal of History ; Eochaidh the Heremonn—The 'Scarlet Thread.'" " The Fact of History ; The Deluge and the Advent—Proof and Guarantee." " The Hope of History ; The Crisis, and the Millennium—At Hand ! " " The Riddle of History ; Paul and Daniel Interpreted." Price, 75 cents. each. Published by " Our Race Publishing Company,' New Haven, Conn., U.S.A.

America, that when he came all the way from New Haven, Connecticut, in the morning to see the Father, he was prevailed upon to stay. Throughout the Father's address, he was repeatedly interrupted by bursts of loud and continued applause.

Taking for his texts Isaiah xlix. 8, " In an acceptable time have I heard Thee, and in a day of salvation have I helped Thee; and I will preserve Thee and give Thee for a covenant of the people to establish (raise up) the earth, to cause to inherit the desolate heritages," and Deut. xxxii. 8, " When the Most High divided to the nations their inheritance, when He separated the Sons of Adam, He set the bounds of the people according to the number of the children of Israel "—the Father proceeded: "I have been asked to speak to you, to-night, on 'America, Her Past, Present, and Future.' *Now*, throughout our land many are interested, and eagerly enquiring into the Anglo-Israelitish Theory, recently so ably set forward in Professor Totten's works on 'Our Race.' You know the interest with which many now study this subject. God Almighty made the two promises taken for our text, to the children of Israel of old. Then and for many thousand years, America was wrapt in the mysterious silence of God's Sabbath of Rest. Her very existence was unknown to man. Guarded by the mighty Atlantic and Pacific Oceans, kept as God's secret *until* the *appointed* time, she was indeed a desolate heritage. While empires rose to the utmost climax of magnificence in the far East, and then passed away, *where* was the mighty continent of America? Wrapt in the magnificent Sabbath hush of obscurity, for a people the *Lord* would provide. For thousands of years, her marvellous mountains, her primeval forests and spanless prairies, her birds of gorgeous plumage, and wild beasts were scarcely disturbed, and *then* only by the whoop of the Aborigine, who must originally have come over the Behring Strait from Asia, ' the home of humanity!' Though this great continent almost touched the rest of the then known world, it did so at its most desolate point; hence the silence, and hush of mystery in which it rested for ages. It was a desolate heritage *indeed* for hundreds of years, as were also the vast continents of Australia and India. Now the Sabbath hush is ended, and God has given them to the people for whom He kept them, and they are, one and all, peopled by the Anglo-Saxon race, or in the hands of the English Kingdom. France in the North, in Canada and in Louisiana, Spain in Florida, touched and tried to colonize America. Though they all *tried*, they failed; for the land was *not* for them, but was kept for a Race of such prolific power, that America should, as she does to-day, double her population in such a short time.

"At last the appointed time was come (for we Christians do *not* believe in chance or accident), and in the early part of the seventeenth century the Anglo-Saxon race began to touch and colonize the coasts of Virginia; then New England, and in the next century, Canada. Look at America of to-day! She is made up of every nationality, and daily receiving her quota of citizens from all portions of the globe. Yet the moment they reach her shores they *lose* their nationality, and, being immersed in American citizenship, become speakers of the English tongue. They all *cease* to be what they *were*, in the common brotherhood of Anglo-Americans. When Archbishop Ireland, the other day, was petitioned to appoint foreign-speaking Bishops for his various congregations, he refused. America is Anglicising the world wherever her children go, in fulfilment of the prophecy: 'When the Most High divided to the people their inheritance, He set the bounds according to the number of the children of Israel.' America of the present day is a *startling, magnificent, ethnological wonder*. Is there anything like, or approaching, the Anglo-Saxon race in its uniqueness and numerity? She dominates the world, and in all quarters of the globe she owns possessions. Look at America, and her fast increasing Anglo-Saxon population! Behold Chicago! —a perfect *miracle*, though but in her *babyhood*, for 60 years ago she did *not* exist. What is she now? A miracle of greatness and magnificence—the greatest city of the day! *What* city *ever* grew like the cosmopolitan Chicago?

"Chicago is, indeed, the most wonderful city in the world, for its cleanliness, its people, its boulevards, and magnificent parks, are unapproachable on the Continent or elsewhere. One is used to hearing so much about the wickedness of Chicago; but now that I have seen her, taking her on the whole, I do not think she is *any* 'wickeder' than other large cities of her size; and she is but in her *childhood*. I do not see that she is any worse than others, and when she has had as much time as New York to settle down, very likely she will be *better*. I think New York should stand up for Chicago, instead of running her down.

"I am grieved to hear that political votes can be bought, and that the system of bribery is extensively carried on. Americans, *can* this be true? Are you thus dimming the glittering stars on 'the star spangled banner' of your magnificent country? Is it not excruciating and painful, to hear it is done. No one can shine, as a bright star in the banner of America, unless he reflects the light of America's Sun—Jesus Christ, and *true* liberty in its pristine purity. Listen to your Pilgrim forefathers, in days now long gone by. Were they to come to life again, what would *they* say? Would they not point you to Jesus, 'America's Sun,' and show you Zion? By finding Him as your Saviour, you may shine as bright stars and stripes in America's banner *for ever !*

"Look at America's future. What is it? Mexico

will soon be annexed as a State; then Central America, and before long South America also. There are no States at the present day, able to compare with the United States of magnificent America. The great vision of her future seems entirely English, and that England and America shall bring true light and liberty, satisfaction, rest, and peace to the *whole* world.

"Thoughtful people must be startled by what meets them in America's rapid growth, doubling its population every 23½ years! As we behold and contemplate the greatness and vastness of magnificent America, no need have we to blush, when we remember that the Americans' great grandfathers *first* came from British shores. Now in these latter days, in *our very midst*, the prophecies in the Old Testament respecting Israel, the chosen children of God (which for so long, on account of their nonfulfilment, have been spiritualized only), are being fulfilled *ad literam*. Let us contemplate them, slowly and thoughtfully. To-day, revolution socially, politically, and religiously, in all parts of the world, is restlessly disturbing the human race.

"Yet, that such should be the case, is foretold in the Word of God, and it is but a key-note of the liberty of 'the Golden Age,' ere long to dawn upon us all. God's scheme for man, is now being evolved before our very eyes. For centuries, as these promises to Israel have been apparently unfulfilled,

Christians have put them on one side, as only capable
of a spiritual interpretation. Thus they have played
into the hands of the Infidels. It is, indeed, most
interesting for us, poor units in this magnificent race,
to consider 'the Golden Age' which is coming, that
golden age when war shall be no more, and the
Prince of Peace shall reign in righteousness 'before
the Ancients gloriously;' when Jerusalem, 'the City
of our God,' long trodden down by the Gentiles, shall
be restored once more to her pristine glory, and sin
and sorrow shall flee away. When we, as Christians,
consider that these promises of God to man are fast
being fulfilled, does it not, indeed, behove us to lift
up our heads, and listen attentively for the signs of His
coming?

"But before this era of joy and peace for which we
look, we are told there shall be a terrible catastrophe,
great distress of nations, a waning of the Faith,
men's hearts failing them for fear. It approaches
with giant strides. Behold! all the nations of Europe
preparing for a tremendous strife, concentrating all
their thoughts and skill on the manufacture of the
most elaborately destructive instruments of war, to
massacre thousands of their kinsmen and neighbours.
The whole of Europe is waiting and watching, in
eager expectation, for what is coming next. Every
religion in the world at the present time is looking,
expecting, and awaiting the *speedy advent* of this
'Coming Man.' He is our great and loving Elder

Brother, Who, when He came before, came to raise us from the pit of sin and corruption to the 'glorious liberty of the Sons of God.' It is He Who, as He stood on the steps of Pilate's Judgment Hall of old, crowned with the crown of thorns, exclaimed : ' Behold *the* Man !' This is *the* Man Whom most of the civilized world accept as *the Pattern*, *Perfect Man* without the *possibility* of a peer. To-day the work of the Gospel is still going forward to take out a people for God, and when the last is gathered in, *this* Man, our long-expected Jesus, will come once more. Consider the promises made of old to Israel, God's chosen race, ' They are to be a nation and company of nations.' Behold America! made up of every nation of the globe, yet already being fast Anglicised, every nation being welded into one. The process is fast going forward. Look at the eight million Africans who find a home on your shores, they all speak English. Though every nationality is represented here, English is the tongue they use. Even the Chinese themselves are now intermingling with other races, and fast settling down and becoming Anglicised. Japan, too, is just beginning to send her children to your shores. Oh, America! such a rush of business, whilst thou art yet but an infant, renders you unable to realize the marvellous process in the strange silence of success.

"Look at 'the promises of God' to His chosen people regarding wealth. They are to be a wealthy nation, lending to others, but never borrowing. Look at the silver of Asia pouring into America's treasury. Out of the world's public debt at the present day of 36 millions, only six attaches to the Saxon race, and that, too, is in *native* hands! 'Their dominion in the sea,' mistress of the sea, 'possessing the gates of her enemies,' are not these signs of the Israelites of God, being fulfilled by the Anglo-Saxon race? 'Britannia rules the waves,' and were the ships of her navy placed but one day apart, they *would* belt the world! Look at Gibraltar, Malta, Cyprus, the Cape of Good Hope, Singapore, Egypt, all in the hands of the English, and are not *they*, indeed, the gates of their enemies? America, *once* in subjection to England, when old enough, naturally wished to walk alone. Soon Australia will wish to follow her example; yet her doing so whilst thoroughly Anglicised fulfils, as it were, the prophecy that 'Israel should be a nation and a *company of nations*.'

" The Anglo-Saxon shall dominate the world, for the world is now all discovered, with the exception, perhaps, of some unimportant islands. They are, indeed, 'a people of merchants'—yes, and settled by great waters. Consider quietly for a few moments the position of America and the Anglo-Saxon in the world, and see if the prophecies made by God of old to Israel are not being fulfilled before your very eyes. We are all *one* family *here*, for your ancestors were mine, and when I come across my American cousins I do not feel at all like a foreigner (as the papers call me); for they are flesh of my flesh, and bone of my bone. Let all Americans realize, if for the first time, how *one* they and the British *really* are.

"When I first reached your hospitable shores, I was remarkably struck with the different impressions I formed to what I had expected, and when I get home I hope to open my countrymen's eyes to the wrong light in which many regard 'magnificent America' and her citizens. What I have seen in the past year has proved to me how unfair it is, to judge a people or a country by what one reads of them. We English expected to find America an irreligious country, like our neighbour France. But what do I see? The Sabbath of God kept as in the old country. Thousands of temples to Jesus Christ, and people trooping off in crowds on Sunday to hear the Word of God. The very atmosphere of America, 'the Land of Liberty,' makes one feel free to stand up for what is *right;* so when I heard of a man, and a *clergyman*, DISHONESTLY taking your money—as the New York Rector of All Souls, Dr. Heber Newton—for undermining the grand old 'Faith, once delivered to the saints,' I felt free to attack him, and call him to account.

"As to my own reception in America, I don't think there is a Christian sect that has not held out to me 'the hand of fellowship'; and I have, indeed, had a practical illustration of 'By this shall all men know that ye are my disciples, if ye *love* one another.'"

Our stay in "the Land of Liberty," under the Star-Spangled Banner of America, was fast drawing to a close. A hall had been hired in Montreal for the next Sunday's service, as we were to sail by "The Lake Superior" the following Wednesday. We had hoped by these means, to be able to see and admire some of the beauties of the River S. Lawrence, but now all our plans were suddenly altered. A friend had obtained first-class berths, at a very reduced price, on the Guion Line steamer "Arizona," sailing on the Saturday, which, though curtailing our stay on the hospitable shores of America, enabled the New York citizens to possess us longer. So the Father decided to go by this route, and a Boston cousin of his took Sister Annie's place, as she preferred sailing from Montreal, on account of the scenery, and on the chance of seeing some more glorious icebergs, unapproachable in their beauty as they glisten in the sun. So Thursday and Friday were given up to packing, and a *packing*, indeed, it was, as all who have ever experienced the packing of one's boxes to return home after a year in a foreign country can imagine. The curiosities, books, etc., that had accumulated since the 21st June, 1890, when we first set foot on the shores of America! You should have *seen* them! I was quite sorry to leave "the land of the Stars and Stripes," so fond had I grown of her people, and all

I found and saw there. In the midst of this interesting work of packing, people were continually calling to say " Good-bye," and to bring thank offerings. Many a sad leave-taking had to be gone through, with those we should probably never again see, till we meet them in our Father's home on the Eternal Shore.

On the Thursday, when the farewell meeting of "the Bond" was held, the following letter was received :—

" DEAR FATHER,—It is with great sadness that I pen these lines, knowing that you are soon to leave my beloved country, perhaps never to return.

"Your going away from this city is like the *going out* of a *great light*; for although we have many brilliant and eloquent preachers, we have no Ignatius —you stand alone. I never knew a minister fit to place beside you, *especially* among any of our eminent divines of New York City.

"Your almost unique character would naturally isolate you in the midst of a generation of *hypocritical, impure,* and *heretical* preachers. They know only too well that you are the *true* messenger of Jesus Christ—that you are as much inspired as ever Paul was. That is *why* they fear you. If you were a lesser personage, *without* the courage of your convictions, they would receive you with *open arms*; but because you possess the fine discriminating knowledge which enables you to distinguish between the true and the false, they cry you down. Your pure celibate life is a source of rebuke to them. Your blessed Master was hated because he told the truth to the Jews.

"There are men who gain the applause of the multitude, who ought to be loathed, despised, and discarded. Social ambition, wealth, and intellect are exalted above simple truth and purity; ministers who would be popular in this age must dilute the truth to suit the craving of the pulpit appetite. One day the crowns will be taken from those unworthy heads.

" To say that I have been benefited by your blessed work only faintly expresses what you have done for me *personally*. Your words have proved my very *life*. I had never really known Jesus until I was brought under the influence of your preaching. No one before had ever been able to convince me of the truth of those vital questions, thereby bringing comfort and ease of mind to me in my unhappy state. The lives of *most* preachers are so *contrary* to their *teaching* that I could only wonder and doubt; for you know, as the Greek writer said : ' When one learns to think, one is miserable.'

"Bishop Potter confirmed me six years ago, and I have never taken communion in all these years. I consulted our pastor—who is now dead—and he said, 'Read certain books and pray—that is all that is required.' Of a class of forty, I was the only one who walked out at communion, which was administered four days after confirmation. I could *not* take it, feeling as I did; and I am glad I refused it then. There was no change of heart, no *conviction of sin* and indwelling of the Holy Ghost. Pray! It was like telling a starving man to read a bill of fare and be filled.

"The moment I saw and heard you speak from your heart, I felt satisfied and comforted. I knew then why I had been starving all these years. Your blessed words were like a light from heaven; something within me revealed to me your true character. I knew you were His true disciple; Jesus spoke to me through you. I was electrified by the force of some of your sayings, radiant with truth. My confidence was yours from the moment you offered up your first prayer in my presence.

"If some of the New York *clergy* had *known* Jesus Christ, they would have known *you*—' His sheep hear His voice.'

"I shall always regret that I did not push my way through the crowd, and thank you for the beautiful way in which you spoke of my native place—Chicago.

"When you left New York I telegraphed my family to be sure to hear you. If you could only hear the beautiful things that are said of you, instead of all the 'falsehoods in the newspapers'! To have been privileged to hear your wonderful sermons, and take part in your prayers, is the happiness of my life; and although I have never met personally any of your devout followers, of which there are many I hear, it has not been through a lack of desire on my part. I should think a little society could be formed of those persons who have derived so much benefit from your teaching, to meet together and carry out your work, and learn more of your faith, the blessed Catholic Apostolic Religion. In the future, that is the church I have chosen. I have always been censured for leaning toward the church. I intend to study several of your works to help me.

"And although we lose you in person, you will be with us in spirit. We shall never forget you. So when you sail from these shores on Saturday, you will carry away the undying devotion and admiration of many earnest and prayerful Christians; who will ever remember you, as a man full of gladness, of love personified, always sacrificing self for others, an exotic transplanted from an angelic nursery.

"The remembrance of what you *are*, and *have done*, will make us strong to battle for the Blessed Faith. There are hundreds of your followers who love and respect you, and appreciate what you have done in this city. There are some people that we meet with, but once in a lifetime; contact with them is like a benediction; they flash across our pathway and are gone, before we realize what we have lost, but the spirits remain. We can commune with our great thoughts, stars to lead us, were we but equal to following them.

"It is a struggle to let such a one depart from us, when we felt so secure under his blessed teaching. But the work will live on.

"God bless you for what you have done for this wicked city. That you may have a safe voyage to your beautiful and quiet retreat in Wales, and think and pray often for your faithful ones on this side, as well as for those ungrateful souls who never knew you, is the earnest prayer of your faithful follower.

"I shall never cease to pray for your safety on the great deep till you arrive at your haven beyond. Good-bye, and God be with you."

One dear old blind lady from Orange, New Jersey, who had listened with blessing to her soul, to the words of peace, joy, life, comfort, and rest that fell from the Father's lips, sent her husband, all the way to New York, to give the Welsh Monk a small book as a thankoffering. Partings are *always* sad, but there is a day in store for us, when we shall *meet* to part *no* more.

It was seven o'clock on S. Benedict's Day, July 11th, that we went on board "The Arizona." The morning was clear and bright, the air sharp and crisp.

In spite of the earliness of the hour, some hundreds

who owe their eternal salvation to the Father's visit to America, had gathered on the dock to see us off. "The Bond" presented the Father, just before sailing, with a magnificent basket of fruit, while a husband and wife now reunited *in* the Lord, gave him some diamond jewelry as a thankoffering. Episcopalians, Presbyterians, Salvation Army soldiers, and members of all denominations, were gathered there in sorrow, and in sadness, to bid farewell to the Welsh Monk. Tears were unrestrainable and many were the cries of "*Come back! Come back!*" It was not till eight o'clock that the anchor was weighed, so that for the last hour, the Father moved about amongst his spiritual children, *comforting* them in their sorrow, and strengthening them in their Faith.

After an absence, of a little over a year in the New World, where he was the instrument in God's Hands of bringing many into the new life, and the peace of God which passeth understanding, the Father was now returning to his cloister home, amongst "The Black Mountains" of Wales. Many an American cousin thanks God, that the Father ever visited their shores, as through his missions, husbands and wives, who for years have never spoken, are now reunited, sinners of the deepest dye are rejoicing with their sins forgiven, atheists and sceptics have bowed down their human wisdom and scientific knowledge before the simple message of the Gospel, and highly religious professing Christians, having been led to find they were *not* Christians *at all*, have come as little children home to the feet of Jesus.

As the steamer left the wharf, some hundred or more, who had gathered to bid farewell to their spiritual father, broke out into "Praise God from Whom all blessings flow," in a *shout* of praise and thanksgiving, its sounds being wafted away down the river to us, as we stood waving farewell on the steamer's deck, the Father proving *himself* especially patriotic, by waving a small "Star Spangled Banner" just given him, till we were out of sight and hearing. The faithful and enthusiastic hardworked Rector of S. Edwards, who had been the *first to welcome* the Father to the American shores, was the *last* to bid him farewell, with a hearty kiss and a hug, just as the passengers' friends were put off the steamer. How *greatly* HE felt the parting, was apparent to all around.

As we slowly steamed out into the ocean, we had time to look round, and survey our fellow-sailors. Many a passenger of the ill-fated "Servia," including the Dean of Georgia* and his party, were on board, once more *en route* for the shores of old England. An Episcopalian Rector, two Roman Catholic Priests, a Methodist, and Presbyterian Minister, made up the religious part of the passengers. The day was beautiful as we got out towards Nantucket Island and Martha's Vineyard, the sea smooth as a mill

---

* Dr. A. S. Barrett.

pond, the wavelets looking like dancers sparkling in the sunlight, while behind us Bartholdi's magnificent statue of "Liberty enlightening the World," was the last fair glance we had of *beautiful America*. Very soon after we were afloat, a most cordial and kind letter of good wishes was handed me from a Chicago Rector, who wished me to receive it *just* as we were sailing, and so directed it to the ship.

It was not very long, when we once went on deck, before we all got acquainted—(such a charming, thoughtful, friendly set of passengers)—for they were true Americans, who wave the stiff introduction ceremony deemed necessary in England, and before many days were over, the whole set of passengers seemed like *one* great, happy family. No one stood on ceremony, but each seemed thoughtful for the other's comfort. After the first day the number of those on deck basking in the sunlight, and enjoying the saline breezes, *gradually diminished*, for several began to suffer from the unpleasant but inevitable pangs of sea sickness.

The Episcopalian priest on board, who was a Brooklyn Rector, was *the one* who stood up for the Father in January, when inhibited by Bishop Littlejohn, of Long Island, and whose daughter had constantly attended the Father's services, and derived great blessing therefrom. This priest, a very strict churchman, did not quite agree with the Father's views of conversion, (except in infancy) being necessary

U

before baptism. He was a great upholder of sacraments, and held that a *baptised* person was safe. The very first day on deck, he endeavoured to enter into an argument with the Welsh Monk. I only mention this now, as before the voyage was over, the Holy Spirit spoke to him, when at the point of death.

As we neared "The Banks of Newfoundland" the customary fogs became dreadful—so bad, in fact, that for two days and three nights the captain was unable to leave "The Bridge," but had to have his meals taken there to him. All day Sunday, the foghorn was going regularly every two minutes, and though service was held in the morning, Captain Brooks would *not allow* a second one in evening!

In the morning the Brooklyn Episcopalian Rector, Mr. Tighe, took the service at ten o'clock, in the first-class saloon, and asked the Father to preach, which he did for fifteen minutes on, "They did all eat and were filled." The purser was obliged to limit the time of the sermon, as the stewards wanted to come in, to lay the tables for dinner. The saloon was full, and numbers in the doorways, *all* the ship's passengers being allowed to attend *this* service. We were very surprised to find it had been arranged to sing, "Abide with Me, fast falls the *event*ide," at the commencement of this MORNING service, but at the Welsh Monk's request, "Praise God from Whom all blessings flow," was substituted for it. After the service, on going on deck, everyone was most profuse and enthusiastic in their congratulations, thanks, and expressed desires of another sermon, which the Father consented to preach in the evening, if the captain's permission was obtained. A message was consequently sent to him on " The Bridge " to know when he would receive a deputation of ladies, which he regretfully stated his inability to do, until the fog had cleared away.

Whilst on deck, I obtained a splendid view of a shark, quite close to the ship. Sailors, who are of all men the *most* superstitious, consider a shark following a ship to be the *sure* sign of a death. Before our voyage was o'er, we saw shoals of porpoises and dolphins playing in the sunshine, and several large whales throwing up magnificent fountain-like jets of water. On Monday, a gloom was cast over the ship by the sudden death, from heart disease, of a second class passenger, who had come out solely and entirely to nurse a friend, who was also ill, and unexpected to live. The funeral was taken by the Roman Catholic priest, though, at the request of the invalid that was left, the Father subsequently visited and comforted her. Oh! the awful solemnity of a funeral at sea, when the body of the dead, covered with the Union Jack, is committed to the deep, till the vast oceans at the Resurrection Day (when our Lord comes to claim His Own) shall give up their dead.

I must not forget to tell you the pleasant surprise

the Father had soon after embarking, to find one of his own cousins was the ship's doctor; and also a gentleman on board, with whom he often used to play as a little boy, and whose mother was a very great friend of his mother's, and another who had been a chorister at S. Martin's Church when the Father preached at Canterbury, as also a chorister of that time at the Cathedral.

Most delightful it used to be on deck in the early mornings, and through the day when it was sunny. When the Father first set foot on the ship's decks at New York, it was said he would prove a second St. Paul on board, and so it came to pass, for besides preaching twice, our Lord allowed him to do a great work for His glory amongst the passengers, both by talking to them on deck, and visiting the sick in their cabins. A few days before reaching Ireland we had a second death, and funeral on board, a birth and a wedding, besides which a woman lost her senses from the effects of the voyage, and had to be confined in a strong room with guards. Altogether the voyage was most eventful and anxious.

On the Monday, not having been able to hear the Father preach the previous day a second time, the wife of the Dean of Georgia started a petition to the captain (which all of the first-class passengers signed), asking for a special service and sermon on Wednesday evening. Such a thing, as a service on board on a week-day, had never been heard of before, but the captain granted it, and stated he should himself attend, and was glad to get a chance to hear the Father, as he was unable to be present on the Sunday, though on that day he generally took the service himself. So the service was held, and well attended and appreciated by the passengers—a playwright and a well-known actress being amongst the first to thank the Father.

On the Friday night a concert was got up for "The Liverpool Sailors' Home." Programmes were sold at 1s. each, and a fair sum netted for that admirable institution. The whole thing proved a great success. The Father, who had been asked to sing, was now worn out with his work among the passengers, and consequently unable to do so. But I must return to the Monday; we were then off Sable Island, on the coast of Nova Scotia. This island, on the shores of which a cargo of ponies was once wrecked, is now noted for its small ponies, similar to the Shetland, which are highly prized and in great demand for children.

Those who have had any experience at all on the mighty ocean, know full well the scene on deck at noon, when the sea is calm and the sun bright—they know full well the rows of chairs, the crowded state of the deck, the eager seeking for the most sheltered sunny corner. This time our decks were overcrowded with chairs of all descriptions, owing to "The Arizona" having so many extra passengers from the ill-fated

"Servia" on board, amongst whom was a little girl of ten, who, with her Kodak, had photographed Prince George of Greece, and now wanted to "Kodak" the Father. Knowing the Father's love for children, this little girl was frequently sent by the passengers, to ask him to play and sing something, when he generally chose :—

" I hear the voice of Jesus speaking,
    'Tis speaking now to me ;
  Oh, *come*, poor sinner, come and *trust* Me !
    Have I not died for *Thee ?* "

Or, "O, King of Beauty," both being "Llanthony Monastery Hymns" composed by the Welsh Monk himself.

The Welsh element was fairly well represented on board, for besides ourselves, the purser, first mate, and another were Welsh. The captain himself knew Llandrindod Wells well, and there was a Welsh lady amongst the second class passengers. On a clear, moonlight night at sea—to stand on the deck and watch the moonlight kissing the waves with silver, carries one's thoughts (involuntarily perhaps) above to the Almighty, and makes one wonder how any human being in his senses can behold such a sight and *doubt* the existence of a God.

Before reaching our journey's end (for the Father had decided to disembark at Queenstown) the Brooklyn Rector was one evening suddenly struck down with heart disease, and, thinking he was dying, at once sent for the Father. For hours the Welsh Monk sat with him, telling him the glad message of "the Love of Jesus," and was glad to find him better and recovering when he left him for the night. Next day, by the mercy of God, he was once more on deck, basking in the summer sunshine. Just as we were getting in sight of land again, on the south of Ireland, everyone was on deck in a state of excitement, eager for the first glimpse of *terra firma*. When it was indeed sighted, coloured fires and limelights were lit in various parts of the ship. That night few went to bed, as many of the passengers were to leave the ship, and the happy, homely party to *break* up in the early morning hours.

CHAPTER XX.

IRELAND.

QUEENSTOWN—CORK—DUBLIN—TARA.

IT was a little after three o'clock on Sunday morning, July 19, as the day was just breaking over the hills in the Eastern sky, that the Rev. Father and his party landed on Irish soil at Queenstown, after an absence of little over a year across the Atlantic in the New World, where he had been the instrument in God's hands of bringing many into the New Life and "the Peace of God which passeth all understanding."

On leaving the Guion Line Steamship "Arizona," at Roches' Point that Sunday morning, and embarking on the Tender that had come out to the steamer to take the Queenstown passengers into the harbour, cheers were raised in the quiet early morning hour, by the departing passengers, for the "Arizona" and her captain. Many who had been blessed by the Father's ministrations on board, and who were going on to Liverpool (some of whom had sat up all night), had risen to say farewell, and to wave their handkerchiefs as the Tender left the side of the ship.

On entering the harbour, the view of the town, built on the side of a hill, is very pretty and picturesque—the

Catholic "Cathedral of S. Colman," with a statue of "Our Lady Star of the Sea," being conspicuous in the centre of the city. The entrance to the harbour is guarded by two forts built on rocky hills, whilst in front of the town is Spike Island. Queenstown Harbour is not only the finest in Great Britain, but one of the best in Europe. It could shelter the whole of the British Navy, and the largest ships may at all times of the tide lie a short distance from the shore. The town is built on an island, which is five miles from east to west, and two from north to south. The city, with its streets rising one above another, like the parallel courses of some great amphitheatre, looks out upon the islands and the sea, upon ports and lighthouses, and upon great ships at anchor or under sail; while yachts, pleasure boats, and fishing craft pass swiftly to and fro.

It is a question, says one, whether even Killarney, with all its lakes, mountains, woods, and waterfalls, presents brighter scenes or loftier images than those we witness here.

On landing at Queenstown, the ordeal of the Custom House had to be gone through, at a time when, having been up all night, one was longing to get to rest. Troublesome though the ordeal of unpacking the baggage for examination is to *most* passengers, the chief officer in attendance immediately passed all the Father's things without so much as wishing them unlocked, or asking any questions. The Monastic habit commanded his respect and proved a pass, as well as an object of great respect and veneration, from all with whom we came in contact, wherever one went in the "Emerald Isle." The Custom House passed, the next thing was to find rooms, but at that hour in the morning, the steamer being unexpected, everyone at the hotels was slumbering in bed, though the Father and Brother David soon managed to rouse someone at "The Queen's Hotel,' facing the harbour, and before very long he was able to breakfast and rest. Most conspicuous round the Custom House, early though the morning hour, was the number of Paddys, and their persistency in wanting to carry all you had, no matter how small, in hope of a gratuity.

Here, in the neighbourhood of the far-famed Blarney Castle and Lake, where the Blarney Stone of Ireland lies, the brogue of the peasants and the Irish style of their dress was *most* pronounced, whilst "jaunting cars" appeared to be in great demand; though it was not until we visited the Ancient Halls of Tara, that the Father first rode on one, when it proved far more comfortable than it looked.

On going down to breakfast on Sunday morning, the first thing noticeable in the Hotel coffee-room was a very old banner with a fine embroidered figure of St. Patrick, Apostle and Patron Saint of Ireland. At 12 o'clock noon, Mass at the Cathedral was attended, and a vigorous sermon for the abolition of wakes, on account of the drinking bouts attending them, was listened to. This Cathedral, which is but a new one and in the *process* of building, promises to be a grand one, if we may judge by the portion already erected. The statues on the pinnacles of "Our Lady Star of the Sea," with a star of electric light behind her head, the figure of Our Lord, and also one of S. Helen, were very handsome.

In walking through the streets to and fro from the Cathedral, blessings, hats off, and curtsies from the passers-by were of frequent occurrence.

After service, we walked back through some of the narrow courts below the Cathedral, to see *how* the poor live. The hovels or cottages were wretched, while outside was a litter of straw, old rags lying about, a donkey and some fowls, but though Paddy is generally supposed to have a pig, none was visible. The majority of the children of the poor about Queenstown were barefooted and barelegged, whilst the girls were also either bareheaded or with an old shawl thrown over their heads and wrapped round their shoulders. The women also wore extremely short dresses. It is *generally* said that Irish children are pretty. They may be, for those who like a flushed high colour, but though a really ugly one is an exception, they are *generally* not more than bright and pleasant looking. On the Sunday evening the Father attended the evening service at S. John's (the Irish Church), which was both an ugly modern edifice outside, and bare inside. The whole appearance of the church and its service pronounced it to be " Protestant." Next morning, having attended the early mass at the Cathedral, and taken several photographs, we left for Cork in the middle of a terrific downpour of rain, which turned the streets into "rivers of water." Floating calmly down one of them, as we drove to the station, we saw an old Irish fruit woman's basket, while *she* was sitting by her stall, trying to shelter herself under an old umbrella.

On Sunday the crowded state of the Cathedral, as well as that of the street outside, at the early Masses was most edifying.

En route for Cork, several old ruined castles, &c., were seen, some nestling amongst the trees, while others crowned here and there a hilltop, and the country round was dotted with many a straw-thatched home of an Irish peasant, whitewashed, and glistening in the sun. Some of these were poor and wretched indeed, proclaiming poverty and misery to all beholders, whilst others might compare with English country cottage homes. We arrived at Cork, in a little over an hour after leaving Queenstown. The Father wanting to get on to Dublin the same evening, a covered car was secured at once, in which to visit the two Cathedrals of the City, and her chief churches. Alas! before very long (the shaft of the car being broken, and the driver *knowing* it when taking us) we found ourselves gradually falling out backwards into the muddy street, so refuge had to be taken in the Church of S. Patrick, whilst Brother David went to find a fresh conveyance. This having duly arrived, we soon started for S. Fion Bar's Cathedral*, hoping to find his shrine and relics there, but were doomed to disappointment, for instead of even finding the *old* Cathedral, as we expected, we learnt it had been pulled down recently, and a new one erected in its stead, which indeed was most fine, stately, and massive for a *modern* building. High on the East End Pinnacle, was a golden angel with a trumpet, whilst the figures of the Saints round the doorways at the West End were very grand.

The Roman Catholic Church of "S. Peter and S. Paul" was next visited and greatly admired, the carving of the angels throughout the church, holding the lights, as well as the carving of the confessionals, with its fine high altar, procuring for it the place of honour as the handsomest Roman Church seen in Ireland, though *also* quite modern. From here we went to the Franciscan Priory Church, erected as a memorial to Father Mathew, the great temperance champion, whose statue stands in the centre of S. Patrick Street, just after crossing S. Patrick's Bridge, and at whose grave, by his intercession, miraculous cures are stated to have been effected. Here were most beautiful pictures, of the Rapture of S. Francis, S. Francis receiving the Stigmata, and

---

*Commonly known as S. Finbar's Cathedral.

several others, besides an altar to S. Anthony of Padua.

The Father being tired, and it being too late to get on to Dublin, a room for the night was secured at "The Imperial Hotel" (round which a sentry was kept on guard, and several police, as the Judge Barry was at that time staying there, whilst holding the Court at Cork. He was escorted to and from the Court and the hotel by a guard of troops and mounted police, so you see, whilst in Cork, *we* were WELL guarded.)

Whilst here, curious it was to meet some American friends, who had been passengers on the "Arizona" with us, and blessed by the Father's preaching. So pleased were they to see him, that they said, *had* they been in their own country, "Magnificent America," they would have given him plenty of money; but as the letter of credit they had brought was so small, their thank-offering was smaller than they would have liked.

Next day the journey was resumed to Dublin; passing on our way several Irish Round Church Towers, and many a fine old ruin. These old towers (Sir John Forbes says) have existed 1,000 years, and *may be* twice or thrice as old. Passing Dundrum, the fine range of the Galtee Mountains, including some of the loftiest in the South of Ireland, comes in view, towering away to the skies in the distance, in front of which stands the long hill known as Slieve-na-Muck, which is more than 1,200 feet high.

Next is the station of "Goold's Cross and Cashel," formerly the residence of the kings of Munster, close to which are the most remarkable combinations of ruins in Ireland, and numerous as are the ecclesiastical remains in the sister isle, they sink into insignificance when compared with those of "royal and saintly" Cashel. Here, in the midst of "the Golden Vale," stands a huge mass of limestone rock, isolated, precipitous, and covered with a beautiful pile of sacred edifices; while all around stretches the richly cultivated but treeless country—a scene that has attracted the veneration and wonder of ages of the past, and will continue to kindle like emotions for ages to come.

The ruins which crown the entire summit of the hill, though roofless, windowless, and shattered, still retain their original proportions, and though the courts are lone, and the aisles are voiceless of Cathedral Chapel and Palace, "the rock-throned battlements and towers" defy the further attacks of "Decay's effacing fingers."

The most ancient of the ruins are the Chapel and Round Tower, the former of which is built of hewn stone. The doorway, adorned with zigzag and bead ornaments, is Saxon, the ceiling of stone, groined with square ribs springing from stunted Saxon pillars, with enriched capitals. The Cathedral, built in the Pointed style, is of later date, and about 200 feet long. All these buildings are of limestone with the

Round Tower, 90 feet high, which stood here for ages, before "the Rock of Cashel" was made the abode of S. Mary's monks, or the fortress of the kings of Munster.

Leaving Cashel far behind, we speed on in our journey towards Templemore, and soon see in the near distance the Devil's Bit Mountains, which have an evil reputation, in consequence of a gap, in the summit of the highest of the range, concerning which the legend of the country is, that the devil, being out amusing himself with his imps, and in a hungry mood, bit a mouthful out of the ridge ; but finding it unpalatable and not easy of mastication, he dropped it on the plain, where it now forms the celebrated "Rock of Cashel."

The next object of interest, comes between Maryborough and Portarlington, where the interesting and picturesque Rock of Dun-a-mase is visible—a solitary and perpendicular mass of limestone, accessible only on *one* side, and rising from the plain to a considerable altitude, crowned by the ruins of a castle, once the stronghold of the O'Mores, and the *locale* of many turbulent and bloody deeds during " the Wars of the Pale." From Portarlington, once more the train steams on to Kildare, where many antiquarian associations gather round its Round Tower, which is 110 feet high, and also round its Abbey Church, *now* being restored.

Hard by, was a stone cell known as "The Fire

House," where the sacred fire—" the bright lamp that shone in Kildare's holy fane"—lighted by S. Bridget, the foundress, is said to have continued to burn, from the fifth century to the thirteenth. Last, but not least, we reach the pretty little village of Clondalkin, four miles out of Dublin, with its Round Tower, 86 feet high, surmounted by a conical top, which can be ascended by a series of ladders.

Sir John Forbes, speaking of these towers, says, " No one, who sees their beautiful lofty and slender shafts shooting up into the sky, and dominating in solitary grandeur the surrounding landscape—all strikingly resembling one another, and resembling *nothing* else—but must be struck with admiration and curiosity of the liveliest kind." Their origin and object remain a secret, though they add considerably to their mysterious interest, hidden away deep in the recesses of the past.

Arrived in Dublin at six o'clock, the first thing to do was to find a roof, under which to rest for the night. Russell's Temperance Hotel in S. Stephen's Green was selected, and glad, indeed, were the people there (who were scared at us at first, thinking us to be Roman Catholics) when they discovered we belonged to the British Church. Across the Green from our hotel, was the palace of His Grace the Archbishop of Dublin.

After resting and refreshing the weary travellers, at 8.15 the Father started out on a pilgrimage to the
v

three cathedrals and chief churches. Having hired a nice old Catholic Irish coachman, who could hardly speak for excitement, and scarcely cared whether you paid him or not, we soon—passing *en route* Trinity College and the General Post Office—found ourselves at the Roman Catholic Cathedral in Marlboro' Street, which was open, though the two Irish *Protestant* Cathedrals of Christ Church and S. Patrick's we subsequently found closed. The Protestant's were closed, but in the dim religious light and solemn hush of the *Roman* Cathedral, in the Real Presence of Jesus in the Blessed Sacrament, "*verily and indeed*" enshrined in the Tabernacle on the altar, were numbers of people at their private devotions, many, doubtless, after a hard day's work; while, in one part of the Cathedral were a Sodality, reciting aloud their Compline office.

From here we drove to the Dominican Church, which, though late on a week-day evening, was *packed to the doors*, with people listening to a vigorous and earnest sermon by a Friar of the Order. Here (seeing the Father in his monastic habit), as elsewhere, everyone made room for him, doubtless believing him to be a Roman Catholic.

It is interesting here to note that a Roman *Priest*, who *knew* the Father to be but an English Deacon, directly he heard the Father was in Dublin, came to see him, and before leaving knelt and asked his blessing. A Roman *Priest* kneeling and seeking the blessing of an Anglican *Deacon!!!* Yet so it was, his reverence for the Monastic life being so great.

From S. Dominic's we drove to Christ Church Cathedral, a fine Early English and partly Norman edifice, which was admired outside, though the inside was invisible, being shut at that hour. In this Cathedral are the tombs of Strongbow and his wife, the vaults dating back to the very days of S. Patrick himself. *This* was the Abbey Church *without* the walls, while S. Patrick's was the Cathedral *within*—the two Cathedrals being in the same position to each other as Westminster Abbey and S. Paul's are in London.

On driving on to S. Patrick's fine Cathedral, with its lofty tower and spire, we were more fortunate, for though it was shut for the night, on calling at the sexton's house, he at once came and conducted us round by the light of a single taper. As we made our pilgrimage 'neath the groined roofs and betwixt the stately pillars of the aisles, and the choir hung with old banners of the Knights of S. Patrick, it was solemn indeed. Though our light came but from *one* small taper, yet *everything* seemed visible. Among the ancient relics from the old Cathedral, were the ball that killed S. Ruth, a very old image of S. Patrick, some of the old tile flooring and arches still *in situ*. On the south side of the chancel is the Holy Well of S. Patrick, from which, seeking his most powerful intercession, we enjoyed a drink of water. Half-way up the nave, on the south side, was Dean Swift's old pulpit of wood; whilst just outside the chancel gates is a new finely-carved stone one.

Behind the high altar is the Lady Chapel, in which there was also an altar. Talking to the sexton as to how they managed with the two cathedrals in Dublin, he told us that the Bishop's Throne in S. Patrick's was really the seat of the Archbishop of Armagh, Primate of *All* Ireland, but that, when the Archbishop of Dublin visited and officiated there, *he* did so *under the Dean*, though he was recognised as Bishop in his own right at Christ Church. Fancy a Bishop and a Primate of Ireland under his Dean!!! In the Lady Chapel was a chair, made of the wood from the roof of the old Cathedral founded by S. Patrick himself, A.D. 450. Driving to this Cathedral, misery and want seemed rife on *all* sides in the back streets. At S. Patrick's and Christ Church Cathedrals, we were pleased to learn, that daily choral services were held both morning and afternoon. The altars might, indeed, be improved, and the solemnity of the choir increased, by the introduction of a cross, candlesticks and flowers, as with only frontals, they produce a *very* bare appearance.

After a night's rest, the Father decided to visit *the ONCE stately Halls of Tara*, the ancient seat of the first Houses of Parliament in Ireland, and the palace of the Irish kings three thousand years or more ago. *Now*, alas! they are no more. The glory of Tara is departed, and Ireland's chiefs and leaders, who met there to transact the business of the country, have passed away. The name of Tara, so dear to the hearts of the Irish people, will live on *for ever*, and the *day* may come when *thousands of Christians throughout the world* will have reason to *bless* the ruined Halls of Tara, for the preservation of relics, a thousand years and more lost sight of. Dear to the poet Moore, were her *once* stately halls, to which he dedicates a poem, from which the following familiar lines are taken:—

> " The Harp that once in Tara's Halls
> The Soul of Music shed,
> Now hangs as mute on Tara's walls
> As if that soul were fled.
>
> So sleeps that pride of former days,
> So glory's thrill is o'er;
> And hearts that once beat high for praise
> Now feel that pulse no more."

Having left Dublin soon after midday, in a little over an hour we found ourselves at the small country station of Kilmessan, the nearest starting point for Tara. Though a car had been previously telegraphed for to meet the train, there was none there, and we had to wait whilst one was being procured. The sky was darkening overhead, and rain began to fall, but soon it cleared away—and a good thing for us it did, as there was no train back to Dublin till four o'clock, and it would not have been pleasant, had we been obliged to wait till then, on a little country platform. From the stationmaster, whilst waiting, some interesting information about Tara was obtained. Amongst other things, he told us that numbers of people were *continually* coming to visit the sacred spot of Tara, where *many* believe the Ark of the Covenant, the Urim and Thummim, and the Roll of Baruch, are buried, *they* having been brought over from Egypt by the Prophet Jeremiah, in the time of Zedekiah, when his daughter, Tea Tephi, (known as and spoken of in legendary lore by Armegen, chief Bard to King Dermon, Monarch of Ireland in the sixth century, and the celebrated Bard Cu—an o'Cochlain, 1024, and others, as well as the Irish peasants of the present day, as "the fair-haired beauty,") married an Irish king in the Halls of Tara. Besides which, the stationmaster stated that some time ago, £17,000 was collected by subscriptions to excavate the ancient and historical mounds, but that the treasurer *ran off* with the money.

Though these assertions may seem strange to many, we *know* from the Bible, that the tribes of Israel were *lost* in *Media*, and from history we learn that *from* Media the Irish first came. The Coronation Stone of Scone was carried, as we all know, from the Halls of Tara (Eochaidh and Tephi) to Dunstaffnage, from thence to Scone, and finally to England, where it now is in Westminster Abbey. There are many who state, and believe *this* to be "the King's Pillar," the stone on which Jacob slept at Bethel, that was brought over to Ireland by Jeremiah in the days of Zedekiah. It is a curious coincidence, that no one has ever attempted to state, *where* Jeremiah died and was buried, but that after he went to Egypt, he is lost sight of entirely.*

After a drive of three miles on an Irish jaunting car, through picturesque green lanes, decked in the summer garb of beauty, roses, and honeysuckles, filling the air with their fragrance; delicate ferns, foxgloves, and purple harebells peeping their heads through the leaves on the mossy banks, we soon find ourselves approaching the Hill of Tara, once the Capital of all Ireland, where the King held his Courts. On the way up, nestling among the trees, many a peasant's cottage, straw thatched and whitewashed, added to the general picturesqueness of the scene.

Arrived at Tara, and the jaunting car discarded for the time being, a start was made, with a very old Irishwoman, bent double with age, for guide, to inspect *those* mounds and remains, of which we had heard so much, and which are now creating *such* an interest and excitement all over America, owing to some recent books on "Our Race," written by Professor Totten, of Yale University.*

---

*Since writing the above, I have been told that Jeremiah's grave has been shown from time *immemorial*, in the Isle of Davenish, Lough Erne, Ireland.

†Especially the volumes entitled "Tea Tephi," "The King's Daughters; or, the Flight of David's Line," and "Eochaidh,

Whilst the Father inspected the mounds and trenches, which were far more numerous and considerable than we expected, Brother David went to call on the owner of the property. First the site of the old Banqueting Hall, now overgrown with grass, was visited. It was originally five hundred feet long, by forty wide, though now its width is little more than twenty. Tradition states that three hundred goblets of gold were used therein.

Next in interest, came the mound where the King's golden chair used to stand; then our steps were wended to the Coronation Mound and the Royal Mound, surrounded by trenches, on the top of which is a stone pillar—of a stone quite foreign to the country. This, some years ago, was dug up, and the natives declare it to be the *true* "Lia Phial," and state that the stone we have in Westminster Abbey, is *not* the right one. It is asserted in Scripture, that the House of David should *never* want a representative to sit on the throne. If the Tara Legends *are* correct, they would *prove* our Queen Victoria to be the descendant of David's Royal Line. Whilst on the Royal Mound, on "the Lia Phial," and also on the Coronation Mound, the Rev. Father wrote a letter to Professor Totten, whilst doing which he was photographed. *Very* superstitious are the Irish peasants, for our old guide did not want the Father to write on "the Lia

---

the Heremon," price 75 cents each, obtainable from "Our Race" Publishing Company, New Haven, Conn. U.S.A.

Phial," declaring *no good* EVER came to people who *touched* those things. As an example, she declared that a Mrs. Preston, who some time previously owned the land, had had one mound removed, *but died within a fortnight.* We learnt that a gold brooch and a massive gold belt, some time ago, with other things, were discovered there, and are now in the Museum at Trinity College, Dublin.

Far away in the distance, some three miles off, on the top of a hill, was the old Shrine of S. Columbkille; also the hill where S. Patrick lived, and from whence, once when he had lit the Holy Fire, before the King did at Tara, where custom commanded it to be first lit, he was summoned to appear before his Majesty.

Tara Church is a new building, built almost on the site of the old Church of S. Patrick. A piece, though very small, of the old church walls is *still* standing. It belongs to the Irish Church, and our old Irish peasant guide informed us that the rector had three churches, in each of which he held an afternoon service *once* a month, though there were but *ten Protestants* in the *whole* neighbourhood. On the previous Sunday afternoon, we learnt that the ruined grass-grown Halls of Tara had been visited by a thousand members of the Archæological Society of Dublin.

A wholesome country lunch having been partaken of by us at the village inn, a start was made for the station in order to catch the four o'clock train back to Dublin. As the Father came out to mount his car, the peasants knelt round the door in knots and rows for him to bless them, and solemn, indeed, was the picture in that rustic Irish village on the mountain side. One old dame brought him a present of the true shamrock, to take home to Wales.

On the way back to the station, the little Catholic Parish Church of Kilmessan peeping through the trees, with its churchyard cross, like those of the Franciscans, with the spear and reed, was noticed. At the station the Father and his group of pilgrims, who had visited the sacred mounds of Tara, were photographed *on* the jaunting car.

Having caught the train, in an hour we found ourselves in Dublin, where, after a rest and some refreshment, we drove out to Kingstown (the town was gay with its regatta fireworks), to be ready for the mail packet for Holyhead *next* morning, when we crossed to Wales. Glad, indeed, were we all to land at last on British soil once more, but with hearts *full* of loving memories of America.

CHAPTER XXI.

Return to Wales.

Bala—Llangollen—Abergavenny.

AFTER a short and uneventful passage across the Irish Channel, the Father once again landed on the shores of Cambria. Returning from a year's journeyings in a foreign land (although it *was* "Magnificent America"), welcome indeed was the cloud-kissed crest, towering up into the heavens, of the queenly "Y Wyddfa."

Once more "the language of music" sounded in our ears, once more the memories of Cymry's Saints, Druids, and Bards were reawakened in our hearts, by the name of many a village hamlet, many a fertile vale, nestling among her hills.

Landing at Holyhead, guards, porters, &c., all began to welcome the Father home, and to be of what assistance they could to him. From now, it was very pleasant to see the way in which the Father was greeted. The true Cymro throughout the land loves the Father, as do the Welsh in America, for they *know* his love for, and interest in Wales, and *everything Welsh*. All our luggage having been transferred from the steamer to the train, the journey was resumed, passing *en route* the Tubular Menai Bridge, Bangor, S. Asaph, Rhyddlan, Corwen, and many other historical sites, still living in the legends and traditions of the Cymric peasants.

A few words about some of these places may be of interest here, culled from a Welsh guide book.

St. Asaph or Llanelwy, as it used to be called until the beginning of the 12th century, is built on a hill in the picturesque Vale of Clwyd, overlooking the marble church of Bodelwyddan. The tower of the cathedral is square, and it is the smallest of the Welsh Cathedrals, besides being the only one *not* built in a *hollow*. Its first founder is universally admitted to have been Cyndeyrn (Kentigern), the exiled (A.D. 560) Bishop of the North Britons, inhabiting Strath Clyde. His ablest disciple, Asa or Asaph, succeeded him, and the monastery was converted into a cathedral by Maelgwyn, King of Gwynedd.* Before reaching S. Asaph, we came to Rhyddlan (with its ancient castle), where the waters of the Clwyd and the Elwy unite. Then Denbigh, with the ruins of the old castle crowning the summit of the hill, upon the steeps of which the town is built, was passed.

In Rhyddlan Castle Richard II. was once imprisoned in 1399, but this great fortress was eventually dismantled in the period of Cromwell. Here also, of later years, the saintly John Elias, the promoter of Welsh Calvinistic Methodism (when the *Church*

---
* North Wales.

throughout the country lay *dead in worldliness* and *formalism*) preached a campaign against, and put a stop to, the Welsh and Border custom of hiring harvestmen on a Sunday afternoon, when they might bɔ found in the streets, reaping-hook in hand. John Elias, Rowlands of Llangeithio, Charles of Bala, Howell Harris of Trevecca, and Williams of Pantycelyn!! *Great Apostles* by the Grace of God, in the *latter* days, to the Cymry—*your* names will live FOR EVER in the hearts of the children of Wales, in grateful thankfulness, for the work ye did, for Jesus and Eternity. The Church of Wales was dead, and *but* for *you*, must have *remained* so. The Welsh Church *owes* a debt to the promoters of Welsh Calvinistic Methodism, she can *never* sufficiently repay. "Between the town of Rhyddlan and the sea, is Morfa Rhyddlan, where the armies of Offa and Caradog once met in battle, and the Saxons defeated the Cymry."*

Having changed trains at Denbigh, we steamed away through a lovely valley until we reached Corwen, *i.e.*, "The White Choir," which is situated at the eastern extremity of Merionethshire. The old church here with its square tower (and Wales indeed is rich in ancient churches and ruined abbeys and castles) is dedicated to SS. Mael and Sulien.† In the outside of

---

* "*Gossiping Guide to Wales.*"

† Two brothers from Armorica in the 11th century. S. Sulien was Archbishop of Menevia, *i.e.*, S. David, and S. Mael, who, when the Sons of Cunedda had delivered Wales from the

one of the church walls is cut a rude cross, now forming the lintel of "the priest's door," "which of course is the true mark of Owain Glyndwr's dagger"—spiritualised, I suppose. Standing in the churchyard is a rude column called "Carreg y Big yn y Fach Rewlyd."* S. Sulien's Holy Well, on the N.W. side of the River Dee, near Rhug Capel, was *once* even *more* sacred than the Dee itself. In olden times water was fetched therefrom to fill the Corwen Baptismal Font. Corwen was a great centre for Prince Owain Gwynedd, who ruled in 1165, and on the mountain N.E. of the town is Caer Drewyn, an encampment of his during the invasion of Henry II. Caer Drewyn is considered by antiquaries to be very ancient work, probably of the Bronze Age. In 1845 the pretty little town of Corwen, nestling as it does on the hillside, beneath the shadow of the rugged cliffs, was nearly destroyed by a great flood. With the mountain cliffs at the back of the town, at her feet lies a panoramic view of the *far-famed* valley of Llangollen, with the sacred Dee winding its serpentine way through the green meadows, glistening like silver flashes in the bright noonday sun.

Corwen passed, we resumed our journey to Bala,

dominion of the Irish, received Dinmael in the eastern part of Merionetteshire as his portion.

* Curious visitors may *here* trace, in fancy or reality, the Eisteddfod emblem, *the three beams of light* on the southern walls of the Church.—"*Gossiping Guide to Wales*," published by Messrs. Woodall, Oswestry.

that little town situated on the banks of Lake Tegid, now famed throughout the land, as the home of Thomas Charles,* the Welsh Evangelistic Priest, whom a *Saxon* Bishop DROVE out of his Mother Church. When we arrived at the station, the station master was there to meet and welcome the Father. The guard and the porters all expressed their pleasure at seeing him again. It was some time before we could leave the platform, and before doing so a leading member of the Calvinistic Methodists invited the Father to preach in their large Memorial Chapel to Charles, next Sabbath. This chapel will seat a thousand persons. The Father, having explained that *Church* rule would *not* allow him to accept the invitation in *Great Britain*, stated, that if he was asked by the new rector of Bala, to preach in the Parish Church, he would be *glad* to do so and redeem his promise made last time he was here. The promise came to be made in this manner. The old rector, directly he heard the Father was at "Plas Goch,"† called on him and invited him to preach; but the Father only having one day to spare, and being obliged to hurry on for his mission in Glasgow, promised to come back. Numbers were anxious to hear the Welsh Monk, and day after day callers at the Plas Goch, to know if the Father was going to

---

* Those interested in this great Patriarch of the Welsh Church should read " *The Life and letters of Charles of Bala,*" by *Rev. Wm. Hughes, Vicar of Llannwchllyn.*

† Red House.

preach, were numerous. It was the same this time, but Friday and Saturday passed, and the rector *never* called, nor *even* wrote to invite him to preach ; and it was not until two o'clock on the Sunday afternoon, that, at the *instigation* and *prompting* of an influential layman, the vicar called, and invited the Father to preach in the evening. But I am rather anticipating, and so must go back to our arrival at Bala, which place the Father was visiting, on a pilgrimage to the tomb of blessed Charles of Bala, and to obtain a little rest and refreshment, before returning to the Abbey.*

A few notes on the town, its situation and picturesqueness, will not, I am sure, be without interest here. On entering the town from the new station, the first things that catch the eye are the " Tomen-y-Bala,"† the Mwnwgl-y-Llyn Bridge over the waters of the " Sacred Dee," and the large Methodist College standing on the slope of the hill behind the Welsh Church. The Tomen-y-Bala is a round mound of earth covered with grass and trees (*near* the Village Green), supposed to have been raised by the ancient Druids of the Cymry. From the summit of this mound a fine view is obtainable. The Welsh Calvinistic Methodist Chapel, erected in

---

* Llanthony Abbey is situated in the Vale of the Honddhu, between the Towns of Hay and Abergavenny, being 14 miles from the latter. Llanfihangel Crucorney, 10 miles off, is the nearest railway station.

† " The heap of Bala."

memory of Charles, is the finest modern building in the town. In front of the chapel is a large white stone statue of Thomas Charles himself,* which our Queen specially visited, as well as his grave in Llan-y-cil Churchyard, when in 1889 she came to Bala. In memory of that eventful sojourn here, three shops in the little town are now able to put up the Royal Arms, the great descendant of Owen Tudor having purchased her meat, groceries, and Welsh flannel there. The cook at the Plas Goch Hotel had also, we learnt, cooked for Her Majesty while here; we felt indeed highly honoured in having our food dressed by the same hand. Having had tea, the first evening we arrived the Father went for a stroll in the summer gloaming, along the shores of Lake Tegid (generally known as Bala Lake), 4,084 acres of water, the largest natural lake in Wales, to visit the grave of Charles in the little churchyard of Llan-y-cil on the lake side. Here also is buried the Rev. Evan Lloyd, of Vron, a once popular Welsh poet. Close to the humble tomb of Charles, beneath the east window, where he lies in peace awaiting the resurrection of the just, is an 18th century cross. In the church itself are some 15th century bench ends. Llan-y-cil is really the old Parish Church of Bala restored; the new edifice in Bala being but the Chapel of Ease thereto. Legendary tradition states, that the *old* town of Bala is buried beneath the lake, even going so far

---

* The work of a *Welsh* artist.

as to state that in parts, on very clear days, the tops of houses are visible.

"Bala aeth a Bala aith
A Llanfor aith yn Llyn."*

Magnificent indeed is the view all along the shores of Llyn-Tegid, bounded in the distance by the peaks of Arran Benllyn (2,962 feet), and Arran Fawddwy (2,975 feet), the latter being one of the chief of the Welsh mountains. To the right, and further off, in the purple distance, stands out Cader Idris in *all* its glory, *as* it is seen from few other spots. To the right and nearer are the Arrenigs. The lake abounds with perch, pike, trout, roach, and shoals of a fish called "gwyniad" from the extreme whiteness of its scales. It is a gregarious fish found in the Alpine lakes, more especially in those of Switzerland.

To revert once more to the Patriarch of Bala, Thomas Charles. Behold a man persecuted by one appointed TO BE a shepherd of the sheep, and driven out of the Church, by the man who *should* have been his spiritual father. The memory of Charles still lives, as keen as yesterday, in the hearts of thousands. Pilgrims from all parts visit his grave at Bala. The word of the Scripture, " the righteous shall be had in

---

* Anglice—
  Bala has become a lake,
  Bala will become a lake,
  And Llanfor will also become a lake.

A similar legend is attached to Llangorse Lake in South Wales.

everlasting remembrance," is in his case fulfilled. But what of the Bishop who persecuted him? WHO goes to visit *his* grave? WHO cares *one* straw about him *now*, or where *he* is buried? Charles will live on *for ever*, and hearts *full* of gratitude for his revival of the great Sunday School and Bible Society movement will *never* cease. " The old, old story " of the simple Gospel is *never* fashionable. It is *too* simple, and those *who* preach it, must *always* look for persecution and calumny.

The second day of our pilgrimage at Bala, a most delightful walk was enjoyed along the Corwen Road to Llanfor, where the vicar, directly he heard the Father wished to see the church, came out himself and took us all round. He told us, he had heard the Father many years ago, when he was conducting a mission at Llangollen. This little village of Llanfor was a picture of rustic beauty, with its old yews and thatched cottages overgrown with creepers. It was a restored church, and welcome was the news that the services were "yn Cymræg." Several curious old monuments, etc., had been re-erected in the walls of the new church, whilst the old oak carving of the screen had been used once more, and most adroitly mended where broken.

After the church (in which the Father played and sang an " Oen Dduw "*) had been inspected, twilight

---

* The Welsh for the "Agnus Dei," or, "O Lamb of God," in "The Communion Service."

was creeping on all around. In spite of this a climb was started up "The Lover's Hill" at the back, from the summit of which a magnificent view, on all sides, was obtained for miles around. In the rector's garden was the old font, in use as a flower pot, while a new one had taken its place in the church! Close to the churchyard was the mound of an old British encampment.

Back once more to Bala, and its Green, so famous in Wales for the great religious assemblies, called "Sassiwn," that meet there every June. As many as twenty thousand persons have been gathered there at *one* time.

On the Saturday we had our first sight of a Welsh woman in the ancient costume of red shawl and tall black hat, as she, an old woman of over eighty, was going to get her Sunday dinner. Having learnt that she was the clerk's wife of Llan-y-cil, she was subsequently visited and photographed. The same evening another old lady of 89, in the garb of the ancient Cymry, was seen.

In the afternoon, a very pleasant drive was enjoyed all round the lake, going one side and returning by the other. The woodland lanes and moss-grown banks sparkling with the various coloured flowers of spring were lovely, the scenery *en route* being past the pen of man, to adequately describe. The first stoppage was made at Llanuwchllyn* to visit the old church,

---

* The Church above (*i.e.* at the top of) the Lake.

in which, on the north side of the high altar, is a perfect specimen of a recumbent knight in armour. The drive was then resumed to Llangower Church, a very small, quaint, little place. Noticeable in the churchyard, was the fact that whilst the majority of the *older* tombstones were inscribed with English, the *newer* ones were almost *all* in the soft musical language of Wales.

On Sunday morning the Father was enabled to get to the early celebration at Bala Church, and at ten o'clock to walk out to the morning service at Llan-y cil, which, with the sermon, was all in Welsh. It was on his way to this service that the gentleman met him who subsequently influenced the vicar to invite him to preach. In the afternoon, a visit was paid to the Methodist College, but, finding no service there till five, it was determined to return home and rest for the event of the evening. When we got to the Welsh service at 6.30 there was a very fair congregation, but it was not till 7.30, when the services at Llan-y-cil and the chapels were over, that the crowd began to gather, and pour in, in such numbers that soon every seat was occupied, the aisles and porch blocked, and crowds in the churchyard trying to *push* their way in ; and this in spite of the church being a fair sized one; and the people only having had a few hours' notice. *Such* a crowd had probably never before been gathered to listen to one man *since* the days of Charles himself. The sermon was on " God so loved the world," etc., and the Father, having both prayed extemporaneously, and announced his text in the tongue of the Cymry, proceeded to preach an eloquent, earnest sermon, *perfectly* riveting the attention of his congregation throughout, in spite of the number of children, young boys, and men. The singing of the *Welsh* hymns before and after the sermon, was a treat *never* to be forgotten, one and all helping to swell the immense volume of sound continuously rising and falling like the waves of the sea.

Well may it be said of Cambria, "Mor o'gan yw Cymru i gyd."* After the service, both the vicar and curate heartily thanked the Father for his sermon, and when the Father left next morning for Llangollen, he left behind many a grateful, loving heart *just* breathed upon, by the love of Jesus. Throughout our stay in Bala, the children used to delight in coming all day long to our window, to peep in, and try and get a look at the monks. Attempt to speak to them, and they would scamper off, proving how "excessively silly" and "skeered" they were, and *very* different to their little American cousins.

Before leaving the town, we visited the house and room where Thomas Charles died. On Monday morning, just before starting for Llangollen, the Father received a letter from its rector, stating *how delighted* they were to hear the Father was coming,

---

* "A sea of song is Wales altogether."

and begging him to telegraph, if he might secure the Assembly Rooms, and placard the town for a service, which the Father agreed to hold, and so telegraphed him accordingly. Our travelling companions were a rector, his wife, and little boy, from a village near Harlech, and most pleasant companions they proved, begging the Father to let them know if he ever was their way.

On arriving at Llangollen, as we drove from the station, at the door of a small china shop was one of the Father's converts of seven years ago, ready to welcome him, and waving her hand in delight. The luggage and birds safely deposited at "The Hands Hotel," a carriage was procured, and we started off *at once* for Valle Crucis to see the old ruins, and the recent discoveries there—a Cistercian Abbey dedicated to Our Lady about 1200, A.D., by Madoc ap Gryffydd Maelor, Lord of Dinas Bran and Bromfield, grandson of Owain Gwynedd, Prince of Wales.

Valle Crucis* is so called, after the large cross known as Eliseg's Pillar, which lies in a meadow at the foot of Bronfawr. The Abbey was dissolved in 1535, and very little now remains, with the exception of the Chapter House (in which the Father once preached to a large congregation), still complete, the Dormitory, a piece of one of the transepts with groined roof, and

* In the record of the foundation of the Abbey in 1200 by Madoc, it is called " the Monastery of Llanegwistle, near the old cross in Yale."

the west end. At the east end, under the east window, is the monks' fish pond, still full of fish. The foundations have just recently been dug out on the north side, and the tombstone, in perfect condition, of a Knight Templar has been discovered. Many a piece of old stained glass, and many a skull have been brought to light.

The clergyman in charge, asked the Father to sing an old monkish hymn in the ruined sanctuary, so, in the old chancel, just in front of the site of the High Altar, "*O Salutaris Hostia,*" once more floated through the ruined pile, on the balmy, summer air. Some ladies, now arriving, began to sing with heart and voice "*Faith of our Fathers.*" So once more, amidst the ruined pile, for centuries mouldering in silence to decay, the praises of the Creator ascended.

From Valle Crucis, we proceeded past Eliseg's Pillar to the farmhouse on the mountain side, where the Father lodged seven years ago. Glad indeed were the landlady and her family to see the Father again, and the last we saw of them, they were standing in the doorway, waving their farewells as we drove away.

Eliseg's Pillar,* or Llwyn-y-Groes, in a meadow a short distance from the ruins, was erected to the memory of Eliseg, father of Brochmael, Prince of Powis, by Concenn, his great grandson. It *was* a cross

---

* This is amongst the earliest lettered stones that succeeded the Meini Hirion and Meini Gwyn.

twelve feet high, but the shaft only now remains, and is but eight feet. The tumulus on which it stands, when opened many years since, disclosed remains of bones lying between broad flat stones.

Soon home again at the hospitable "Hands Hotel," with its lively and picturesque outlook, we passed on our way the ruined castle of Dinas Bran, which is very prominent for miles round, crowning the summit of a *lofty* hill overlooking the town. It appears to have been 290 feet long by 140 feet broad, and was the residence in 1390 of Myfanwy Fechan, descendant of the house of Tudor Trevor.

Soon after reaching the hotel, the rector called to say, he was sorry he had been unable to arrange a service for *that* evening, as there was not time, and begging the Father to stop and preach twice next day, which he, having consented to do, the rector went off, got a number of bills printed, and the town placarded before five o'clock. Here, when we arrived, the welcome notes of the Welsh harp, played by the lame harper, greeted us, and daily throughout our stay, the strains of "Hen gwlad fy nhadau," "Y Codiad Haul," and many a Welsh air once more sounded in our ears.

In the evening, at seven, we attended evensong in the parish church of S. Collen, where the Father once held a mission. After service, the Father went with the rector up to Plas Newydd, where a surprise was in store for him, for he was to meet a member of his Kensington congregation, who subsequently offered him the use of the furnished hermitage in her grounds, whenever he came to Llangollen. The parish church is without any peculiarity of architecture, but with several old arches and the porch doorway still standing.

Up to now, the Father's return to Wales had been, indeed, a pleasant journey homewards. He had as yet, met with nothing but kindness and expressions of joy from all, at seeing him again; but *now* he was to receive the exact opposite experience.

Next morning, by a special messenger from S. Asaph, in the form of a lawyer's clerk, he received an inhibition from the young Bishop of that city. The inhibition stated, that he was not to preach in Llangollen Church (by the bye, he had not been *intending* to do so) nor in any parish of the Diocese. Merely the formal inhibition was sent, without any explanatory reasons or accompanying note. The Bishop had lost very little time, considering that the Father had not been a week in the country.

It fell to my lot, to see to the Hall, and the preparations for the services in the Assembly Rooms at 4 and 8. The sermon at 4, when the congregation was small and fashionable, was on the word " Kept," but when the Father preached in the evening, on " I have found my sheep that was lost," every inch of standing room was packed, and there were crowds at the doors and outside on the stairs. Men and boys, some who had never entered a place of worship before, many without hats, some in rags and tatters, the *élite* of the neighbourhood, clergy, ministers, theological students, *all* helped to swell the throng, who drank in with avidity the words that fell from the Father's lips. The clergy and rector's daughters were heard to say afterwards, that the service was *just* what was *wanted*. As the Father left the Hall, numbers begged him to come back again.

Happy and pleasant indeed were the days spent in the picturesque Vale of Llangollen, with the veritable " Maid of Llangollen " for our hostess, and sorry we were to leave it and our kind friends. Llangollen Bridge, spanning the waters of " The Sacred Dee," is regarded as one of *the seven wonders of Wales*.* It was erected in the 14th century, by Dr. Trevor, Bishop of St. Asaph, and consists of four irregular narrow pointed arches. The Dee, a broad and shallow river, here rolls its turbulent waters over a rocky bed.

Wednesday morning, having bid Llangollen farewell, we started for home, arriving in Abergavenny at half-past four. On the way—once more at Shrewsbury and Hereford, the guards welcomed the Father, and were most anxious to know *what they could do* for him. As the train passed Llan-fihangel-crucorney,†

---

* "The Seven Wonders of Wales" are : 1, The Tower of Wrexham Church; 2, Llangollen Bridge ; 3, St. Winifred's Well; 4, Overton Churchyard ; 5, Gresford Bells ; 6, Pistyll Rhaiadr Waterfall; and 7, Snowdon.—" *Gossiping Guide to Wales.*"

†The Welsh for "The Church of St. Michael with the Horn."

and the Father looked out of the window, there was the station master waving a welcome home, though his joy, at the sight of the Father once more, was *almost* too much for him.

At Abergavenny, nothing but welcomes greeted the Father, and when we arrived at "The Angel Hotel" we found a carriage ready, and Sister Annie and the proprietress just going to meet us. After a night's rest, the journey was resumed to Llanthony. We were told, that when Sister Annie walked up the street, everybody stopped her, to inquire how the Father was.

As we drove home in an open carriage, many came out to their doors, to welcome the Father, as we passed. When we got to the Old Priory at Llanthony, we found a triumphal arch erected, with "Welcome Home," and a crowd collected, while cheer after cheer rent the air, and bouquets of wild flowers were thrown, from the windows of the village inn, into the carriage. Arrived home, a flag of welcome had been erected at "The Abbot's Gate," and was floating in the breeze, whilst Father Cadoc and Brother William were glad indeed to get their dearly-beloved Father home after his long absence, and everyone had much news to tell one another. That night, I think, no one was sorry to sleep in the cosy bed of their monastic cell, and cheerily welcome was "The Angelus" once more, as it rang out next morning at six, on the great Abbey bell, "Big Bernard." On Saturday two visitors arrived, and the next day, Sunday, we were enabled, by the goodness of God, to have two celebrations of the Mass, Brother Ernest, an associate of our Order, taking the early one, when all communicated *together* once more, and Brother Dunstan, an old novice, singing the eleven o'clock choral Mass. At this latter service the Father preached on " Jesus weeping over Jerusalem," dwelling on how *she* had *wasted* " her day." In the evening, after Vespers, he preached again on the same subject, *this time* dealing with the great love of Jesus for the sinner.

CHAPTER XXII.

CONCLUSION.

EVERYONE goes to America nowadays. *Many* cross backwards and forwards several times a year, and talk of their voyage across the mighty Atlantic as, a century ago, an Englishman would have spoken of a journey from London to Edinburgh.

Well may the worn-out business-man of our vast cities, steal a few weeks in the summer months, to explore the hidden beauties, and gaze on the magnificent cataracts, and glorious lakes that stud her verdant valleys, as well as the rocky and snow-capped mountains of magnificent America! The *half* of her beauty is *untold.* The average Englishman who lands upon her shores for the first time, as a rule, is full of preconceived ideas of America and her citizens, which, ere long, are doomed to be scattered to the four winds.

Instead of finding (as one is led to expect) everyone talking through their noses, and "calculating and guessing," and the towns poor and dirty, (none of which objections we came across during our year's delightful sojourn on her hospitable shores), the foreigner will experience *quite* the reverse. He will find people "*refined* to a degree," highly cultured, delightful, and to be surpassed *nowhere* for hospitality, —cities and buildings without a peer for size, magnificence, and variety of architecture,—palatial hotels, a most picturesque and romantic country, and *wherever* the traveller goes, kindness and attention.

But ours, as you know, was not solely a visit of pleasure or exploration. God had work in the Episcopal Church for the Rev. Father to do, and as His Messenger, he landed on the shores of the New World. It was a *strange* event—the advent of this Monk,—who claimed to belong to the Church of England,—in the great cities of the States! " Popery in its *worst* guise" many a dear old Protestant now feared had come among them. " A Papist," " a Jesuit in disguise," " preaching the dear old Gospel," but "only to lure the poor, deluded Protestants into the Church of Rome." Such was the opinion of many when we *first* arrived, and we were to have many a trial, many a repulse, from those who *should* have been as our fathers in Christ, representing, as they did, the Apostles, in the Dioceses of America. Strong in the Power of Jesus, strong in the Faith of Christ, remembering the words, " If God be for us, *who* can be against us?" the work for Him and for Eternity was commenced.

Of the fourteen bishops, with whom the Father's Mission work brought him in contact, six opposed him (though even one of these was wavery), while the other eight realized the immense showers of blessings and numerous conversions his services brought about. The Bishops of Massachusetts, Rhode Island, Long Island, Montreal, Florida, and Pennsylvania were unable to see their way to sanction his preaching in their dioceses, where *countless thousands* of *immortal souls*, for whom the Saviour died, were *starving* for "The Bread of Life," "The Star of Bethlehem!"

While these six Bishops opposed the Father's work, the Bishops (Potter) of New York, Quebec, Niagara, Minnesota, Ohio, Wyoming and Idaho, Chicago, and Newark, realizing their responsibility as "Shepherds of the souls of men" they had been called to guide and teach, and for *whose* souls they would be called to account at the last, either quietly sanctioned the Rev. Father's preaching, or openly gave their blessings on his work for their Master's glory. I need not deal specifically with these apostolic overseers here, as I have already done so in the preceding chapters.

Throughout our journeyings, from Quebec in the North, to Myers in the South, and out Westward to Chicago, we learned, *indeed*, a lesson of *true* Christianity; for our Blessed Lord's words, "By this, shall all men know, that ye are *My* disciples, if ye love one another," received a striking illustration. Though it was always *well known* that the Rev. Father was a Monk of the Church of England, with the *highest* Ritualistic and Catholic views, yet Christians of, I think, *every* denomination in the country, placed their places of worship at his disposal. Even the strict *Quakers* of Philadelphia begged him to prolong his stay, and address them at their Annual Meeting last April (1891). The *Roman Catholics* in Quebec welcomed him most cordially to their Seminary*, where he was privileged to speak for our Coming King. In Chicago an *orthodox Jewish Synagogue* (!) and a *Swedish Church* were among those, whose pulpits the Welsh Monk was solicited to occupy.

Dr. Hale's *Unitarian* Church in Boston received the Messianic message of the Gospel, and its walls echoed and re-echoed with the hymn, " All hail the power of Jesu's Name ! " when the Rev. Father preached there in Nov. 1890. In New York, by special request, he several times addressed the *Salvation Army*, many of whose soldiers might often be seen (as in England) at our services throughout the States. The *Methodists* everywhere, were specially friendly and *anxious* that Jesus might be *exalted*. At Myers in Florida, the Rev. Father held a Mission—the *like* of which I have NEVER seen, and shall remember for *Eternity !*—in one of their churches. The *Presbyterians* of Boston, St. Augustine in Florida, Chicago, and Cornwall-on-Hudson, threw open their church-doors wide to the preaching of the Welsh Monk. Nor were the *Baptists*, in anywise, behind them. In Chicago, the Rev. Father preached for them to an

---

*The Seminary of " The Christian Brothers."

enormous congregation in Mr. Moody's large Church, La Salle Avenue.

The *Congregationalists* and *Reformed Dutch* in their turn also listened to a monk's words from their own pulpits! Was it *not* a strange experience, but a lovely example, to find external differences of dogma and ceremonies *entirely put aside*, that "the Faith once delivered to the Saints," and *now* so *slightingly* regarded, might be upheld and proclaimed amongst their congregations. You have seen in'the past pages, the countless blessings brought to souls at the Rev. Father's services, so I shall pass on, to a few remarks I wish to make, concerning American home life, customs, and outdoor amusements.

Though America sets *us* an example in *many* ways, *yet* to us English it would be an improvement, if the heating of her hotels was not marked so high on the thermometer. It is customary over there, to heat the houses and all rooms, with either furnaces or hot-water pipes, fireplaces being rarely seen. Our American cousins are accustomed to bear a great amount of heat in all their rooms, *night* AND day. *We* found it TOO hot, even in winter there, to bear *more* than a sheet over us at night. Such a temperature naturally renders the Americans, when they go out, extremely susceptible to cold.

The arrangements of her tramcars and elevated railways, which thread a regular network through the streets, and over the houses of her chief towns, would be the better for enlarging or the adding of more cars. It is now the rule to find them *too* crowded, even to secure safe standing room, and packed in a way NOT allowed in England. The height of some houses in Chicago is terrific, one foundation being made to do for so many stories skyward. NOT being satisfied with houses of eighteen stories which already exist, they are now building one of twenty-two !!

It was sad to find it very customary, especially amongst the fashionable world, to have weddings solemnized in the evening, and in private houses. When we were in Chicago, I am sorry to say, *one* was celebrated in the MIDDLE of a game of tennis. I also heard of one at a balloon ascent. As I mention tennis, we used to go out walking in the morning at six o'clock and find whole families enjoying the game at that early hour. The Americans are early risers, one of their good examples, which the English might with *great benefit* adopt.

The churches are, as a rule, entirely carpeted. The collection or offertory is taken in silence, so that the congregation may not be disturbed by the singing of any hymn whilst making their *freewill* offerings to God, from Whom they receive *all*.

Oh, the glorious winter games American boys and girls enjoy!—in fact, all ages enjoy alike. Coasting on hand sleds, down the steep inclines of frozen snow, the sleighing through the evergreen woods to the music of silver bells, and wrapped in luxurious furs, or the dash down the tobogan slide—all these unite to make the winter's frosts and cold, a most enjoyable season for the American born. It was at Yonkers, on the Feast of the Epiphany, 1891, that I first witnessed the picturesque scene of coasting; and watching the enjoyment of youths and rosy maidens, gave one quite a pleasure. Children of all ages join in the upward ascent, hauling their sleds, then, pausing a moment on the top of the incline, they are gone *like a flash of lightning* to the bottom, and so on for hours. They rest on the sled and guide it with one foot and a rope attached in front, this, *oftener* than not, while the glass stands at zero and even lower. Being dressed in sliding or Indian costume they feel no cold. This costume consists of a blanket suit either white or bright, caps and belts of contrasting colours to suit the trimmings of the blankets, thick woollen mittens and mocassins of moose hide. Everyone who goes sleding, coasting, or snow-shoeing, dresses in this manner. Sleighing in the snow to the soft, sweet music of countless tiny bells, attached to both sleigh and harness, on the clear bright nights of cloudless moonlight, flying, as if on wings, through the sharp frosty air, which makes one's cheeks like rosy apples with its kiss. WHY need I describe this, for none who have *experienced* it, can EVER forget it. Skating, too, *such* skating, *vast* expanses of glassy ice " *unsoiled by the foot of man* " all go, towards making a transatlantic winter *truly* enjoyable.

Now, as I draw my American experiences to a close, let me say how *thoroughly* pleased I was with all I *saw* and *found* on that great continent; and while never forgetting how I enjoyed my year there, if it is our Lord's will, ever to lead us there again, what *different* feelings shall be mine on landing, to those I had, when first I trod Columbia's shores on the 21st June, 1890.

THE END.

LIST OF BOOKS
PUBLISHED AND SOLD BY JOHN HODGES.

Always the Same; a Love Story. By M. E. S. Crown 8vo. 2s. 6d.

Antrobus.—History of the Popes from the Close of the Middle Ages. Drawn from the Secret Archives of the Vatican and other Original Sources. By Dr. LOUIS PASTOR, Professor of History in the University of Innsbruck. Translated from the German. Edited by FREDERICK ANTROBUS, of the Oratory, with a Preface by His Eminence, Cardinal MANNING. Vols. I., II., III., and IV. Demy 8vo. 12s. each.

Avrillon.—A Guide to Advent, being a Guide to the Holy Observance of the Season of Advent; containing A Practice, A Meditation, Affections, Sentences from Holy Scripture and the Holy Fathers, and a point of the Incarnation. From the French of AVRILLON. Sewed, 6d.; Cloth 1s.

A Guide from Lent.—In the press.

Autobiography of an Alms-Bag, The; or, Sketches of Church and Social Life in a Watering-Place. By the Author of "John Brown, the Cordwainer," "Recreations of the People," etc. *Second Edition.* Crown 8vo. 2s. 6d.

"A clever book. Sketchy, anecdotic, chatty, humorous and suggestive. We read of many topics, all full of interest."—*Literary World.*
"The author is a kind of ecclesiastical Dickens and Thackeray combined, and the work has all the trace of Dr. Holmes' 'Autocrat.'"—*Oldham Chronicle.*
"Overflows with good stories effectively told, and most of them brought into good and useful purpose."—*Guardian.*

A Lapide.—The Great Commentary upon the Gospels
of Cornelius à Lapide. Translated and Edited by Rev. T. W.
MOSSMAN, D.D., (B.A., Oxon.), assisted by various Scholars.
6 Vols. Demy 8vo. 12s. each.
    SS. MATTHEW AND MARK'S GOSPELS. 3 Vols.
    Fourth Edition.
    ST. JOHN'S GOSPEL AND THREE EPISTLES. 2 Vols.
    Third Edition.
    ST. LUKE'S GOSPEL. 1 Vol. *Third Edition.*

The Acts of the Apostles.—*In the Press.—The whole of the New Testament is in hand, and will be issued at an early date.*

A Chronicle of the English Benedictine Monks, from
Renewing of their Congregation in the days of Queen Mary
to the Death of James II. ; being the Chronological Notes
of Dom. Bennett Weldon, O.S.B., a Monk of Paris. Edited
from a Manuscript in the Library of St. Gregory's Priory,
Downside, by a Monk of the same Congregation. Demy
4to. Handsomely printed. Price 12s. 6d.

Benedictine Calendar, The.— From the Latin by Dom
EGIDIOUS RANBECK, O.S.B., edited by JOHN A. MORRALL,
O.S.B., Sub-Prior of Downside.

This remarkable work was first published in 1677, at the
cost of the great Bavarian Monastery in Augsburg.

The Life of a Benedictine Saint is given for every day in
the year. The great merit of the work, however, consists in the
beautiful engravings which illustrate the lives.

In the new Edition these Engravings have been most
effectively reproduced by the Meisenbach Process, and the
accompanying Lives, which will be adaptations rather than
translations of the originals.

The work will be issued in Twelve Parts, beautifully
printed by the Messrs. Dalziel on fine plate paper.

*** Part I., containing the Month of January, with Thirty-
One illustrations, price 3s. 6d., post free. *Ready.*
Part II., February. *In the Press.*

Bernard, St.—The Works of St. Bernard, Abbot of
Clairvaux. Translated into English from the Edition of
DOM JOANNES MABILLON, of the Benedictine Congrega-
tion of St. Maur (Paris, 1690), and Edited by SAMUEL J.

iii.

EALES, D.C.L., Vicar of Stalisfield. Vols. I. and II., containing the Letters of St. Bernard. Demy 8vo. 12s. each. *Vol. III. in the Press.*

Beardsley, E. E.—The Life of the Right Rev. Samuel Seabury, D.D., First Bishop of Connecticut and of the American Church. By E. BEARDSLEY, D.D., President of the General Convention of the American Church. Crown 8vo, 5s.

"He has told in a calm and simple style, with much dignity and restraint of panegyric, the story of a great and good man whose deeds live after him to remote generations."—*The Literary World.*

"He was a man who was in advance of his age, to whom the Church must always look up with admiration and reverent thankfulness, and be grateful also to Dr. Beardsley for this tribute to his memory."—*The Guardian.*

Benedict, St.—A Sketch of the Life and Mission of St. Benedict. With an Appendix, containing a complete List of the Benedictine Churches and Monasteries in England, with the date of their foundation. By a Monk of St. Gregory's Priory, Downside. Third Thousand. 1s.

Biographies.—Price 2d. each; 12s. per 100.
THE REAL MARTIN LUTHER. *Twenty-fifth Thousand.*
LUTHER'S REAL TEACHING ON CONFESSION, BAPTISM, AND THE SACRAMENT OF THE ALTAR. With his Preface. *Fifth Thousand.*
THOMAS CRANMER, an English Reformer and sometime Archbishop of Canterbury.
THOMAS CRANMER, Archbishop of Canterbury, an English Reformer. *Fifth Thousand.*
THE TRUE JOHN WYCLIFFE. *Second Thousand.*
THOMAS CROMWELL AND HIS OFFICER.
These biographies are very useful for Missions.

Bowden, C.—Life and Martyrdom of St. Cecilia and her Companions. Edited by FR. CHARLES BOWDEN, of the London Oratory. Limp cloth, 1s.; wrapper, 6d.

Burke, S. H.—Historical Portraits of the Tudor Dynasty, and the Reformation Period. By S. HUBERT BURKE. Complete in 4 vols. Demy 8vo. 12s. each. "Time unveils all Truth."

Ireland Sixty Years Ago, being an Account of a Visit to Ireland by H.M. King George IV. in the year 1821. By S. HUBERT BURKE. Price 1s.

The Catholic Standard Library.

Under this title is now issuing a Series of Standard Works, consisting of Foreign Translations, Original Works and Reprints, printed in the best style of the typographic art, bound in cloth, in demy 8vo, of from 450 to 500 pages, and issued at short intervals, price 12s. each Volume, net ; *post free to any part of the world;* or twelve Vols. may be selected for £5 5s.

The Great Commentary on the Gospels of Cornelius à Lapide. Translated and Edited by the Rev. T. W. MOSSMAN, D.D. (B.A., Oxon), assisted by various Scholars.

SS. MATTHEW AND MARK'S GOSPELS. 3 Vols. *Fourth Edition.*
S. JOHN'S GOSPEL AND THREE EPISTLES. 2 Vols. *Third Edition.*
S. LUKE'S GOSPEL. 1 Vol. *Third Edition.*

"It would indeed be gilding the finest gold to bestow praise on the great Commentary of à Lapide. It is a work of unequalled—we should say unapproached —value. We specially entreat the clergy not to neglect obtaining so vast a treasure of saintly wisdom, even if, in so doing, they are obliged to sacrifice many volumes far inferior to it in real helpfulness.'—*John Bull.*

"Mr. Mossman has done his part as an able and sympathetic scholar might be expected to do it, and the volume, both in translation and execution, is worthy of its author."—*Saturday Review.*

"It is the most erudite, the richest, and altogether the completest Commentary on the Holy Scriptures that has ever been written, and our best thanks are due to Mr. Mossman for having given us, in clear, terse, and vigorous English, the invaluable work of the Prince of Scripture Commentators."—*Dublin Review.*

"Really the Editor has succeeded in presenting the public with a charming book. We have been accustomed to regard à Lapide for consultation rather than to be read. But in the compressed form, clear and easy style, and excellent type in which it now appears, it is a book we can sit down to and enjoy."—*The Month.*

"We set a high store upon this Commentary. There is about it a clearness of thought, a many-sided method of looking at truth, an insight into the deeper meaning, and a fearless devotion which lend a peculiar charm to all that he writes. The great value which his commentaries have for Bible students is in the fact that nowhere else can they find so great a store of patristic and scholastic exegesis."—*Literary World.*

Henry VIII. and the English Monasteries.—An Attempt to illustrate the History of their Suppression, with an Appendix, and Maps showing the situation of the religious houses at the time of their dissolution. By FRANCIS AIDAN GASQUET, D.D., O.S.B. 2 Vols. *Fourth Edition.*

"We may say in brief, if what we have already said is not sufficient to show it, that a very important chapter of English history is here treated with a fulness, minuteness and lucidity which will not be found in previous accounts, and we sincerely congratulate Dr. Gasquet on having made such an important contribution to English historical literature."—*Athenæum.*

"The old scandals, universally discredited at the time, and believed in by a later generation, only through prejudice and ignorance, are now dispelled for ever."— *Academy.* Signed, JAMES GAIRDNER.

"A most valuable contribution to ecclesiastical history."—*Saturday Review.*

"A learned, careful and successful vindication of the personal character of the monks. . . . In Mr. Gasquet's skilful hands, the dissolution of the monasteries assumes the proportions of a Greek tragedy."—*Guardian.*

Historical Portraits of the Tudor Dynasty and the Reformation Period. By S. HUBERT BURKE. 4 Vols. *Second Edition.* "Time unveils all Truth."

"I have read the work with great interest, and I subscribe without hesitation to the eulogy passed on it by the *Daily Chronicle*, as making, as far as I know, a distinct and valuable addition to our knowledge of a remarkable period."—*From a Letter by* MR. GLADSTONE.

"We do not hesitate to avow that, in his estimate of character and events, Mr. Burke is seldom wrong. . . . We heartily wish it a large sale and an extensive circulation."—*The Academy.* Signed, NICHOLAS POCOCK.

"They are full-length portraits, often so life-like, that when placed beside each other, we feel no difficulty in realizing the relations which Mr. Burke aims at establishing between them."—*Annual Register.*

"The author writes history as it should be written. The men and women that pass before us in these portraits are no hard lifeless outlines, but beings of flesh and blood, in whom, and in whose fate we feel a keen and absorbing interest."—*Tablet.*

"We attach great importance to Mr. Burke's work, as it is, we believe, the first attempt on any considerable scale, to collect and arrange in a living picture, the men and women who made the England of to-day . . . This effort, seriously and conscientiously undertaken, and aided by a graphic and attractive style, must do immense good."—*Dublin Review.*

"No honest student of a most memorable period can afford to neglect the aid of Mr. Burke's long and laborious researches, while the general public will find in his pages all the interest of a romance, and all the charm of novelty about events more than three centuries old. He is also what is rare—an historian of absolute impartiality."—*Life.*

Piconio (Bernardine a). Exposition on St. Paul's Epistles. Translated and Edited by A. H. PRICHARD, B.A., Merton College, Oxford. 3 Vols.

"The learning, the piety, the spiritual-mindedness and loving charity of the author, which deservedly earned for him a high reputation in France, are everywhere conspicuous, and there is a freshness in the mode in which he presents much that is suggestive, hopeful and beautiful."—*National Church.*

"We desire to recommend this book to all. Of course to the priesthood any commendation of it is unnecessary: but among the laity there are many souls, one of whose greatest drawbacks in the spiritual life is unfamiliarity with the Word of God. Let them read the Scriptures daily, if only for a few minutes, let them bear along with them such guides as Piconio, and the Spirit of God will illumine their minds and inflame their hearts with a freshness and vigour of Divine life altogether peculiar."—*New York Catholic World.*

The Dark Ages: A Series of Essays illustrating the State of Religion and Literature in the Ninth, Tenth, Eleventh, and Twelfth Centuries. By the late Dr. MAITLAND, Keeper of the MSS. at Lambeth. Fifth Edition, with an Introduction by FREDERICK STOKES, M.A.

"The Essays as a whole are delightful; although they are full of learning, no one can find them dull or heavy; they abound in well-told stories, amusing quotations, and clever sarcasm. Whatever the previous knowledge of a reader may be, he will be stirred up by these essays to learn more of a subject they treat so pleasantly."—*Saturday Review.*

"No task could be more worthy of a scholar and divine so eminently distinguished as the author of this volume, than a vindication of institutions which had been misrepresented for centuries, and a defence of men who had been maligned by those to whom they had been generous benefactors. We have read this work both with pleasure and profit."—*Athenæum.*

The History of the Popes, from the Close of the Middle Ages. Drawn from the Secret Archives of the Vatican and other Original Sources. By Dr. L. PASTOR, Professor of History in the University of Innsbruck. Translated from the German and Edited by FREDERICK ANTROBUS, of the Oratory. Vols. I., II., III., and IV.

"It would be difficult to name any great historical work written with so obvious an anxiety to tell the truth and nothing but the truth, and should these volumes not meet with a favourable reception, we should regard the event as little short of a literary calamity."—*Daily Chronicle.*

"It is no exaggeration to say that this work is one of the most important historical studies of the present century."—*Tablet.*

The History and Fate of Sacrilege. By Sir HENRY SPELMAN, Kt. Edited, in part from two MSS., Revised and Corrected. With a Continuation, large Additions, and an Introductory Essay. By Two Priests of the Church of England. New Edition, with Corrections, and some Additional Notes by Rev. S. J. EALES, D.C.L.

"All who are interested in Church Endowments and property should get this work, which will be found to be a mine of information on the point with which it deals."—*Newbery House Magazine.*

A Commentary on the Holy Gospels. In 4 Vols. By JOHN MALDONATUS, S.J. Translated and Edited from the original Latin by GEORGE J. DAVIE, M.A., Exeter

College, Oxford, one of the Translators of the Library of the Fathers. *Vols. I. and II. (St. Matthew's Gospel).*

" I have often consulted Maldonatus in the original with advantage, and I am glad to see it in English."—*W. E. Gladstone.*

" Maldonatus is as yet but little known to English readers, yet he was a man of far more ability than à Lapide, and is by far more original in his remarks and explanations."—*Month.*

" To those who may not with facility be able to read the Latin, this English version will be a great boon. The Commentary is certainly one with which a Biblical student should make himself acquainted."—*Guardian.*

The Complete Works of St. Bernard, Abbot of Clairvaux.
Translated into English from the edition of DOM JOANNES MABILLON, of the Benedictine Congregation of St. Maur (Paris, 1690), and Edited by SAMUEL J. EALES, D.C.L., Vicar of Stalisfield. Vols. I. and II., containing the Letter of St. Bernard. *Volume III. in the Press.*

" In his writings great natural powers shine forth resplendently, an intellect more than that of the subtle Abelard, an eloquence that was irresistible, an imagination like a poet, and a simplicity that wins the admiration of all. Priests will find it a most valuable book for spiritual reading and sermons. The printing and binding of the work are superb."—*Catholic World* (New York).

" We wish Dr. Eales and his publisher all success in what may be called a noble undertaking."—*Church Quarterly Review.*

" No writer of the Middle Ages is so fruitful of moral inspiration as St. Bernard, no character is more beautiful and no man in any age whatever so faithfully represented all that was best in the impulses of his time or exercised so powerful an influence upon it. . . . There is no man whose letters cover so many subjects of abiding interest, or whose influence was so widely spread."—*Athenæum.*

" It is not a little strange that a man of intellect so powerful, and character so noble and self-denying, should have had to wait seven centuries for his works to be rendered into English. . . . The letters are of great historic interest, and many of them most touching. The simple earnestness of the man, and his utter freedom from ambition, strike us on almost every page."—*Notes and Queries.*

" We congratulate both the publisher and the editor upon the issue of these volumes, which we predict will be warmly appreciated by English readers, and which we can thoroughly recommend."—*Literary Churchman.*

" The task which Mr. Eales has undertaken of bringing out an English edition of Bernard's works is one that is deserving of every praise, and we hope that it may be carried to completion by the appearance of the remaining volumes without undue delay."—*Literary World.*

" English readers of every class and creed owe a debt of gratitude to Dr. Eales for the great and useful work which he has undertaken. It is strange that now for the first time has such a task been even, as far as we are aware approached. . . . In this, the earliest complete English edition of Bernard's works, a reparation tardy indeed, but ample, is about to be made for the neglect or indifference of so many bygone generations of the English-speaking race. . . . We have, indeed much to be grateful for to the first English translator of St. Bernard's works."—*The Month.*

Edward VI. and the Book of Common Prayer.
Its Origin Illustrated by Hitherto Unpublished Documents. With Four Facsimile Pages of the MS. By FRANCIS AIDAN GASQUET, O.S.B., (*Author of " Henry VIII. and the English Monasteries,"*) and EDMUND BISHOP.

"A more accurate history of the changes of Religion and the motives of the statesmen of the reign of Edward VI. than has ever before appeared ; and as regards the antecedents and the compilation of the Prayer Book, we have no hesitation in saying this volume is the most valuable contribution to its history that has appeared since the time of Dr. Cardwell."—*Athenæum*.

"We cannot refrain from expressing our admiration of the method in which the author has conducted his whole inquiry. It ought to have a large circulation, for it contains by far the best account we have ever seen of the changes introduced in Edward VI.'s reign."—*Guardian*.

"This book will occupy a place of special importance in the library of every liturgical student."—*Saturday Review*.

"We may say, without hesitation, that the second, third, and fourth appendices are the most valuable contributions to the early history of the Prayer Book that have yet appeared."—*Church Quarterly Review*.

"This volume is one of the most interesting and valuable contributions to the study of the Reformation in England that has appeared for many a day." —*Academy*.

"The book deserves great praise for its learning and fairness." *Spectator*.

"We gladly acknowledge our gratitude to its authors, and willingly bespeak for their labour the earnest attention of every priest and layman."—*Church Times*.

"The publication of this book has done more for the elucidation of the history of the first Prayer Book than any writer since Proctor."—*English Churchman*.

"A volume of hardly less than national importance, and most opportune at this moment for the sake of all interested in the Lincoln judgment."—*The Month*.

The Hierurgia; or the Holy Sacrifice of the Mass. With Notes and Dissertations elucidating its Doctrines and Ceremonies. By Dr. DANIEL ROCK. A New and thoroughly Revised Edition, with many new Illustrations. Edited, with a Preface, by W. H. JAMES WEALE. 2 Vols.

"We hope the 'Hierurgia' may find many readers and command a wide and extensive sale. It is very serviceable as a book of reference."—*Dublin Review*.

The Relations of the Church to Society : A Series of Essays by EDMUND J. O'REILLY, S.J. Edited, with a Biographical Notice, by the Rev. MATTHEW RUSS: LL.

The Church of Our Fathers, as seen in St. Osmund's Rite for the Cathedral of Salisbury. By the Rev. Dr. ROCK. A new and Revised Edition. By the Benedictines of Downside. 4 Vols. *Preparing.*

Change in Faith or Development. A Critical Exposition of St. Vincent of Lerins. *Quod ubique quod semper quod ab omnibus.* Addressed to Anglicans. By C. TONDINI DE QUARENGHI, Barnabite. 8vo. 1s.

Central London : Ten Years' Experience of Church Mission Work by EMILE ISHERWOOD, with a Preface by the REV. R. ISHERWOOD, Senior Curate of St. Martin-in-the-Fields. Price 6d.

Church Congress Reports. Swansea, Leicester, Newcastle-on-Tyne. Demy 8vo. Cloth. Each 10s. 6d.

Church Congress—Complete Set of Church Congress Reports. 32 Vols. in Half-Calf Antique. Red edges. Price £24 net.

This would make a handsome present to a Home or Colonial Library.

Gentlemen having incomplete sets of the Church Congress Reports, and being desirous of completing them, should apply to Mr. Hodges, who has several of the Volumes that are out of print. Sets can be uniformly bound in any style at moderate charges. Back Vols. purchased or exchanged for others.

Church and Cottage Tracts. A Series of Leaflets for General Distribution, Nos. 1 to 48. A Specimen Packet, 1s., post free.

Come to the Woods, and other Poems. By C. J. CORNISH, M.A., Prebendary of Exeter. Cheaper Edition, cloth, gilt edges, 1s. 6d.

Conscience, H.—The Popular Tales of Henry Conscience (the Walter Scott of Flanders). Translated from the Flemish. To be issued in Volumes. In Wrapper, 1s. each.

  Vol. I. THE HAPPINESS OF BEING RICH.
  Vol. II. THE IRON TOMB.
  Vol. III. FISHERMAN'S DAUGHTER.
  Vol. IV. WOODEN CLARA AND RICKETICKETACK.
  Vol. V. THE LOST GLOVE.
  Vol. VI. THE PALE YOUNG MAIDEN.
  Vol. VII. LUDOVIC AND GERTRUDE.
  Vol. VIII. THE YOUNG DOCTOR.
  Vol. IX. THE BLUE HOUSE.
  Vol. X. THE FATAL DUEL, etc., etc., etc.

"In simplicity and purity of tone, it leaves nothing to be desired: and like all that Conscience wrote, there is nothing that ordinary people cannot understand. Should have a place in every parish library."—*Church Times.*

Copinger, A. E.—A Short and Easy Catechism on the Creed. For the Young. Price 4d.

Creedy.—Mr. Daniel Creedy, M.P. An Extravaganza. Price 6d. Post Free.

Devotional Readings.—Being selected passages from the Rev. H. E. Manning's Anglican Sermons. *Second Thousand.* Limp cloth, 1s.; cloth, bevelled boards, 1s. 6d.

Divine Counsels; or, the Young Christian's Guide to Wisdom. Translated from ARVISENET, by Rev. W. B. CAPARN, M.A., with a Preface by JOHN SHARP, M.A., Vicar of Horbury. Cloth. 1s.

"A welcome addition to devotional literature; it should be in the hands of all young persons of an age to be preparing for Confirmation and First Communion. The style of the work is suggestive of the *Imitatio Christi*, and the teaching it contains is thoroughly plain and practical, while full of religious earnestness and devotion."—*Church Times.*

Drexelius, J.—**The Heliotropium; or, Conformity of the Human Will to the Divine.** By JEREMY DREXELIUS. Translated from the original Latin. With a Preface by the late Bishop FORBES. Second Edition. Crown 8vo. 5s. net.

"A rational and simple-minded piety runs through the whole work, which forms excellent material for devotional reading, especially for men."—*Guardian.*

"An excellent book, and one that deserves to be more used than it is."—*Literary Churchman.*

Edward VI. and the Book of Common Prayer. Its origin illustrated by hitherto unpublished documents. By FRANCIS AIDAN GASQUET, O.S.B. (author of "Henry VIII. and the English Monasteries"), and EDMUND BISHOP. Demy 8vo. 12s. *Third Thousand.*

Evans, A. B.—**Reflections Delivered at the Mid-Day Celebration of Holy Communion in the Church of S. Mary-le-Strand.** By A. B. EVANS, D.D., Rector. Crown 8vo. *Third Edition in the Press.*

"Let a man, before preparing his own sermon, sit down and read through carefully and slowly one of these 'Reflections,' and he will certainly derive a lesson in method, and instruction how to reflect, from a true master of the science, which he could not easily learn elsewhere."—*Ecclesiastical Gazette.*

Gasquet, F. A.—**Henry VIII. and the English Monasteries.** An Attempt to Illustrate the History of their Suppression, with an Appendix, and Maps showing the situation of the religious houses at the time of their dissolution. By FRANCIS AIDAN GASQUET, O.S.B. 2 Vols. Demy 8vo. 12s. each. *Fourth Edition.*

Good Friday—How shall I keep it? With picture of the Crucifixion. 5s. per 100.

Hancock, T.—Christ and the People. Sermons on the Obligations of the Church to the State and to the People. By THOMAS HANCOCK, M.A., Lecturer at St. Nicholas Cole Abbey. Second edition. Crown 8vo. 6s.

"As compared with the general run of pious, feminine, hazy sermons, they are as a breeze on the hill-top to the close atmosphere of a sick-room, with its faint smell of medicines and perfumes."—*Church Times.*

Headlam, S. D.—Priestcraft and Progress. Lectures and Sermons, by STEWART D. HEADLAM, B.A. *Fourth thousand.* 1s.

Headlam, S. D.—The Service of Humanity, and other Sermons. Price 2s. 6d.

"Almost every page contains suggestive hints which all will do well to ponder, especially those brought into contact with secularism and infidelity."—*Ecclesiastical Gazette.*

"Our advice to the clergy and laity is to get this book, read it, and preach it, and live by it."—*Church Times.*

Headlam, S. D.—The Laws of Eternal Life, being Studies in the Church Catechism. Price 2s.

Headlam, S. D.—Lessons from the Cross, being Addresses given on Good Friday. 1s. 6d.

Headlam, S. D.—The Theory of Theatrical Dancing. Edited from CARLO BLASIS, with the Original Plates. 8vo. Cloth. 3s. 6d.

Headlam, S. D.—The Function of the Stage: A Lecture. Sewed. 6d.

HEROES OF THE CROSS.

Under this title is now publishing a series of biographies of eminent Christians, who have lived in all ages of the Christian Church. The lives will aim to be historical rather than devotional, and controversy will be avoided. Each biography will be complete in one vol., crown 8vo, cloth, 3s. 6d.

St. Gregory the Great. By the Right Rev. ABBOT SNOW, O.S.B. (*Ready*).

Christopher Columbus. His Life, Labours and Discoveries By MARIANO MONTEIRO. (*Ready*).

Hugh of Avalon, Bishop of Lincoln. By Rev. GEORGE G. PERRY, M.A., Rector of Waddington and Canon of Lincoln. *In the Press.*

St. Stephen Harding. Founder of the Cistercian Order. Reprinted from "Newman's Lives of the Saints." *In the Press.*

The Most Rev. Robert Grey, D.D., Bishop of Cape Town and Metropolitan, by S. J. EALES, D.C.L., Vicar of Stalisfield. *In the Press.*

Holy Communion, the Service for the Celebration of, Commonly called the Canon. According to the use of the Famous and Illustrious Church of Sarum in England, being the only office authorised for use at the Celebration of the Most Holy Eucharist. Price 6d.

Holy Men of Old. Being Short Lives of the Saints, with Meditations for Every Day in the Year, by R. W. LOWDER. To be issued in twelve monthly parts at 1s. each, October, November and December ready. Each part is complete in itself, and contains one Month of the Calendar. Admirably adapted for reading at Family Prayer.

Hours of the Passion, Including in full the Daily Office for Morning and Night, chiefly after the Ancient English Use of Salisbury, with other Devotional Forms, for private and household use. Compiled and Edited by a Priest of the Church of England. Second and Revised Edition. Cloth. Red edges. 2s. 6d.

Ignatius.—Father Ignatius in America. BY. FATHER MICHAEL, O.S.B. Crown 8vo, with frontispiece. 6s.

In the Light of the Twentieth Century. By INNOMATUS. Crown 8vo. 2s. 6d.

"This book is undeniably clever, full of close and subtle reasoning, lighted up with keen epigrammatic wit."—*Literary World.*

Jones.—Dishonest Criticism. Being a Chapter of Theology on Equivocation, and Doing Evil for a good cause. An answer to Dr. RICHARD F. LITTLEDALE. By JAMES JONES, S.J., Professor to Moral Theology in St. Beuno's College. Crown 8vo. 3s. 6d.

"Nothing like it has appeared since Newman's reply to Kingsley.'—*John Bull.*

Justorium Semita (The Path of the Just), being the Lives of the Saints commemorated in the Calendar in the Book of Common Prayer, a new edition of a book which has been many years out of print. *In the Press.*

Lights and Shadows.—Stories of Every-day Life. One vol., containing Thirteen Stories. Cloth. 2s. 6d., or in 3 parts, 6d. each.

Maitland, S. R.—The Dark Ages : A Series of Essays illustrating the State of Religion and Literature in the Ninth, Tenth, Eleventh, and Twelfth Centuries. By the late DR. MAITLAND, Keeper of the MSS. at Lambeth. Fifth Edition, with an introduction by FREDERICK STOKES, M.A. Demy 8vo. 12s.

Mermillod, Cardinal.—Lectures to Ladies on the Supernatural Life. By Cardinal MERMILLOD, Bishop of Lausanne and Geneva. Translated from the French, with the Author's sanction, by a Lady. Crown 8vo. 3s. 6d.

"These addresses are fine specimens of compilation which seem to stand midway between that of a meditation and a sermon. The spiritual teaching is most direct and excellent."—*Literary Churchman.*

Maldonatus, J.—A Commentary on the Holy Gospels. In 4 vols. By JOHN MALDONATUS, S.J. Translated and Edited from the original Latin by GEORGE J. DAVIE, M.A., Exeter College, Oxford, one of the Translators of the Library of the Fathers. *Vols. I. and II. (St. Matthew's Gospel).* Demy 8vo. 12s. each.

Manuals for the People. Nos. 1 to 21. A Specimen Set. 1s. 9d.

Montifeore, A.—Life of Christopher Columbus. By Miss MONTIFEORE. Crown 8vo. 3s. 6d.

Mossman, T. W.—Mr. Gray and His Neighbours. By T. W. MOSSMAN, D.D. Second Edition. 2 vols. Crown 8vo. 9s.

"Mr. Gunter, the very unspiritual Rector, who cares less for principle than for preferment, and who makes his Laodicean principles pay, is a clever caricature."—*Standard.*

"The entire absence of goodliness or sentimentality in the way the matter is handled, and the mode in which Mr. Gray and his daughter are depicted as dealing with it, deserve warm praise."—*Academy.*

"Bishop Stubblegrass is equal to Bishop Proudie himself, which is saying not a little."—*Nonconformist.*

"Alice Gray is a finely-drawn character with all the virtues of a sincere Christian and the heroism of a Grace Darling. The style of composition is that of an accomplished scholar "—*Stamford Mercury.*

By the same Author.

Latin Latter, A. (with an English Translation) to his Holiness Pope Leo XIII., Successor of St. Peter, and Primate of the Catholic Church. By THOMAS W. MOSSMAN D.D., Rector of Torrington, Lincolnshire. 1s.

The Relations which at present Exist between Church and State in England. A letter to the Right Hon. W. E. GLADSTONE, M.P. 8vo. Price 1s.

New Musical Works. By HENRY F. HEMY. Author of " Hemy's Pianoforte Tutor."

The Children's Musical Longfellow, Containing about 400 Songs. The Words from Longfellow. To be published in Shilling Parts, each complete in itself, and sold everywhere. Part I., containing 25 Songs. Price 1s.

The Westminster Hymnal for Congregational Use. Part I. containing 52 Hymns for Advent and Christmas. Price 1s.

Notes on Ingersoll. By the Rev. L. A. LAMBERT, of Waterloo, New York. Revised and Reprinted from the 50th Thousand. American Edition, price 1s. 6d.

"*By far the ablest antagonist infidelity has met with.* Every possible objection brought by Ingersoll against Christianity is completely crushed by Lambert."—*Guardian.*

" We hail with gladness the appearance of this volume, and heartily wish it the extensive circulation in England it has had in America."—*Rock.*

Our Vicar's Stories. In Six Numbers, 6d. Each. Illustrated. Edited by Rev. H. C. SHUTTLEWORTH, M.A. Also the First and Second Series. Cloth, 1s. 6d. each. And the Six Numbers in 1 Volume, Cloth, gilt, 2s. 6d.
    No. 1.—RHODA ST. BARB.
    No. 2.—TRUE AS STEEL.
    No. 3.—SUNFLOWER COURT : A Christmas Story.
    No. 4.—THE PEARL MERCHANTS.
    No. 5.—IN THE NEW FOREST.
    No. 6.—JEM, A REAL REFORMER.

" Well adapted for lending libraries and school prizes, and very like our old favourite ' The Curate's Budget.' "—*Church Bells.*

Peacock, E.—Narcissa Brendon, A Romance. By EDWARD PEACOCK, F.S.A., etc. 2 vols. Crown 8vo. 12s.

Pathway, The. A Practical Guide to Instruction and Devotion in the Elements of Christian Religion. Demy 18mo. Limp Cloth, 1s. Cloth Boards, 1s. 6d. Limp Persian, 2s. 6d.

"It is truly a pathway to the practice of devotion on the lines of the teaching of the Church of England, and is just such a book as we should like to s e in the hands of every boy and every girl in the kingdom."—*Church Times.*

Perry, G.—Life of Hugh of Avelon, Bishop of Lincoln. A new and revised edition by GEORGE PERRY, M.A., Canon of Lincoln. Crown 8vo. *In the Press.*

Piconio (Bernardine a). Exposition on St. Paul's Epistles. Translated and Edited by A. H. PRICHARD, B.A., Merton College, Oxford. 3 Vols., Demy 8vo., 12s. each.

Public Health.—A Popular Guide to the Rights and the Duties of the Inhabitants of the County of London. By W. ADDINGTON WILLIS, LL.B. (Lond.), of the Inner Temple, Barrister-at-Law. Price 1s.

Rock, D.—The Church of our Fathers, as seen in St. Osmund's Rite for the Cathedral of Salisbury. By the late Rev. DR. D. ROCK. A New and Revised Edition. By the Benedictines of Downside. 4 Vols. *Preparing.*

Rock, D.— The Hierurgia; or, the Holy Sacrifice of the Mass. With Notes and Dissertations elucidating its doctrines and ceremonies. By the late Dr. DANIEL ROCK. A New and thoroughly Revised Edition, with many new Illustrations. Edited, with a Preface, by W. H. JAMES WEALE. Demy 8vo, 12s.

A Large Paper Edition, limited to 250 copies, printed on fine laid paper, with red rubric lines, price £2 10s., to secure copies of which, immediate application is necessary.

Spelman, H.—The History and Fate of Sacrilege. By Sir HENRY SPELMAN, Kt. Edited in part from two MSS., revised and corrected. With a Continuation, large Additions, and an Introductory Essay. By two Priests of the Church of England. Fourth Edition, with Corrections, and some Additional Notes by Dr. EALES, Demy 8vo.

Snow, T. B.—St. Gregory the Great, His Work, and his Spirit. By the Right Rev. ABBOT SNOW, O.S.B. Crown 8vo. Wrapper 2s. 6d., cloth extra, top edge gilt, 3s. 6d.

Sacristy, The, A Review of Ecclesiastical Art and Literature. Two vols., handsomely bound in cloth, top edge gilt, 12s. 6d. each ; or, One Guinea the Two Vols. on direct application to the publisher. Only a few copies remain.

"Such a contribution to the folk lore of Europe cannot but be welcomed by all antiquarians. . . . We do not know when we have experienced greater pleasure, or learned more from the perusal of any book. As in matter it is excellent, so in its get-up it reflects the greatest credit upon its publisher."—*Weekly Register.*

Salvation—How shall I gain it? By LESLIE MAXWELL. Price 4d.

Staniforth, T. W., Carols, Hymns and Noels for Christmastide. 20 Selected and Edited. By THOMAS WORLEY STANIFORTH. Price 1s. Already the book has been adopted for use in several Churches.

"Some of them are very beautiful, and certain to become popular."—*Morning Post.*

Thoughts for Those that Mourn. Eleventh Thousand. Cloth, 1s. Roan and Red Edges, 2s. 6d.

The Treatise of St. Catherine of Genoa on Purgatory. Newly translated, with an introduction of Hell and the Future State. Price 2s.

Thoughts and Suggestions for Sisters of Charity, and for those desirous of becoming Sisters, with Heads of Mental Prayer and Consideration. Second Edition. 2s. 6d.

Winter, A.—Problems of Life. By Alexander Winter. Crown 8vo. Limp Cloth. 2s.

Order in the Physical World and its First Cause according to Modern Science. From the French by T. J. SLEVIN. One Vol. 3s. 6d.

The Life of Pope Adrian IV. (Nicholas Brakespeare), *The Only English Pope.* By the Right Rev. EDWARD TROLLOPE, D.D., Bishop of Nottingham, Suffragan of Lincoln. One Vol. *In the Press.*

JOHN HODGES, 7, AGAR STREET, CHARING CROSS, W.C.

Short Manuals of Canon Law.

EDITED BY

OSWALD J. REICHEL, B.C.L., M.A., F.S.A.,

Some time Vice-Principal of Cuddesden College.

A Series of Short Manuals of Canon Law is about to be issued, in which not only the law will be laid down, but references will be given to authorities for every statement, so that readers may be able to verify the law for themselves.

The following subjects will be among the first issued :—

The Canon Law of the Sacraments,

Containing the Sacraments generally, the nature and essentials of a Sacrament, Sacramental signs and their uses.

The Canon Law of Baptism,

Containing Baptism, Confirmation, the position and duties of Laymen.

The Canon Law of the Eucharist,

Containing the law of the Sacrifice, of Communion, of the Liturgy.

The Cannon Law of Penance,

Containing the Ministry of Reconciliation, the Discipline of Reconciliation, Extreme Unction.

The Canon Law of Order. The Law of Matrimony, &c., &c.

The whole Series forming a complete Manual of Canon Law and a handy Book of Reference for Theologians and Students.

Part I., demy 8vo, containing Baptism, &c., price 1/-, post free, IN THE PRESS.

JOHN HODGES, Agar Street, Charing Cross, London.

HENRY VIII.

AND THE

ENGLISH MONASTERIES.

An attempt to illustrate the History of their Suppression, with an Appendix and Maps showing the situation of the religious houses at the time of their dissolution.

BY

FRANCIS AIDAN GASQUET, D.D., O.S.B.

2 Vols. 12s. each. Fifth Edition, now ready.

In reply to a desire from many quarters, and with a view to bring this important historical work within the reach of a larger circle of readers, it has been decided to issue an

Illustrated Edition in Monthly Shilling Parts.

The sale of four large Editions in so short a time, of a work of the kind, is almost unprecedented, and it is certain that no other book since the appearance of Dr. Maitland's "Dark Ages" has done so much to dispel prejudices resulting from falsified History.

The Publisher respectfully solicits the aid of the Clergy, and every one interested in spreading abroad historical truth, in making this issue of a valuable work as widely known as possible.

PART I. to X., price 1s. each, post free.

A Specimen part, post free, on receipt of Three Stamps for Postage.

SOME OPINIONS OF THE PRESS.

"A learned, careful and successful vindication of the personal character of the Monks... In Mr. Gasquet's skilful hands the dissolution of the Monasteries assumes the proportions of a Greek tragedy."—*Guardian.*

"We do not feel the least hesitation in saying that it is by far the best book in existence on the religious changes which took place in England during the period between Henry's desire to put away his wife and the accession of Elizabeth."—*Tablet.*

"The book is a valuable contribution to church history, and one which throws a flood of light on the real cause and actual methods and results of Henry VIII.'s high-handed treatment of the English Monasteries."—*Standard.*

"It is no exaggeration to say that it would have been a national misfortune if anything had happened to hinder the completion of this book."—*Month.*

"Mr. Gasquet's great work is before us. We call it great without hesitation, for the first volume was admitted on all hands to be the fairest book that had yet been produced concerning the great Tudor revolution."—*Notes and Queries.*

"We may say in brief, if what we have already said is not sufficient to show it, that a very important chapter of English history is here treated with a fulness, minuteness, and lucidity which will not be found in previous accounts, and we sincerely congratulate Mr. Gasquet on having made such an important contribution to English historical literature."—*Athenæum.*

JOHN HODGES, 7, Agar Street, Charing Cross, London.

www.ingramcontent.com/pod-product-compliance
Lightning Source LLC
Chambersburg PA
CBHW022114290426
44112CB00008B/667